SMUGGLED

The Underground Trade in Australia's Wildlife

SMUGGLED

The Underground Trade
in Australia's Wildlife

RAYMOND HOSER

APOLLO BOOKS

Published by Apollo Books
P.O. Box 87
Mosman NSW 2088
Sydney Australia
Tel: 61 48 691 550
Fax: 61 48 691 551

First published 1993

Hoser, Raymond T. (Raymond Terrence), 1962-   .
Smuggled: the underground trade in Australia's wildlife.

    Bibliography.
    Includes index.
    ISBN 0 947068 17 1.
    ISBN 0 947068 18 X (pbk.).

    1. Wild animal trade. 2. Poaching — Australia. 3. Smuggling —
    Australia. I. Title.

364.187

Author's Note:
On 18th June 1992, material from this book was tabled before Federal
Parliament by Senator Meg Lees. It subsequently became the basis for
a Senate inquiry into wildlife smuggling and official corruption,
which commenced in September 1992. The manuscript of this book
has been edited and some material has been deleted for legal reasons.

CONTENTS

NOTES TO THE READER

SCIENTIFIC NAMES: In this book, scientific names appear only once after their common name. Thereafter, the animal is referred to by its common name only, in the interests of avoiding tedious repetition.

MONEY: Unless otherwise stated, all amounts of money in this book refer to Australian dollars. In specific instances, foreign currency is indicated, for example US$1 000, for American dollars.

PRICE LISTS: Price lists from animal dealers are reprinted in this book only to illustrate a demand for wild animals. With the exception of the Atlanta Wildlife Exchange, NO illegal activity is stated or implied by the other dealers.

PHOTO CREDITS: These appear with the photos. Uncredited photos are by the author.

ABOUT THE AUTHOR

Raymond Hoser was born in the U.K. in 1962 and came to Australia in 1967. He grew up and studied in Sydney. From the age of four, he kept reptiles as pets and began his research into these animals early, publishing many scientific papers in journals worldwide from the age of thirteen. Raymond is now internationally regarded as an authority on Australian reptiles.

Following his allegations of official corruption in State wildlife authorities, Raymond's reptile facilities were broken into on several occasions by wildlife officials. Reptiles, computer disks, files, camera equipment and other valuables, were stolen.

Most of the author's claims regarding corruption have since been vindicated by other, independent sources. Many officials named by him as being corrupt, have since been removed from their positions.

Raymond has become an authority on wildlife smuggling, and has featured in documentaries on the subject, including the widely acclaimed British series, 'Animal Traffic — Out Of Australia'. He believes that present laws and the public service structure actually facilitate smuggling and perpetuate corruption.

Raymond's previous books, *Australian Reptiles and Frogs* and *Endangered Animals of Australia* are extremely detailed and regarded as definitive works in their fields. This book represents a summary of Raymond's search for the truth in wildlife smuggling.

FOREWORD

'The law goes hard on man or woman,
Who steals the goose from off the common,
But lets the greater sinner loose,
Who steals the common from the goose.'
                                    — *English proverb*

Those words point to two massive problems facing the Earth's wild creatures.

Habitat destruction and degradation of the Earth's natural systems — stealing the common from the goose — are on-going and global problems which are proving a basic threat to biodiversity and all the future options that biodiversity affords us in scientific, aesthetic, cultural and moral terms.

And the actual removal of species (either dead or alive) from their natural ecosystems — stealing the goose from the common — is also threatening that biodiversity, and the options and enjoyment of this and future generations.

We all get angry when something is stolen from us. We all get angry when someone deprives us of something which is rightfully ours, either in the personal or communal sense.

Wildlife smuggling is theft. Theft from the ecosystems, and theft from fellow human beings, who can rightly claim deprivation of common heritage, as we are all mere custodians for others, and theft from future generations.

A tragic irony of this smuggling is that, in many cases, the rarer and more endangered the species, the higher the price gained on the smuggling market, and, therefore, the greater the smuggling threat.

This vicious circle, if allowed to continue unabated, could wipe out some species, especially when combined with widespread problems such as habitat destruction.

I have heard a particularly good analogy to illustrate the plight of the world's environment. It involves rivets being removed from an aeroplane; a certain number of rivets can be removed, without apparent effect. Alas, there is a critical point when, suddenly, only one rivet more is removed, and the plane breaks up. The removal of one too many a species, or one too many an individual bird or animal, may spell the end of an ecosystem.

Species are the rivets of the Earth. They hold the system together. The interactions within and between ecosystems made up of individual species, are finely-balanced and delicately arranged.

There is more than enough pressure on those ecosystems, and the ecologically and aesthetically vital species within them, without the wilful removal of species from their natural homes.

Raymond Hoser's previous book, *Endangered Animals of Australia*, provided a vivid description of the many species we have nearly lost. This book, *Smuggled*, adds greatly to that picture, providing a clear understanding of the magnitude, the cruelty and the threat of wildlife smuggling.

When I was Federal Environment Minister, I quickly realised that such an understanding is vital if we are to solve the problem of illegal trading and maximise the survival chances of the unique species which make up Australia's natural heritage.

One may not agree with everything stated in this book, but it will make all who read it more aware of the problem, and more inclined to help stamp it out.

We must not forget that biodiversity is vital for this planet's sustainability, and species protection is vital for that biodiversity. Let's not get to the situation when, suddenly, the removal of just one rivet — perhaps by smuggling — proves fatal for a species, an ecosystem, or a globe.

Graham Richardson

PREFACE

This excellent book is about wildlife conservation. The protection of Australian native flora and fauna is now a prority for *all* thinking Australians. You do not need to be an extremist member of the green movement or the animal liberation lobby to be anxious about the future of Australian wildlife species.

The Duke of Edinburgh is on record as saying: 'It will not be much use if, after spending so much time and effort cleaning up the whole environment and limiting the population, we wake up to find that, in the meantime, whole lists of creatures and plants have disappeared from the face of the earth.'

Smuggling of wildlife takes a terrible toll on Australian flora and fauna — it is stealing from every Australian.

The Governments of Australia, in their well-intentioned endeavours to stop smuggling, have passed various anti-poaching and anti-export laws. These have not been effective and the future for a large number of Australian wildlife species is bleak.

As a lawyer I note that 'prohibition', in the history of law and order in western litigation, has been a total failure. Ask the Americans about the prohibition of liquor between 1918 and 1933. Clearly the prohibition on drug importation and possession in Australia is also a total failure.

Governments of all levels provide only lip-service to wildlife conservation, including law enforcement, anti-poaching, anti-smuggling, species management, national park management, and captive breeding of rare and endangered species (both publicly or privately funded).

As a solicitor, I have helped to prepare several lengthy, detailed submissions to wildlife authorities of the New South Wales and Federal Governments over the past ten years without result.

These submissions, on behalf of private zoos, dolphinariums, herpetologists and aviculturists, contained proposals for improved wildlife conservation, enhanced animal welfare, improved law enforcement and measures that should be cash neutral or cash positive for the relevant Government agency.

There has been no acknowledgement or response to any submission to date.

Australian Governments are in a position to act but do not. Why is this? I believe the answer lies in their failure to perceive environmental and wildlife issues as *really* important. They allocate priority to schools, hospitals, administration and so forth. After all, koalas, parrots and snakes do not vote.

All levels of Government in Australia need to rethink current legislation regarding wildlife export and the prohibition of captive breeding.

A change in direction, allowing captive breeding and trade in Australian wildlife, would have several satisfactory results, including:

1 The establishment of captive breeding colonies of Australian rare and endangered species, which would ensure the survival of species threatened by extinction in the wild.

2 The establishment of a viable industry in Australian wildlife, easily supervised by Government authorities, which would generate both income and employment.

3 The elimination of extremely cruel current smuggling practices which have a high mortality rate. This in turn creates a greater demand and higher black market prices which encourage smuggling. Legally exported wildlife, on the other hand, has a negligible mortality rate, a high mortality rate being bad for business, financially unviable and attracting the attention of animal protection societies and Government departments.

4 There appears to be substantial evidence that illegal drug traffickers into Australia make the return trip smuggling wildlife out. Legal captive breeding and export of Australian wildlife would significantly undermine this activity.

5 The establishment of an Australian wildlife captive breeding industry would provide several substantial benefits for the people of Australia:

(a) Private monies would be injected into endangered species survival projects in Australia.

(b) The progeny of these programmes would be available for stocking public or private zoos, research and education, both in Australia and overseas. Tourism, one of Australia's major growth industries, would benefit. Species in the wild could also be restocked as circumstances permitted. Properly managed, this could clearly become a renewable resource, unlike many other Australian resources which are merely extractive.

(c) The industry established would provide substantial economic activity involving labour, materials, agricultural products, veterinary products and services, Government services on a user pays basis, freight facilities, etc. It is hard to identify a species of animal that has become extinct after a commercial environment was created around it. Would tourists come to Australia to see koalas and kangaroos if they could go into the bush to see them? I believe not. Tourists pay to see the animals in captive breeding facilities around major cities. Many of these facilities currently have to keep males separate from the females to stop them breeding, as this is considered illegal, yet they are prolific breeders in captivity.

6 Our international profile would improve. Australia is perceived to be very immature amongst overseas wildlife breeders and keepers, with our policy of killing pest native species in the wild which could be sold for export. If the pink galah (*Cacatua roseicapilla*) is worth say, $500 overseas why can't a struggling sheep or wheat farmer establish satisfactory facilities to trap or breed these birds for export for say, $25 per head, the Government receiving $5 per head for certification, etc?

SMUGGLED

Many people in Australia and elsewhere have concluded, after watching the destruction of the environment, that the only future for some species is captive breeding colonies if extinction is to be avoided. This has proven the case for the California condor (*Vultur californianus*), the Lord Howe Island woodhen (*Tricholimnas sylvestris*), the orange-bellied parrot (*Neophema chrysogaster*), and the western swamp tortoise (*Pseudoemydura umbrina*).

How obscene it is that some Australian native species are now prolific captive breeders overseas but at present are rare and endangered in Australia. Yet their importation back into Australia is *prohibited!* This applies, for example, to the palm cockatoo (*Probosciger aterrimus*), the Gouldian finch (*Erythrura gouldiae*) and the parma wallaby (*Macropus parma*). Why is it these species cannot be imported back into Australia where captive breeding colonies could show our grandchildren what was nearly lost forever?

Let's get serious: let's change direction. Let's impose compulsory prison plus heavy fines and forfeiture of private property to the Crown for anyone convicted of wildlife smuggling in Australia (whether it be Australian fauna or otherwise).

At the same time, let's set a world example by establishing a civilised and sophisticated wildlife industry. Let Australia set the benchmark in captive breeding, reintroduction, trade and export of its wildlife.

In 1992, we are still killing our wildlife, both intentionally and accidentally, not putting it to good purpose nor attending to its conservation. We are not husbanding our national heritage.

Does anyone really dispute the philosophy that the current environment and stock of Australian native wildlife is merely held by us in trust for future generations? If this is agreed, then it is also the role of a diligent wildlife trustee to preserve the assets of the trust and if possible, increase them. This book points us in the right direction.

CHRISTOPHER CHAPMAN, Dip Law, Dip C.M., ACIM
Solicitor of the Supreme Court of New South Wales, Victoria and the Australian Capital Territory, and the High Court of Australia.

INTRODUCTION

Conservation of Australia's vanishing native animals has recently become a major concern to our community. Although most birds, mammals and reptiles are now given some form of statutory protection, this itself has often led to more problems for the species than it has solved. With the Federal Government's near total ban on exporting native animals from Australia, and the apparently insatiable demand for our wildlife by overseas collectors and zoos, conditions are highly conducive to a flourishing illegal trade in our wildlife. This has been the case since the late 1960s and early 1970s. Today, wildlife smuggling rackets operating from Australia are among the most sophisticated in the world.

A SENSITIVE ISSUE
Restricted reports such as 'Operation Doughnut' by the Federal Customs Department, detail the web of people involved in these rackets. As early as 1974, journalist Dick Wordley said 'There are allegedly more outwardly respectable people on the syndicate's payrolls — even Government and airline officials, some of whom have already been charged under the Commonwealth Crimes Act — than most Australians would believe.'

'Operation Doughnut' in the 1970s was so sensitive, naming as it did prominent members of the community, that most of the file has since been destroyed. A Member of Parliament was named as a principal, one of many who, by virtue of his public office, was immune from prosecution. Both the former director of Sydney's Taronga Zoo, Sir Edward Hallstrom, and the head reptile keeper, Uwe Peters, were well known wildlife traffickers. Neither was prosecuted although their smuggling activities have been well documented since then. Both men are now dead.

As recently as 1990, both I and the Federal Minister of the Environment, Ros Kelly, were both refused access to the remaining pages of the 'Doughnut' file on the grounds that it was still 'too hot to handle'.

Wildlife smuggling racket principals are as ruthless as any other criminals.

SMUGGLED

In Sydney a doctor was kidnapped after doublecrossing a bird-smuggling syndicate. Ransom of $30 000 was paid on his life in central Sydney in broad daylight.

Another man was jailed in East Africa having been caught on his way back to Melbourne and Adelaide armed with two automatic machine guns with the aim of eliminating the principals of an Australian wildlife smuggling operation.

Some individuals who dared to speak out about wildlife smuggling and related rackets in the 1970s have been killed. According to journalist Dick Wordley, at least 'six men had gone down in eight months in lobster pots behind the Sydney Heads.' The bodies were 'sawn, cut up and dropped behind the Heads. The lobsters took the flesh, the sea lice took the rest and there was nothing left.'

Bird breeder Joseph Mattinson was found dead after a tractor rolled on him at Fairy Meadow, New South Wales. He had been a double agent for Customs officials and it was alleged he'd been murdered before he could expose key people in smuggling rackets.

Many others have been beaten or harassed into silence over the years since then.

MY PERSONAL INVOLVEMENT

Perhaps it was an incident in May 1981 that led me to write this book. After about five years of gathering evidence and tracking down the principals involved in wildlife smuggling, I finally discovered who was responsible for sending vast quantities of wildlife out of Australia. I knew how rare and exotic birds and reptiles were being obtained by traders. In fact my own reptile collection had lost specimens to wildlife smugglers who had broken into my facility on several occasions. I knew how wildlife was being shipped out of the country, more often than not via Mascot Airport, Sydney; and I knew who was buying the animals in countries such as the U.S.A., U.K., Holland and West Germany.

In fact, not only had I obtained a complete picture of who was plundering our natural resources and how, but I also discovered that the wildlife smuggling rackets were often quite different to what was being reported in the media at the time. The rackets didn't usually involve the highly publicised 90% death rate of smuggled fauna, supposedly caused by cruel treatment of the animals. This was mostly a myth. As a bird trafficker once said, 'There's no money in dead birds.' The reality was that virtually all wildlife leaving Australia through illegal channels arrived at its destination alive and well.

However, I did find that wildlife smuggling rackets were in other ways even more cruel than anyone imagined, both to the animals themselves and to the people who spent their time and money either trying to conserve wildlife or attempting to expose the corruption that is part and parcel of most wildlife smuggling in Australia. On 8 May 1981, the smugglers, whom I'd been white-anting for so long, struck back.

Tied to a chair in my lounge room, I witnessed my house being taken apart by five employees of three Government departments. These men had taken more than a passing interest in my desire to expose wildlife smuggling rackets. A week earlier I had been contacted by a journalist to produce a story in the *Australian* newspaper about the illegal trade in wildlife out of Australia and the role of corrupt Government employees.

Unknown to me, my telephone had been tapped for some months and the break-in had been timed to coincide with an overseas holiday by my parents who lived at the house. The journalist's approach had necessitated an earlier break-in. All my files were removed, I was harassed, the house was 'trashed' and as an afterthought, some 14 of my snakes held for research purposes were stolen. The alibi for the break-in was that I had illegally imported a rattlesnake and a viper, although no evidence or reason for this was ever produced by anyone. In 1990, the New South Wales National Parks and Wildlife service admitted in writing that the charge had been trumped up.

It was at this point I decided that those who were promoting the illegal trade in wildlife should come under some form of public scrutiny.

Subsequent legal action against the New South Wales National Parks and Wildlife Service resulted in an out of court settlement between my father and the then director Don Johnstone — some of the stolen snakes were returned to me in July the same year. The remainder I presume to have been sent overseas.

What happened to me later is too complex to detail in a book dealing principally with wildlife smuggling. I was subject to harassment by Government officials in three States and by various Government departments.

Worth repeating here is the story of a female journalist who chose not to be named, and who was investigating wildlife smuggling. She decided to infiltrate the trade and paid a visit to a well-known exporter with official connections. She told the exporter she wanted to get involved in the trade. However, she must have aroused suspicions, as that night she received a telephone call telling her to meet someone with more information at a quiet city location. When the journalist arrived at her rendezvous, no one seemed to be present and the area was dark and quiet. Just as she decided to leave, she was grabbed by two men, who held her down on the roadway while another man ran over her with a car. She was left in agony with two broken legs until someone later found her and took her to a nearby hospital. She left the country as soon as she was able.

These stories illustrate the seriousness of the problem and the ruthlessness of those involved.

SMUGGLING IN AUSTRALIA

Within Australia, about 20 people a year are convicted of wildlife smuggling offences by Australian authorities. Those convicted are usually 'small-timers' in terms of the number of specimens they smuggle, often no more than two or three animals. Most 'big-time' smugglers escape, as evidenced by the continuing flow of wildlife out of Australia. In terms of actual dollars, the penalties awarded by the courts, although rising in value, remain substantially lower than the average value of wildlife smuggled.

Who is Involved?

Despite media reports to the contrary, the illgal trade in Australian wildlife continues unabated. It involves corruption of officials worldwide, with Australia being part of this global network. There isn't necessarily a 'Mr Big' of wildlife smuggling, but there are plenty of 'Big enoughs'.

Due to the enormous sums of money made by wildlife smugglers (sometimes thousands of dollars for a single animal) it is logical that organised crime should become involved in such operations. These people tend to know where they stand in terms of other crime rackets; they keep to their own turf and don't encroach upon one another. However, those involved in different types of criminal operations will seek assistance from one another in combating those who seek to expose their operations. So, for example, corrupt fauna officials engage the assistance of corrupt police, judges, magistrates, Telecom officials and others who have no direct connection to wildlife trafficking. Should the opportunity arise, favours may be repaid and the cycle of mutual help by otherwise-unconnected criminals continues.

The all-pervasiveness of official corruption is amazing. In the late 1980s in New South Wales, Australian Bird Traders (A.B.T.) set up a fighting fund to fight the National Parks and Wildlife Service (henceforth referred to in this book as N.P.W.S.) and their activities in promoting illegal trade in wildlife.

A Reptile Keepers Association (R.K.A.) had already formed in New South Wales to fight smugglers who broke into people's houses and took reptiles for smuggling purposes.

Both these organisations have made lengthy representations to fauna authorities and the Minister for the Environment. They asked for changes to legislation governing the keeping and trading in wildlife, in a bid to remove theft problems faced by keepers and curtail the illegal activities of some enforcement officers. They got nowhere.

The Drug Connection

The connection between drug trafficking and wildlife trafficking has often been noted in the media. Despite this, each operation involves a different type of 'expertise' and criminals taking part in these rackets usually are involved only in one or the other, not both. Occasionally, wildlife smugglers may be found in possession of drugs such as marijuana, but in small quantities for personal consumption.

Cases of drug smugglers using a highly venomous snake to guard the haul have been reported by the media, but the snakes in question are rarely valuable species. For example, during the late 1970s and early 1980s a licensed snake keeper in the Sydney suburb of Turramurra used a highly aggressive and dangerous eastern brown snake (*Pseudonaja textilis*) to guard a marijuana crop growing in the snake's cage, which was a specially converted bedroom in his house. That he never got into trouble with the law, may have had as much to do with having a close friend in the New South Wales police force as the fact that the snake guarded the plants.

Other cases involving wildlife have occurred. Snakes have been transported with drugs in their cages and dead birds have sometimes been opened so drugs could be inserted into their carcasses before being sewn up. The birds were then shipped with live birds so that officials who viewed the consignment would reasonably assume that the dead birds had died in transit rather than being 'plants'. Similar methods are used to illegally export duty-free precious stones and other valuables.

CASE MATERIAL

Many of the cases cited in this book may appear 'old' in that they span the last 20 years. One has to realise the difficulty in obtaining specific case information relating to wildlife trafficking operations at the time they occur.

INTRODUCTION

Subjudice rules and the reluctance of people to talk at the time of the 'incidents' often result in information being concealed for a while. The soothing effect of time allows people to talk about their previous illegal dealings, without fear of prosecution. One example is New South Wales Aboriginal Commissioner Steve Gordon who spoke out about smuggling and official corruption. Honest enforcement officials from Customs departments and wildlife authorities tend to 'go public' about their corrupt associates only after they have left their job, collected their retirement benefits and no longer fear retribution, financial or otherwise, from their former colleagues or employers.

Quite often people are named in this book for their involvement in particular smuggling operations. I have named these people for several reasons. Firstly, so that readers may verify all the information in the book as being true and correct. This may be done from the sources cited in Chapter 16. In particular, case material previously published by Michael Schooley (ex-Customs), Dick Wordley (journalist), Fia Cumming (journalist) and others formed an excellent basis from which to start the research for this book.

In preparing the book, I have also relied on tape recorded conversations made by me or others, often when one or more parties to the conversation were unaware they were being taped. I have retained these tapes and transcripts to indemnify myself from potential legal action, should anyone question the factual nature of some of the material used here.

Secondly, it is in the public interest for wildlife trafficking rackets to be exposed and so stop future rackets before they gain a foothold. Some people named here have certainly paid their penalty to society. Some have reformed and joined the conservation movement. Unfortunately, others have yet to be brought to justice and in the current political climate are unlikely ever to be taken to court.

The preparation of a book such as this has been a difficult task, particularly in terms of dealing with the complex matters involved in a simplified and sequential order. It has been unavoidable that certain themes and names have recurred. It has not always been logical to cover all incidents relating to a given person or organisation in a single part of the book. Consequently people and organisations may be referred to more than once in differing contexts.

Some readers may detect a slight bias in favour of my coverage of reptile-related matters. The reason for this is simple. I am principally a 'reptile man' having been actively involved in herpetology (the study of reptiles) for over 20 years. I have a more distant association with and knowledge of other groups of animals.

THE FUTURE
This book is a correlation of facts to describe a problem that has existed for at least 20 years and some of the later pages attempt to offer, in part at least, a solution to the problem.

Australian problems with illegal wildlife trafficking are related to similar problems elsewhere. It is fair to say that Australia's problems are the world's. Likewise, wildlife conservation problems in other countries are also the responsibility of Australians.

Legalising Fauna Export
Although the export of almost all wildlife to or from Australia is currently

5

illegal, there are several good arguments for legalising the wildlife trade. If overseas buyers wish to keep as pets the kangaroos we shoot as pests, and are willing to pay a lot of money to do so, why should they be stopped? Similarly, galahs (*Cacatua roseicapilla*), which sell in pet shops here for $10, and are shot as pests in their thousands each year, sell in the U.S.A. for US$2 500 each. Surely a controlled export of these birds would be sensible.

The problem at the moment is that while trade in wildlife is illegal, organised crime can and will move in to fill the demand. Once organised crime has established itself as the major wildlife dealer in Australia, it only stands to reason that these people will go out of their way to protect their interests. This includes trying to perpetuate laws that enable criminal rackets to continue and make enormous profits.

On a recent television programme dealing with wildlife smuggling, 'John Laws World', Marie McCaskill of the New South Wales branch of the R.S.P.C.A. summed up the current problem when she said

'We in the R.S.P.C.A. have over many many years had a lot to do with both Customs and National Parks and Wildlife ... it is probably beneficial to keep the laws as they are, because there are a lot of people within Government circles and out of Government circles who are in fact benefiting from the graft of this trade, and I think it is about time it got cleaned right up for the benefit of the animals as well as for the benefit of the Government.'

Before detailing different types of smuggling activity, it is necessary to explain the factors that created the demand for wildlife in the first place: who is willing to pay enormous sums of money for our animals and why?

THE SUN-HERALD, January 19, 1992   7

Sydney search in bird racket breakthrough

By MATT CONDON

CUSTOMS officers issued search warrants in Sydney last night for evidence relating to an international bird smuggling ring which was smashed in the US yesterday.

The operation followed the arrest of a New Zealander in Los Angeles yesterday, when Customs officers seized hundreds of live Australian cockatoos.

US authorities said the arrest capped a three-year undercover investigation into bird smuggling in Australia, New Zealand and the US.

Rare and valuable Australian cockatoos were smuggled into New Zealand, falsely documented as captive-bred wildlife and then exported to the US, the US Interior Department said.

Australian cockatoos sell for $A13,500 to $A27,000 each on the US market.

Customs spokesman Alastair Wilson said yesterday several search warrants had been issued in Sydney and in other States.

"There have been no arrests here but we will be forwarding summonses soon," Mr Wilson said. "This was a very significant smuggling ring which has now been cracked."

The international wildlife trade is estimated at $5 billion a year by the US Fish and Wildlife Service. Nearly 30 per cent of the trade is believed to be illegal.

"The time has come to stop this practice," said service director John Turner. He said the US was also a conduit for rare birds from Africa to New Zealand and Australia.

Australian Customs said no extradition would be sought over the latest arrest.

INTRODUCTION

1 Not all trade in wildlife is illegal. Legal trade in wildlife is commonplace and is not a problem. Throughout Australia and elsewhere, strict laws govern what wildlife may or may not be traded. Well-known, licensed institutions such as public zoos may trade relatively freely in wildlife. Zoos commonly exchange animals for breeding programmes, to replace dead specimens needed for exhibitions and similar purposes. Private individuals and dealers are usually prohibited or restricted in trading wildlife.

2 Wildlife smuggling is taken here to include all illegal trade in wildlife, including species subject to statutory protection: i.e. the trade which occurs outside the laws of at least one given State or country. Wildlife legally obtained by a person or institution may have been illegally obtained by someone else in the first place and is therefore still considered to be smuggled wildlife.

However, wildlife taken illegally from the wild may be kept at the point of capture, e.g. in the case of a farmer who takes a protected possum and keeps it as a pet. Such cases could not be treated as smuggling, but rather as the keeping of wildlife illegally, a separate issue. Wildlife smuggling almost always involves the transportation of wildlife, which is usually illegal.

Smuggling activity usually has a series of stages: obtaining the wildlife, usually by capture or theft from a facility, transportation and sale. Only one stage needs to be illegal for it to be defined as wildlife smuggling. If all stages are legal it cannot be defined as smuggling.

3 Large-scale wildlife smuggling is typically dependant on laws that make the equivalent legal trade in wildlife either impossible or so difficult that going through illegal channels is the far easier option. This is the main reason for the illegal trade in wildlife to and from Australia and in other countries where similar legislation exists.

Wildlife laws usually restrict taking rare or endangered species from the wild other than in exceptional circumstances. Most current keepers of threatened and endangered wildlife hold it with the purpose of breeding in captivity. Some are also interested in financial gain.

4 Endangered animals, although forming a significant proportion of what is smuggled, are not the major portion of it. Most of what is smuggled is regarded as rare in terms of its availability to the purchasers in a particular State or country, and may not necessarily reflect their abundance in the wild. Some parrots, for example, shot in their thousands as pests in Australia, are called 'rare' in the U.S.A. and may sell for thousands of dollars there.

5 Many private individuals who are otherwise law-abiding citizens have participated in wildlife smuggling in order to own otherwise unobtainable wildlife species. These people constitute the overwhelming bulk of the market for smuggled fauna and are the principal reason for the existence of smuggling practices.

6 Large-scale wildlife smugglers are businessmen in the true sense of the word, and their activities are governed by the fundamental laws of business,

including those of supply and demand. Smugglers of wildlife must compete (at the sale end) with other sources of supply, including those who smuggle the same species and others who breed the species in captivity. Elimination of competition is a major objective of smugglers and this is achieved principally by putting other smugglers out of business and by eliminating captive breeding to keep given species 'rare' in terms of availability.

Most major wildlife smuggling operations from Australia carry out undetectable sterilisation of all stock to prevent captive breeding and long-term price declines. The method usually used is to give the animal several doses of X-rays which neutralise the reproductive capacity of the sex cells. This is perhaps smuggling's most harmful side effect on conservation.

7 Australian wildlife is among the most sought-after in the world, with Australian reptiles and birds commonly being the most expensive animals on overseas price lists. With the relatively small Australian domestic market, less than 20 000 000 people, versus a combined total of over 500 000 000 in Europe, Japan and North America, the ratio of wildlife leaving the country to what comes in is far higher. Internationally, Australia is therefore regarded as a 'source' country for wild species and not as an importing nation. Importation of wildlife into Australia is not currently regarded as a major problem.

8 Although most keepers of Australian fauna in foreign countries keep wildlife legally, many don't; others will break the law if it is the only way to keep a given species. The demand for illegal specimens therefore, is nearly as great as the demand for legal ones.

9 Although wildlife smuggling may be and usually is cruel to the smuggled animals, most animals smuggled within Australia and to and from this country, are physically treated very well by those who eventually end up keeping them.

Smuggling isn't always harmful to the species either, or to long-term conservation of wildlife in general. In relation to these issues, each smuggling act must be assessed on a case by case basis.

10 Australia is a signatory to a number of international treaties involving wildlife protection, perhaps most notably the Convention In Trade In Endangered Species (C.I.T.E.S.). The treaty is non-political in that most countries of the world are signatories and it gives some limited legal protection to a nation's wildlife after it leaves that nation. Although originally put in place to reduce smuggling of wildlife, the treaty has apparently failed in that wildlife smuggling remains prolific.

For example, although a signatory of the C.I.T.E.S. treaty, the United Arab Emirates was one of many nations openly flouting the provisions of the treaty in its wildlife trade throughout the 1980s. Notification to parties number 366, from the C.I.T.E.S. secretariat, in the mid-1980s urged all C.I.T.E.S. parties to prohibit trade in C.I.T.E.S. listed species with the U.A.E. The request was ignored by most signatories, and was just one of many examples indicating the limited value of the treaty and the lack of enforcement power by either the C.I.T.E.S. secretariat or participating nations.

11 In many parts of the northern hemisphere there is almost completely free trade in legally held or obtained wildlife. Legally held wildlife may be exported to almost anyone else in other 'open' countries. Consequently, wildlife may be traded freely between, for example, Germany and Holland virtually without restriction. International wildlife protection treaties have little if any relevance to this free trade in captive wildlife.

12 A detailed outline of the methods used to procure specimens from the wild is beyond the scope of this book, but one can say with certainty that at the present time it is possible to remove any specimen of any species from the wild, if there is a will to do so. Collection methods for reptiles and frogs are explained at length in my book *Australian Reptiles and Frogs* and for mammals and birds in the book *The Animal Smugglers* by John Nichol.

Most wildlife is smuggled out of Australia by plane — through the postal system, in luggage on a commercial flight, on a person or by private plane. Reptiles are usually placed in bags inside boxes, while birds are placed either in well-ventilated plastic tubes in suitcases (when tranquillised) or more openly in bird cages. Smuggled fish are usually transported in plastic bags with water. Mammals and birds are tranquillised with a variety of drugs, although Valium ™ appears to be most widely used.

Reptiles are relatively easy to smuggle. Frogs need to be kept moist and fish need to be kept wet. Birds and mammals are most difficult to smuggle being noisy if untranquillised, prone to overheating if confined, (a problem sometimes combated by placing ice packs or similar in the consignments) and often need regular feeding.

13 Wildlife smugglers like to launder their animals, by making illegally held animals legal. The usual means of doing this is to ship animals through an intermediate State or country where permits for re-export may be obtained. Animals smuggled from Australia are usually transhipped through South-east Asia or Europe. From here they are sent legally to the U.S.A. where they either remain or may be legally re-exported again.

As a result of a court case in New Zealand in 1987, New Zealand authorities sometimes issue export permits for species not native to the country, making it a useful transhipment country for smugglers of Australian wildlife.

1
WHO WANTS OUR WILDLIFE?

Aviculture (the keeping of birds in aviaries) has been a popular pastime in Europe for hundreds of years. With European settlement of North America, Australia and elsewhere, this hobby has spread to many parts of the globe. Greater interest in wild animals and more leisure time have also increased the number of people taking up aviculture as a hobby.

Until the 1960s, bird keepers found it difficult to breed most species of birds. To keep their aviaries full, they had to source new specimens from the wild. Therefore those who trapped wild birds for bird dealers acted as a major drain on populations of wild birds.

Although 50 years ago keeping methods were so crude that it was cruel to keep birds in captivity, this is not the case today. Most captive birds now outlive their wild counterparts due to improved cage designs, medical treatment and other husbandry techniques. Through methods such as 'orphaning' and 'fostering', bird keepers can encourage birds to breed far more prolifically than they do in the wild.

The popularity of keeping reptiles, though perhaps incomprehensible to some readers, is nevertheless increasing, and today nearly as many people keep pet snakes and lizards as birds. Native mammals are less popular as pets, but frogs and native fish are kept by other hobbyists. The desire for rarer species is almost universal among hobbyists and is a major source of demand for all these animals.

PRIVATE INDIVIDUALS OVERSEAS
Australia has a relatively small population compared with the U.S.A. or Europe, so there are far more people in these countries interested in keeping wildlife in cages or small private zoos. Since the export of Australian fauna was banned in the 1960s, our fauna has become relatively hard to obtain, apart from a few species which had already been bred overseas. Most Australian birds and reptiles have been sought after by keepers in these countries since the ban.

WHO WANTS OUR WILDLIFE?

To gauge the magnitude of the potential market for Australian fauna, one only has to look at a few statistics. In the U.S.A. alone there are almost a 100 regional herpetological (reptile-keeping) societies, each with an average membership of about 300. It is fair to assume that even allowing for cross-subscription of societies, and taking into account people who either don't keep reptiles or have less than ten live specimens, the actual number of people with reptile holdings in excess of ten specimens outnumbers society memberships by a ratio of at least 5:1. This means that in the U.S.A. there are about 15 000 reptile keepers who may want Australian species. A quick perusal of dealers' price-lists, reveals that Australian species are commonly seen on these lists and are among the most expensive.

To get an idea of the full magnitude of the demand, one also has to consider the markets of Europe and Japan — the rest of the world seems to be less interested in keeping Australian wildlife.

In 1989, about 18 000 ball pythons (*Python regius*) were imported into the U.S.A. from Togo and Ghana in Africa. These each sold for an average of US$80 each. More were sold in other countries. When one considers that a typical U.S. dealer's price list contains an average of 100 reptile species of which about five are usually Australian, even allowing for captive breedings, it is clear that thousands of Australian reptiles are being smuggled out of the country each year.

A price list from a reputable, legal New York dealer dated early autumn 1990, listed three unrelated adult Australian black-headed pythons (*Aspidites melanocephalus*) for US$14 000 the trio. The same price list was offering a diamond python (*Morelia spilota spilota*), a common snake around Sydney and nearby areas, for US$3 750.

People who keep these snakes pay huge prices for them on the assumption that they will breed these 'rare' (i.e. hard to obtain) species and sell the offspring for similar prices, hence profiting immensely from the operation. If the advertised black-headed pythons produced nine fertile eggs per year for two succesive years — a realistic projection — the breeder/purchaser stands to earn up to US$80 000 by selling the offspring. Profits for breeding harder to obtain snakes such as ant-hill pythons (*Bothrochilus perthensis*) or rough-scaled pythons (*Morelia carinata*), both from Western Australia, which would possibly sell for up to US$20 000 each, would be correspondingly greater.

The position with regard to birds is similar to that of reptiles. Hence the assertion by many witnesses in the 1975-76 House of Representatives Inquiry into Wildlife Smuggling that the demand for Australian fauna is 'insatiable'. Some Australian parrots sell for up to US$30 000 a pair. It seems, however, that although Australian birds are commoner in captivity outside Australia than Australian reptiles, the prices paid for Australian reptiles are usually greater.

A media report in 1988 estimated the total American trade in Australian fauna to be in excess of US$100 000 000 per annum, of which between half and a third was illegally imported. On the assumption that about 1 000 diamond pythons are imported illegally into the U.S.A. per year from Australia (a reasonable estimate) and they have an average market value of US$1 000 for males and US$3 000 for females, then the potential market for this snake alone is worth US$2 000 000.

Remembering that Australia has over 20 species and subspecies of python, about 1 000 other species of reptile and frog, and more than 700 bird species, then the potential size of the market can be imagined.

In terms of outright numbers of birds from all countries sold in the U.S.A. and Europe, the figure is in excess of 2 000 000 live birds annually. Over 500 000 birds pass through England's Heathrow Airport each year. About 100 000 are for the U.K. market while the remainder go mainly to Germany, Holland, Belgium, France and Switzerland.

Fewer reptiles are sold than birds, but the number is still enormous.

The power of the overseas demand for Australian fauna is so great that in 1976 after a new species, the Oenpelli python (*Morelia oenpelliensis*) was discovered and scientifically described from a single specimen, multiple specimens were caught and illegally traded within six months.

Those who keep Australian fauna overseas spend thousands of dollars setting up their wildlife-keeping facilities. To pay large amounts of money for the animals themselves is not seen as a major problem.

The first person in the world to breed in captivity Storr's monitors (*Varanus storri*) was Richard Bartlett, a resident of Fort Meyers, Florida, U.S.A., who somehow legally obtained the original specimens after they had been smuggled into the U.S.A. from Queensland, Australia, through a dealer in West Germany. The three offspring (the species produces three eggs at a time) could have been sold for over US$1 000 each.

New Zealander arrested over bird smuggling ring

By LUCY MACKEN

The alleged ringleader of an international bird smuggling ring has been arrested and more arrests are expected this week after raids around Australia, New Zealand and the United States at the weekend.

US officials claim New Zealander Philip Morrison is largely responsible for the bird smuggling syndicate, which has operated from Australia to the US, via a corridor through New Zealand.

Australian Customs officers are considering whether to make further arrests this morning or to wait until more evidence is gathered.

The raids, which took place around Australia on Saturday, seized captive birds and documents, mainly in Brisbane and Sydney.

The international investigation is aimed at breaking a bird smuggling syndicate in all three countries which is worth about $50 million a year, according to Customs authorities.

Special agents of the US Fish and Wildlife Service arrested Morrison in Los Angeles after he arrived on a New Zealand flight.

The US investigations have been conducted over the past three years and Australian authorities have become involved in the past year.

An Australian Customs spokesman in Brisbane, Mr Leon Bedington, said US officials claimed Morrison had been involved in bird smuggling for two to three years.

Information about illegal smuggling in Australia was passed on to authorities through a confidential hotline. People with information can phone (06) 247 6666.

Monday, January 20, 1992 **5**   The Sydney Morning Herald

ZOOS

Most Western cities of over 1 000 000 people have at least one major city zoo. The demand by zoos is as great as that of private individuals or hobbyists and also fuels smuggling rackets. Dallas Zoo is well known as having perhaps the best collection of Australian reptiles *anywhere*. Species that have never been legally exported from Australia are seen in Dallas Zoo. No one at this zoo has ever been prosecuted for illegally importing wildlife from Australia, either directly or indirectly, and it may well have obtained species legally.

Zoos are usually run as commercial or semi-commercial enterprises. If a given zoo has an animal that no other zoo has, it may be able to promote the fact and thereby increase gate receipts and profits. As Australian species are relatively rare in overseas zoos, the demand for them is always great. Even so-called non-profit zoos such as Whipsnade in the U.K. actively seek rare species to help finance operations.

Both Japanese and American zoos have payed huge amounts of money for platypus (*Ornithorhynchus anatinus*), koalas (*Phascolarctos cinereus*) and sugar gliders (*Petarus breviceps*), not always legally imported. It is notable that the money spent on looking after these animals and the relative breeding success of zoos and individuals, rises in direct proportion to the amount of money paid for the original specimens.

Both zoo keepers and private individuals may suffer from the so-called 'stamp collector syndrome'. Just as a stamp collector will attempt to collect as many different types of stamp as possible, so wildlife keepers may attempt to obtain as many different types of fauna as they can.

Overseas Wildlife Smuggled into Australia

Although the illegal trade in wildlife leaving Australia is far more serious than that of wildlife coming into Australia, there is also a significant illegal trade in this area. The demand within Australia for non-indigenous wildlife remains large and, to a great extent, unsatisfied.

Zoo keepers in Australia are as likely as their overseas counterparts to be affected by the 'stamp collector syndrome'. Accordingly, the temptation to illegally import wildlife is great. Private hobbyists are similarly tempted. In 1991 there were some 12 herpetological societies in Australia each with a membership averaging over 100. There were more than 70 avicultural organisations in Australia at the time, again with each organisation having an average of more than 100 members.

Testimony to the demand for overseas wildlife in Australia comes in the form of regular seizures by Customs officials of small numbers of wildlife brought in by people returning from trips overseas. Animals recovered by officials probably only represent the tip of the iceberg in terms of what actually comes into the country. During the 1980s I knew of about ten individual reptile keepers in Sydney's eastern suburbs who went to the U.S.A. each year on holiday with the specific purpose of obtaining reptiles to bring home. They would purchase from pet shops and dealers various species including indigo snakes (*Drymarchon corais*), corn snakes (*Elaphe guttata*), land tortoises of various species, Jackson's chameleons (*Chameleo jacksoni*) and yellow anacondas (*Eunectes notaeus*). These reptiles, presumably smuggled into the country in luggage, were never detected either when being imported into the country, or later by fauna officials.

Worth mentioning is that birds' eggs are also smuggled. Birds' eggs are sometimes collected by hobbyists who collect just the eggs and have no interest in keeping live birds. Other people smuggle the eggs to incubate and hatch at a later stage, finding the eggs easier to smuggle than live birds. As eggs naturally get turned about after being laid, the movement of birds' eggs by smugglers doesn't in itself adversely affect the eggs.

For reptiles, however, the reverse is true. Reptile eggs are usually not moved after being laid, and doing so usually results in their death (if polarity is changed). Therefore smuggling reptile eggs isn't a viable proposition and is rarely, if ever, done.

Products of wild animals, such as skins, teeth, skeletons, and so forth are also illegally smuggled and traded, but this trade is beyond the scope of this book.

Almost all the non-Australian reptiles and many birds held in Australian zoos today have been seized by Customs and wildlife officials and donated to the zoos instead of killing them, or are the offspring of original specimens.

Snake handler in mail offence

A CAIRNS snake handler was convicted and fined after attempting to mail two protected water pythons and a carpet python to Victoria in a cardboard box.

David John Williams, 27, of Bayview Heights, Cairns, was arrested by Police Fauna Squad officers under the Fauna Conservation act.

Williams faced one charge of dealing in protected fauna in the Cairns Magistrate's Court on Thursday.

Williams pleaded guilty and Magistrate Mr Pollick fined him $120 for the offence, $180 royalties for taking the snakes which, as protected species were the property of the Crown, as well as $48.75 court costs.

A police spokesman said the maximum penalty Williams faced was $12,000 or two years imprisonment.

Sunday Sun (Queensland) 16/2/92

14

2
TYPES OF WILDLIFE SMUGGLING

Wildlife smuggling methods and operations can be placed easily into a given category on the grounds of who is doing the smuggling and why.

In explaining how the rackets operate, the following information has been sourced entirely from already published material, usually multiple sources, which are cited in Chapter 16.

There are two main categories.

OFFICIAL SMUGGLING
This accounts for about 90% of fauna leaving Australia. Easily the most sophisticated type of smuggling, it may be distinguished from other forms of wildlife smuggling on the basis that:

1 species smuggled are not kept by those who do the smuggling;

2 particular species are often smuggled to fill orders from potential buyers or dealers;

3 Government officials play a pivotal role in the initial location of specimens and subsequent organisation of the operation, and are well paid for their protection;

4 official smuggling operations tend to be the largest ones, involving numerous animals.

SPLINTER SMUGGLING
This encompasses all other forms of smuggling, including well-organised smuggling syndicates, some of which may still involve corrupt Government officials. Splinter smuggling includes:

Retail smuggling — includes all operations other than official smuggling in which wildlife is smuggled for commercial gain. It usually involves more than one person (e.g. the exporter and the seller/dealer at the final destination) and sometimes very sophisticated syndicates which use violence and other criminal means to protect their enterprises.

There is a 'grey' area in larger retail smuggling operations that may involve

PRICES IN U.S. DOLLARS OF AUSTRALIAN SPECIES OF FROG, REPTILE AND BIRD TRADED IN 1991 AS TAKEN FROM DEALER PRICE LISTS OR SIMILAR
Notes: No indication is given of age or health of specimens. Other factors such as local restrictions on keeping a given species, known sterilisations, etc., are not indicated, although the following list is believed to contain typical prices for adult specimens. It should also be noted that prices for 'pairs' and known breeders tend to be higher as do those for mutations. For some species the price of each sex varies substantially. The list below is not comprehensive and is for illustrative purposes only. Many of the animals in this list are not traded in Australia and often prices in Australia have little in common with prices in the U.S.A.. Australia has over 1 000 species of frog, reptile and bird, excluding known subspecies and other variants.

Cane toad *(Bufo marinus)* $7
Green tree frog *(Litoria caerulea)* $40
Long-necked tortoise *(Chelodina longicollis)* $600
New Guinea long-necked tortoise *(C. novaeguineae)* $400
Murray short-necked tortoise *(Emydura macquarii)* $600
Southern (Sydney) leaf-tailed gecko *(Phyllurus platurus)* $250
Pink-tongued skink *(Cyclodomorphus gerrardii)* $400
Cunningham's skink, Southern Highlands form *(Egernia cunninghami)* $300
Land mullet *(E. major)* $500
Tree skink *(E. striolata)* $80
Shingleback *(Tiliqua rugosa)* $1 000
Blue-tongued lizard (Skink) *(T. scincoides)* $200
Frill-necked lizard *(Chlamydosaurus kingii)* $800
Rankin's bearded dragon *(Pogona rankini)* $200
Common (inland) bearded dragon *(P. vitticeps)* $200
Sand goanna, west N.S.W. form *(Varanus gouldi)* $450
Mangrove monitor *(V. indicus)* $500
Green tree monitor *(V. prasinus)* $2 000
Storr's monitor *(V. storri)* $1 000
Green python *(Chondropython viridis)* $550
White-lipped python, Australian black form *(Bothrochilus albertisi)* $600
Australian water python, unmarked form *(B. fuscus)* $500
Common olive python *(B. olivaceous)* $1 000
Australian scrub python *(Morelia amethistina)* $800
Carpet python *(M. spilota)* $200-$7 000
Black-headed python *(Aspidites melanocephalus)* $5 000
Woma *(A. ramsayi)* $10 000
Sulphur-crested cockatoo *(Cacatua galerita)* $3 000
Major Mitchell *(C. leadbeateri)* $8 000
Galah *(C. roseicapilla)* $ 1 500
Long-billed corella *(C. tenuirostris)* $3 000
Gang gang *(Callocephalon fimbriatum)* $10 000
Yellow-tailed black cockatoo *(Calyptorhynchus funereus)* $9 000

AVIAN MAGIC
Specializing in Hand Fed Baby Psittacines
P.O. Box 55276 • Riverside, CA 92517-0276
(714) 683-4427
FAX (714) 683-3657

RICHARD
AND
PRISCILLA
KEIM

Avian Magic
P. O. Box 55276
Riverside, CA 92517-0276

Phone - 714 683 4427   Fax 714 683 3657

Exotic Bird Pricelist - 1992 season

Hand Fed Babies to Weaning

Citron Cockatoos	$1,000
Lesser Sulfur Crested Cockatoos	$1,000
Umbrella Cockatoos	$1,100
African Greys (Congo)	$ 900

Other Birds

Grey Cheek Parakeets (hand fed)	$ 110
Sun Conures s/s bonded pr	$ 700

17

White-tailed black cockatoo *(C. latirostris)* $9 000
Red-tailed black cockatoo *(C. magnificus)* $9 000
Bourke parrot *(Neophema bourkii)* $40
Blue-winged parrot *(N. chrysostoma)* $100
Scarlet-chested parrot *(N. splendida)* $50
Scarlet-chested parrot, par blue *(N. splendida)* $250
Scarlet-chested Parrot, white-fronted blue *(N. splendida)* $500
Port Lincoln parrot *(Platycercus zonarius)* $300
Princess parrot *(Polytelis alexandrae)* $200
Princess parrot, blue *(P. alexandrae)* $450
Princess parrot, lutino *(P. alexandrae)* $1 000
Princess parrot, albino *(P. alexandrae)* $1 500
Regent parrot *(P. anthopeplus)* $100
Regent parrot, yellow *(P. anthopeplus)* $140
Superb parrot *(P. swainsonii)* $150
Palm cockatoo *(Probosciger aterrimus)* $20 000
Golden-shouldered parrot *(Psephotus chrysopterygius)* $2 000
Hooded parrot *(P. dissimilis)* $800

SCIENCE BAFFLED

Dealers who refuse to disclose their sources may play havoc with museum-based scientists.

Most reptile people in Australia are familiar with two types of freshwater tortoise. Both are common in captivity but until recently no-one knew where they came from in the wild. As there is no 'type-locality', neither can be formally described and given a proper species name. The two are therefore known as *Emydura pet-shop-i* and *Elseya pet-shop-i*. Pet dealers in Australia, and to a lesser extent overseas, have sold these tortoises by the thousand but refuse to say exactly where they can be found.

In 1991, however, Sydney herpetologist and tortoise expert John Cann solved the mystery. Pet-shop tortoises apparently occur in certain Queensland rivers and he is in the process of describing them as new species, with one of them actually being assigned to a new genus. A distinguishing feature of one of the pet-shop tortoises is the unusually long tail in males.

ORPHANING AND FOSTERING OF BIRDS

Increasing the breeding rates of valuable birds is a major pre-occupation of commercial breeders and conservationists.

Many species of birds lay a second clutch of eggs if they lose the first during the breeding season. A rare bird may have her first eggs taken from her so that she lays a second clutch and rears those hatchlings. The eggs from the first clutch are placed in the nest of another, commoner type of bird, whose own eggs are discarded. The rare eggs are incubated and hatched by the foster bird and the young are raised as her own.

corruption of Government officials. The relatively minor involvement of these officials and their immunity from prosecution if caught differentiates large-scale retail from official smuggling operations.

Private smuggling — in which a person smuggles or transports fauna for personal use or for friends, not for commercial sale or gain. Private smuggling is often a 'one-off' operation, commonly the result of efforts by a single person who intends to keep the wildlife himself.

Counter smuggling — where wildlife is directly smuggled by experts and enthusiasts, often well known in their field, specifically for the purpose of breeding rare and endangered species in captivity. This usually takes place in a country where the given species is available from dealers who have obtained the species through official smuggling channels; counter smugglers may decide to source the species directly through their own channels to avoid wasting time and money attempting to breed sterilised stock.

Accidental smuggling — when tourists arrive home with wildlife products which are illegal imports. Their commercial value is not great enough to create a demand for the products here even though few people in Australia may possess them. It is called accidental smuggling because those who do it are usually unaware of the illegality of their acts and are not habitual offenders. Many accidental smugglers actually declare their illegal merchandise to Customs officials upon arrival in Australia. In 1988, Australian Customs officials recovered the following illegal imports: 506 stuffed marine turtles, 1 468 giant clam shells, 375 birdwing butterflies, 409 items of ivory, 500 pieces of hard coral, and 1 500 packets of Chinese medicines containing derivatives of endangered species such as rhinoceros horn and tiger bone.

The following chapters examine each type of smuggling in detail.

3
OFFICIAL SMUGGLING

Prior to the writing of this book, several State wildlife officers and Customs officials were charged and convicted with wildlife smuggling offences and other corruption-related matters. It is presumed that those charged did not represent the total number involved. More corrupt officials have been quietly dismissed or retired when their illegal activities become too much of an embarrassment to their departments.

In the magazine *Australian Birdkeeper*, former Customs Fauna Squad officer, Michael Schooley, details cases in which Government officials involved in wildlife smuggling are either not identified or not charged and convicted. The recent decline in the export of wildlife is believed to stem principally from a decline in the number of wildlife keepers in Australia and from increased overseas captive breeding of Australian species, rather than from the removal of major smuggling rackets.

In elaborating the role of Government officials in wildlife smuggling, it should be noted that most staff in the State fauna authorities, Customs and other Government departments have no involvement in, or knowledge of, such rackets. I will go further and say that the majority of employees of these organisations, in particular wildlife departments, are dedicated people with a strong concern for the environment, endangered animals and possible corruption within their organisations. Subsequent references to corrupt officials and Government departments therefore should not be regarded as attacks on the departments as a whole and, as already stated, reflect a trend worldwide. A common truism is that 'corruption is everywhere'; the potential financial rewards of corruption are as tempting to wildlife officials as anyone else.

Those Government officials involved in smuggling operations are usually placed in strategic sections where they may be useful. To quote Francis Bacon in 1598: 'Opportunity makes a thief.' Schooley documents several cases in which strategically placed Customs, airlines and other officials allowed wildlife smuggling operations to continue.

In one case, Schooley and an honest wildlife officer, Clive Bennett, raided a well-known bird trader for alleged smuggling activities. According to Schooley, the trader was protected by senior N.P.W.S. management: he was let off and Bennett was posted 'out in the wilderness somewhere'.

In another incident, Schooley recalled making a seizure only to have the material returned to the alleged offender by more senior Customs officials without consulting him.

After a number of incidents in which his efforts were white-anted by senior Customs officials, Schooley decided to quit Customs. He said 'When we started cracking the real good cases, we became a bloody nuisance.' Before leaving, senior officials persuaded Schooley not to go to the press with allegations of corruption and misconduct in his department, in relation to which he later remarked 'It was the worst thing I did.'

Licensing and law enforcement sections of wildlife departments are those most likely to have contact with wildlife keepers, dealers and smugglers and so are most likely to be corrupted. Officials are especially hard to catch, by virtue of their position. Generally, the officials are caught only when they make a very serious mistake, which is rare, or if one member of the operation falls out with another and 'dobs them in'.

THE 'SWISS CONNECTION'

In 1973, the'Swiss Connection' was exposed. It was a typical official smuggling operation involving corrupt officials and others in Australia, Switzerland and the U.S.A. The racket came unstuck when a 1.6 m (5′) taipan (*Oxyuranus scutellatus*), one of the world's fastest moving and deadliest snakes, escaped from its container in the U.S.A. and caused quite a stir.

The 'Swiss Connection' was broken up by U.S. Customs officials. A single consignment involved about 150 snakes, lizards and crocodiles despatched from Queensland through Switzerland, where they were laundered to a well-known wildlife dealer in Philadelphia.

The 'Swiss Connection' continued, however. In 1974, Customs officials became suspicious about a shipment of 350 reptiles from Switzerland to Pennsylvania. Australian species featured prominently in the arrivals and included death adders (*Acanthophis antarcticus*) wholesaled at $300 each and pythons of various species traded at about $1 000 each. By the time a Federal Grand Jury in Philadelphia, U.S.A., indicted 12 persons in August 1977, for scheming to smuggle reptiles into the U.S.A., over 1 000 rare reptiles were known to have been illegally imported. Unrecorded shipments could have been significantly higher.

Evidence was also produced which implied that most, if not all, Australian specimens had been sourced from collections within Australia, as opposed to having been recently trapped in the wild. The number of specimens involved indicated that a substantial number of collections must have contributed to the stock of reptiles imported to the U.S.A.

All the animals had been shipped illegally on commercial flights. All 12 men charged were convicted between September 1977 and June the following year. Although no zoo officials were among those charged, eight zoos and their staff were recipients of the reptiles. These included officials from the National Zoo in Washington, D.C., St. Louis and Philadelphia Zoos. The Australian specimens, the major component of the consignment, were alleged to have been initially sourced illegally from a contact at Sydney's Taronga Zoo, who in turn sourced specimens from State fauna officials. Certainly many, if not all reptiles stolen, seized and otherwise obtained by N.P.W.S. officials from collections in New South Wales in the mid to late 1970s were being passed on to Taronga Zoo.

In attempting to distance himself from claims of deliberately purchasing stolen reptiles, Theodore Reed, director of the National Zoo in Washington said 'We purchased these animals from dealers we thought were reputable . . . it was legally.' 'U.S. News and World Report' stated that such disclaimers would not satisfy those 'from whom the reptiles were stolen . . . American Zoos want rare animals so badly that they sometimes close their eyes to the source of their purchases.' U.S. Customs representative Peter Paypool stated that 'the major culprits facilitating these illegal activities are zoos.' After this racket was exposed, another U.S. Customs official was quoted as saying 'We're trying to take the big guys out of the game.' 'U.S. News and World Report' went on to say 'If this happens, it may mean a new lease on life for many animal species threatened with extinction.'

SOURCES OF SUPPLY

In order to obtain wildlife for smuggling purposes, one may either capture it in the wild or use captive sources. The superiority in health and condition of well-kept captive stock is well documented and therefore long-term captive specimens are most desired by wildlife smugglers. Before a House of Representatives Inquiry into fauna trafficking in 1975-76, a long-term investigator of wildlife smuggling operations from a State fauna authority stated categorically that 'I have never come across birds that are actually trapped from the wild and exported.' Schooley also seemed to think that most smuggled birds came from captive sources.

Wild-caught stock are expensive to capture and may be in poor health, often suffering from parasites and finding it difficult to adjust to captive conditions and survive the ordeal of transportation and a variety of handlers.

As the smugglers have no desire to keep large numbers of fauna in captivity for long periods at great expense, an alternative means of obtaining supply is needed.

Unfortunately there is only one other source of supply — other people who have captive stock. As few if any Australian keepers of sought-after species will freely part with their stock, the only remaining way to obtain these animals is to steal them. It is here that problems of wildlife smuggling start and participation by corrupt Government officials becomes essential.

Due to their fear of having specimens stolen, many wildlife keepers become secretive and hesitate to tell anyone what they actually keep. This is particularly true for those who keep reptiles and birds, the most smuggled forms of wildlife.

Licensing Laws

From the late 1960s onwards there has been a progressive tightening of the laws governing the keeping of native wildlife species, resulting in statutory protection of most native species in all Australian States. Licensing systems to cover all keepers have been set up and are administered by State fauna authorities. Consequently, in theory the only people who know who holds what wildlife and where, are the licensing and law enforcement officials in these Government departments. Around the world as statutory protection of wildlife has become more widespread, it is these officials who have become an important link in all major smuggling rackets.

At the time of writing it was reported in the *Age* newspaper that there were about 20 000 fauna licence holders in New South Wales alone and about half that number in Victoria, so the value of access to wildlife registers is quite obvious.

Throughout Australia, a correlation has been noted between new licensing laws for wildlife and break-ins of facilities where these animals were kept. It also became apparent that those without permits for wildlife (who therefore held it illegally) were less likely to have their specimens stolen, regardless of the legality of their activities.

As early as 1979, crime reporter Bob Bottom noted the trend of licensed keepers having their wildlife taken by smugglers. In the August 21 issue of the *Bulletin* magazine that year, Bottom documented a case involving the theft of 400 birds from a pet shop in the southern Sydney suburb of Kogarah. Bottom stated that 'it was obvious that the stolen birds were destined for foreign markets.' Within Australia the birds were worth an estimated $10 000. Bottom had noted 'the birds, mostly exotic parrots, were all said to have been registered with the National Parks and Wildlife Service.'

What specimens are stolen and from which keepers appears to be dictated by demand from wildlife dealers in other countries, mainly in Europe and the U.S.A. Many wildlife dealers outside Australia have proudly boasted that they could obtain anything from anywhere, regardless of the legality of the act. In a 1979 price list, 'Parrot Jungle' a trading operation based in New York advertised 'If it's not extinct we can get it. If it is, we will still try. Time needed for endangered species.' Where the stock came from, clearly wasn't of concern to the trader.

A well-known dealer in Singapore, Christopher Wee, was quoted as saying that he could get any bird or any snake and some animals from Australia as long as people pre-ordered them.

Michael Schooley also documents two cases involving a single well-known smuggling identity who broke into zoos to steal Australian parrots for illegal export elsewhere.

The largest exposed operation that imported and exported wildlife illegally in the history of the U.S.A. was called the Atlanta Wildlife Exchange. It regularly traded in Australian fauna sourced from established channels here. After being exposed in the early 1980s it was discovered that the principals of that operation were none other than officials from the Fish and Wildlife Service, whose supposed enforcement role in that country was similar to that of State fauna officials here. (See Chapter 12 for a detailed account of the Atlanta Wildlife Exchange).

Break-ins to wildlife keeping facilities may be perpetrated either by civilians or by fauna officials themselves. The advantages of fauna officials doing the break-ins are clear.

It is inevitable that if break-ins are conducted on a regular basis, those committing the crime will eventually be caught. While a professional thief would in due course be jailed, a corrupt law enforcement officer can invent an alibi for committing the crime. Corrupt officials can accuse a keeper of having been put in by a mate for stealing animals from the local zoo, refuse to give further details and be unlikely to face any reprisals from either the keeper or anyone in their department.

The fact that the wildlife keeper is dependant on those same officials for the continued issuing of any permits to keep his animals, increases the likelihood of no action being taken against them for fear of later reprisals in the form of no permits.

N.P.W.S.

In 1981, in the *Australian* newspaper, Fia Cumming described at length how officials of the New South Wales N.P.W.S. broke into the facilities of several keepers of native wildlife and stole specimens.

They deliberately turned a blind eye to certain people who kept all their specimens illegally (without permits) in return for favours, such as names and addresses of other wildlife keepers or for information about anyone investigating corruption within N.P.W.S.

Also in 1981, Cumming documented that the same N.P.W.S. officials allowed another snake keeper, Craig Bennett, to keep about a dozen snakes illegally, including species listed as endangered. He had raided a computer at the News Limited head office, at Surry Hills and retrieved a forthcoming article about alleged corruption within N.P.W.S.

By the late 1970s and early 1980s break-ins and thefts of specimens became so bad in New South Wales, that many reptile and bird keepers failed to register their fauna with the N.P.W.S., for fear of losing animals. The average rate of theft of specimens from licensed reptile and bird keepers was estimated at about once every 18 months and although in most cases the person/s who stole the specimens were not seen or caught, fauna officials were allegedly involved in most of these cases.

Useful enforcement activity by the N.P.W.S. officials was minimal, although they vigorously pursued non-official smuggling operations with numerous well-publicised successful 'busts' and prosecutions during the period in question. This usually involved private smuggling netting only a few specimens.

By the late 1980s keepers' refusal to register fauna was causing supply problems of certain species overseas and therefore price rises e.g. diamond pythons tripled in price during this period.

It was alleged in 1984 that, to facilitate successful break-ins, N.P.W.S. employed illegal telephone tapping to monitor the movements of keepers and avoid being caught during a break-in, although the then deputy director of N.P.W.S., John Rex Giles, stated on national television that the service did not bug telephones, having neither the resources nor the inclination to do so.

However, in the *Weekend Australian* newspaper on 21-22 April 1990, senior N.P.W.S. officials Michael Potts and Steven Hillier related how they had monitored the telephone conversations of a person who 'was highly critical of the National Parks and Wildlife Service's activities' during this period when Giles was still in charge of their section. Potts and Hillier even recorded the telephone numbers dialed from the phone in question.

Another N.P.W.S. official John Cook, who contributed to the article in the *Weekend Australian*, led the raid on my house on 10 July 1984 when all my valuable possessions including files and snakes were taken. That the

---

BACK-LOADING

Back-loading is the practice of smuggling material in two directions when the operation initially operated one way. A classic example is when people smuggling drugs into Australia by light plane decide to ship wildlife out of Australia to fill up their empty planes. Although the racket may be profitable smuggling drugs into the country alone, the extra money made by trading in wildlife makes the venture even more profitable.

In 1981 I met a man at Port Hedland, Western Australia who had smuggled arms from Australia by small boat to Fretelin rebels in Timor some years earlier. Timor locals supplied the man with monkeys and other animals which were brought back into Australia and sold to illegal wildlife dealers.

---

break-in took place when it did wasn't a chance event: prior to that day I had planned over the telephone to arrive home from work after 9 p.m. after leaving the house at my usual time of about 8.30 a.m. The break-in took place at about midday.

Telephone bugging is also an excellent way for N.P.W.S. officials to locate other fauna keepers whom they may later 'raid'. Illegal telephone tapping by Australian Government officials, although widely denied, has been repeatedly documented by many well-known investigative journalists.

In 1990, *Australian* journalist Sally Macmillan described the methods used by N.P.W.S. officials to analyse a bird keeper's personal telephone book in connection with telephone surveillance, during the mid 1980s.

Similar activities occurred in other States. In mid-1987, the facilities of licensed Victorian bird keeper Ronald Hastings were broken into while he attended a bird society meeting. He lost over 100 birds, some worth over $6 000 each on the local and overseas markets. Detective Chief-Superintendent Kevin Holliday of the Ballarat C.I.B. who investigated the theft, stated that the birds were probably well on the way to their chosen destinations, indicating that they had been 'specifically ordered'.

Ballarat bird people certainly weren't lucky when it came to thefts. Three people stole a rare Derbyan parrot *(Psittacula derbiana)* from aviculturalist Paul Sperber of Ballarat on 24 May 1990. The thieves themselves weren't initially caught, but two days later the bird was off-loaded to bird dealer Santa Sergio Casagrande, of Willoughby Street, Reservoir, who was also given false documentation to 'authenticate' the bird.

According to Casagrande during a later court case, the 'documentation' was supposed to 'have prevented Customs officers from destroying all his birds if they believed the parrot had been smuggled into the country'.

According to Sperber, the parrot, which had allegedly been 'sold' to Casagrande for a mere $700, was in fact worth $5 000 or more. On Tuesday 20 August, Casagrande was found guilty at Heidelberg Court of receiving the stolen parrot and another pair of birds, Pekin robins *(Leiothrix lutea)* valued at $2 500, stolen from another bird keeper. He was given a $1 000, 12-month good behaviour bond and ordered to pay $3 000 to the court fund.

CUSTOMS INVOLVEMENT

Official smuggling relies on Customs officials. In countries where corruption is more open, including some northern neighbours of Australia, the involvement of Government officials in the successful export of wildlife is well documented. These officials are regarded as 'the middlemen' in the operation, as they neither obtain nor sell the wildlife, but rather aid in its transportation. These are the hardest people to expose.

Schooley documents a major official smuggling operation in which various people including at least one Qantas employee would feed unaccompanied bags containing birds onto planes at Sydney airport destined for Bangkok. These bags were slipped onto the conveyor belt beyond the final baggage check point so that they would not be discovered by security staff at the Australian end before being loaded onto the plane. (Unattended bags are treated with caution because they may contain terrorist bombs.)

Bags unclaimed by passengers at an arrival destination including Bangkok would, under normal circumstances be taken by Customs and opened, which would presumably mean that the bags containing the birds should have been detected. At the Bangkok end, an apparently well-known local official took the bags containing the birds and passed them to the next person in the smuggling chain. The involvement of this official was pivotal to the whole operation, but he was never caught.

A 1975-76 House of Representatives report claimed 'military aircraft, both Australian and foreign, are used to transport fauna, including mammals from the country.'

By having Government officials 'on side' smugglers are able to take greater care of the wildlife at all stages of the export operation and therefore ensure a very low mortality rate. Specimens available for export are always rare, and particularly when individual specimens are being exported to fill an order, there is no room for a high mortality rate. Wildlife smuggled through official channels is physically better treated than most other smuggled fauna.

A major drawback of this style of smuggling is the almost guaranteed high-dose X-raying of stock to prevent captive breeding, discussed earlier (see p. 8).

The wildlife is usually exported to an intermediate country where it is given false papers to ensure its legality in that country. From there it is 'legally' exported to a third country. The final 'legal' stage goes through wildlife dealers and does not necessarily use the same route each time, as a dealer in an intermediate country is able to export to another dealer almost anywhere else.

Schooley documents a number of specific cases of wildlife shipments being transhipped in this way; in one case, Australian birds were smuggled to Indonesia and then given false papers, stating that they had been captive bred in Indonesian aviaries, to be sold to the American market.

The competitive nature of the wildlife trade means that many dealers are willing to overlook anomalies in official papers that may accompany illegally obtained stock.

As officials in many countries are unable to accurately identify many species, it is easy for smugglers to pass off an illegal species as a legal one. Furthermore, there is nothing to stop a dealer mixing legally obtained and illegally obtained stock in a consignment to lessen the risk of detection.

As recently as 1990, a U.S. Fish and Wildlife Service official appealed for help in a herpetological journal in identifying seized reptiles exotic to the

U.S.A. Quite clearly if officials cannot tell the difference between a legal and an illegal species, then traffickers have fewer problems.

INTERNATIONAL OPERATORS

The magnitude of official smuggling operations is detailed in John Nichol's book *The Animal Smugglers*. When discussing wildlife export Nichol states 'I saw a dealer's premises in Singapore with birds worth about U.K. £50 000 000, and 95% of them were illegal and had been brought in from Indonesia and Australia; indeed many arrive quite openly by air.' Nichol also stated 'no one is in the least bit interested in trying to stop it.'

Nichol cites the case of the frill-necked lizard *(Chlamydosaurus kingii)* to demonstrate the capabilities of official smuggling rackets. In early 1984, a Japanese television commercial screened a shot of a frill-necked lizard. Overnight the lizard became a star, and the Japanese became frill-necked lizard mad.

Quick-thinking entrepreneurs promptly tried to obtain these lizards realising their now immense value if obtained live. Previously they had not been a sought-after species outside Australia, due to the relative difficulty of keeping the animal, so there was no available source of supply outside Australia or New Guinea, where the lizard lives. The fact that frilled-lizards are rarely seen in large numbers in the wild, except during the height of the wet season which was at that time effectively over, meant that the chances of trapping wild specimens were remote. Furthermore the lizard is afforded statutory protection everywhere it occurs. Japan like Australia is a signatory to the C.I.T.E.S. treaty, making both the import and export of the lizard illegal.

Certain licensed keepers in Australia who held this species suddenly found their facilities broken into; and among other things, their frill-necked lizards went missing. At least 50 frill-necked lizards were imported into Japan and put on show to the public very quickly. They were used in shopping centre displays, enabling promoters to make up to $6 000 a day in entrance fees, an amount that soon covered the substantial initial outlay for the lizards.

One of the promoters, the director of the Insect Museum in Utsunomiya, though legally entitled to import insects only, managed to get hold of 12 frill-necked lizards. Nichols alleged that another importer, Mr Naotsugu Shoji, associated with a reptile and amphibian dealership in Tokyo, managed to acquire animals which were imported via the Netherlands, while other specimens came into Japan via European countries which were apparently intermediate countries for these smuggling rackets. Nichol noted that as he tried to piece together the exact route from Australia that 'everyone started laying down smokescreens to confuse the issue.' He summed up by stating that it 'demonstrates how easily protection laws can be flouted when large profits can be made by commercial exploitation of an animal'.

MOLES

Schooley cites an interesting case involving a film crew that wanted to make a documentary about the illegal exportation of birds from Australia to Bangkok. Following a tip-off, a suitcase containing parrots was found by Customs officials at Mascot on a flight bound for Bangkok. Schooley and his fellow officers cross-checked the names and numbers on the suitcase tag with both the flight list and the names of all known smugglers, to find out who had put the bag on the flight, but all they discovered was that the film crew had been on the same flight.

Some time after the incident, Schooley recalled 'I was shocked to learn that they had been informed that they were on our computer list by their producer via a Customs officer in Canberra.' Schooley refers to the problems of a 'mole' in his Customs department more than once. In one case he failed to catch a 'mole' after a lady arrested with a suitcase full of Malaysian long-tailed parrots *(Psittacula longicauda)* admitted to the presence of an 'inside man' at the airport. In a lengthy article Schooley relates how another 'mole' was eventually caught for his role in wildlife trafficking.

In another case, Schooley noted that he accidentally caught an employee from his own Customs department driving around an alleged fauna trafficker after this person had been under surveillance by the department. Schooley said that subsequent events 'turned out to be better than any James Bond film.'

'Moles' inside the system make the prosecution of major wildlife smugglers much harder. Schooley refers to a case where papers mysteriously disappeared so that an alleged smuggler couldn't be charged. In a separate case, Schooley alleged an ex-Customs, ex-narcotics officer involved in an aborted smuggling attempt was tipped off and fled before he could be charged. Another man charged with smuggling by Schooley managed to beat the charges after engaging a prominent barrister in a case that apparently hinged on whether birds seen in two separate containers were in fact the same specimens. Two others charged in relation to the same incident had already been convicted.

Schooley wasn't the only Customs officer to allege corruption in his department. Peter Joseph Marzol, a Customs officer, told the Stewart Royal Commission that as early as 1978 a Customs officer was corruptly giving information to the Mr Asia drug syndicate.

Subsequently it was alleged by witnesses involved in the Mr Asia syndicate that Marzol's colleague, Richard Spencer, was the officer concerned and it was further alleged he had been hired by the syndicate for $25 000 per year.

On a later separate matter, Marzol and Spencer were both alleged to have committed perjury during an inquest into the murder of heroin addict Dale Catherine Payne.

In 1981, Marzol, with two other Customs officers, Smith and Watson, N.P.W.S. official Clive Jones, and Taronga Zoo official Terry Boyland, admitted to entering premises to illegally seize snakes. Each of them, other than Marzol, subsequently admitted that the reason used to enter the premises (illegal possession of exotic snakes) was fabricated. N.P.W.S. and Customs subsequently returned stolen snakes and other possessions. Marzol and Spencer later left their department on the grounds of ill health.

Another Customs official Colin Maclean was charged and jailed for importing heroin into the country inside footballs.

Within Australia, defamation laws prevent most allegations against officials ever being reported in the media, although once aired by one source, they are usually widely reported, particularly when followed up by a court case and subsequent conviction.

A Cinecontact documentary on animal traffic out of Australia carried an interview with a wildlife keeper from Sydney's western suburbs, Mr William Bennett, who stated quite clearly that traffickers relied on an 'inside man' to make their operations successful.

No decision yet on charges against former narcotics agents

The NSW Attorney-General, Mr Sheahan, has still made no decision on whether charges should be laid against two former Narcotics Bureau officers who deliberately withheld knowledge from a coronial inquest.

Mr Kevin Anderson, who earlier this year conducted the second inquest into the death of Dale Catherine Payne, sent papers from the inquest to Mr Sheahan in July. Mr Sheahan was to consider whether charges of perjury, conspiracy or attempting to pervert the course of justice should be laid against the two men.

Counsel assisting the inquest, Mr Chester Porter, QC, had asked Mr Anderson to recommend that Richard Spencer and Peter Marzol be charged. A spokesman for Mr Sheahan said yesterday that the delay in making a decision was due to the volume of material which Crown Law officers had to examine. Dale Payne, a heroin addict and police informant, was found dead in a private hotel in 1978. The first inquest found that she had died accidentally from an overdose of heroin. SMH 8/10/85 Page 3

The coroner, Mr Len Nash, rejected the evidence of a journalist, Mr Brian White, who alleged that Payne had been murdered.

In 1983 the Royal Commissioner, Justice Stewart, recommended that the State Government consider a royal commission into the circumstances of Payne's death.

But on the advice of Crown Law officers, the Government decided instead to seek a second inquest which concluded that "it is likely she was murdered", although Mr Anderson returned an open finding.

Mr Anderson found that Spencer and Marzol had deliberately withheld knowledge which could have changed the course of the first inquest and led to an inquiry into two men who had motives to kill Payne. One of those men, Anthony Eustace Anderson, who had also declined to answer questions at the inquest, was shot dead at Arncliffe two weeks after appearing at the inquiry. The other man, Rodney Rowe, who was Payne's boyfriend at one stage, has not been seen since absconding on bail four years ago.

— ANDREW KEENAN

SMUGGLED

Things Don't Seem to Change
Where major wildlife smuggling rackets involve licensing and law enforcement officers, it is reasonable to expect exposure to come from some source other than fauna authorities themselves. Sometimes, however, staff are involved.

In 1989, after a highly publicised vote of no-confidence in senior management of the New South Wales N.P.W.S. by other staff, and an Independent Commission Against Corruption (I.C.A.C.) inquiry into 'irregularities' in the Service, the director of N.P.W.S., Mr. John Whitehouse left his job. The deputy director, Jack Giles, also left his job and accepted a position at Sydney's Taronga Zoo. Several officers from N.P.W.S. became the subject of corruption allegations.

New South Wales Aboriginal Commissioner, Steve Gordon, himself a very senior public official, has allegedly admitted that in the early 1980s he was involved in a number of activities including gold smuggling, illegal bird trading, kangaroo rackets and selling birds to N.P.W.S. officials.

He alleged that N.P.W.S. officials were very corrupt, and that directors of the service, including Johnstone and Giles, were paid $20 000 and $30 000 bribes by kangaroo harvesters to keep potential competitors out of the industry. He also alleged bribes were paid to N.P.W.S. officials to overlook permit violations and said that officers 'had standover tactics'.

He also alleged that three friends of his who threatened to expose N.P.W.S. rackets were killed before they had a chance to speak out. Two were the Judd brothers, whose bodies were found inside a car at the bottom of a dam near Bourke, New South Wales, some time after they had disappeared. Gordon said he was aware that the two men had been murdered and dumped in the dam shortly after the incident occurred but was too afraid to go to the police. Another friend of his, Andrew Komarnski, was killed and put through a pet meat mincer at St George in Queensland. Gordon was allegedly shown the remains of his minced friend. Gordon said to me 'I was the next bloke and I bowed out.' He also said to me 'I was gone. If I'd said any more I'd have been gone! . . . I got very sick, I stopped dead in my tracks and I just walked off.' He subsequently maintained his silence for several years.

It is to be hoped that the practices of N.P.W.S. directors and officers have improved. Unfortunately, this doesn't seem to be the case. Licensing officer Gary Ellis came under I.C.A.C. attention in May 1991 after it was alleged that he issued a permit to Chris Weinholt, the son of his family doctor, in violation of a N.P.W.S. ban on issuing new permits. It was alleged that Ellis subsequently allowed Weinholt to import a valuable bredl's python *(Morelia bredli)* from the Northern Territory before a permit was issued. Another allegation against Ellis was that he was demanding cash bribes in return for issuing licences to certain people.

N.P.W.S. officer Gary Sims was also the subject of an I.C.A.C. complaint in 1991 for allegedly taking legally held snakes from a licensed keeper and failing to account for their disposal.

After Steve Gordon
In mid-1992, a series of events occurred which put wildlife smuggling under the public spotlight. The authorities stopped several major smuggling operations, including a major bird smuggling venture in New South Wales, Victoria and Western Australia. Several men were caught attempting to

smuggle birds and eggs back to the U.S.A. Two people were fined, $6 000 and $5 000 respectively, while the third, John Rivera, was jailed for 12 months in Sydney.

A separate gang of Germans and Australians were caught trapping reptiles in the Northern Territory for export overseas. After enormous publicity, two men were fined $7 200 each. A group of Victorians was also caught by officials in Melbourne after trapping reptiles in Queensland and selling them to keepers in Victoria.

However, the most significant events stemmed from Steve Gordon's allegations. Journalist Fia Cumming, while researching wildlife smuggling for a newspaper article, uncovered more extensive corruption within various authorities than anyone had realised. Cumming wrote a 3 000 word story which she sold to various newspapers around Australia, due to be published as a scoop on 21 June 1992. However, parts of the story were leaked by Democrat Senator Carin Sowada, to a journalist on 18 June. As a result, no papers ran the story, which remains unpublished.

After another Democrat Senator, Meg Lees, tabled documents received from Cumming, before Federal Parliament, and some newspapers publicised the allegations Cumming had intended to make, Senator Michael Tate (ALP) announced a Federal inquiry into wildlife trafficking.

In mid-1992 Cumming spoke to many people, who corroborated various claims made by Steve Gordon, and provided specific information relating to corruption by officers of the fauna authorities in New South Wales and Queensland.

In her investigations, Cumming uncovered several rackets in the Australian meat industry, including drug running, asset stripping, meat substitutions, workers' compensation frauds, international arms trafficking and laundering stolen goods. A secret 1992 report by the Australian Bureau of Criminal Intelligence, which substantiated this information, had obtained data from various authorities in all States.

Three officers of the New South Wales N.P.W.S. corroborated Steve Gordon's allegations and provided substantial new evidence of corruption among senior officers in the department, again naming Don Johnstone, Jack Giles and Clive Jones, among others. The three officers, Clive Bennett, Les McQueen and Ken Blade provided tapes and documents to back up their claims.

Elaine Patterson of the New South Wales Bird Protection League, also gave specific evidence of senior N.P.W.S. management aiding and abetting bird smuggling operations as well as mafia-style harassment of herself.

Sydney barrister, Janet Coombes, provided information indicating that Queensland N.P.W.S. officer Melino, found dead in 1980 from gunshot wounds, had been murdered, presumably for the risk he posed to smuggling operations.

Several cases in 1989-92 alleging corruption in the Queensland N.P.W.S. also came to light. Perhaps most significant of these was official tolerance of fauna law breaches by a reptile exhibitor, David Williams. In one case launched against Williams by apparently honest officers Veron Harris and others, the file for the case was lost by a senior employee of N.P.W.S., so most charges had to be dropped and Williams was convicted only of a minor charge. From material provided in relation to the David Williams case, it appears there was an ongoing battle between corrupt and honest officials in the Queensland N.P.W.S.

In a separate case a fauna park owner in Brisbane allegedly escaped prosecution for illegally killing 400 native mammals and stuffing them, due to his connections within N.P.W.S. The Criminal Justice Commission of Queensland was examining allegations of corruption in fauna authorities in that state when this material was written.

The allegations against officers of the New South Wales N.P.W.S. have been referred to the I.C.A.C. as well as being the subject of a Federal inquiry. In July 1992, Don McDowell of the Australian Institute of Criminology in Canberra, announced an investigation into wildlife smuggling and related corruption in Australia and called for all available information to be submitted to the Institute.

'OPERATION UNCLE'

In 1973 a bird enthusiast called Bert Field was approached by senior officials in the South Australian N.P.W.S. Field was asked to act as a double agent on behalf of the N.P.W.S. to sell birds to smugglers and inform on them. In Field's words, he was 'approached by people who make the laws' and he was to be 'trapping the birds to trap the dealers.'

Field had trapped birds most of his life so he could move among smugglers without creating suspicion. As trapping is the logical first step in a smuggling chain, the job seemed plausible.

Field was offered 'good money, enough to retire on', and perhaps more importantly to him, 'the finest collection of birds in the country'.

Throughout the period 1973-78 Field trapped about 2 000 of the rarest Australian birds he could find. Field claimed that they were worth over $1 000 000 on the export market. Judging by the species trapped, he travelled in South Australia, New South Wales, Victoria and the Northern Territory in search of birds or to sell what he'd caught. No one has offered evidence of authorisation from fauna authorities in any States allowing Field to trap birds. Field was either acting illegally and without the knowledge of these State authorities, or more probably certain officials were co-operating with the South Australian N.P.W.S.

Field gave N.P.W.S. officials in South Australia, including Brian Eves, the then deputy director with whom he taped conversations, 'names, places, dates . . . everything!' but N.P.W.S apparently didn't act on the information. Field told '60 Minutes', 'I liked doing it and I thought I was doing something that would bring the goodies against the baddies. I thought I was doing something right.'

The only 'bust' that could possibly have been correlated with the information supplied by Field was that of a small-time dealer known as 'Happy Walker'. That single charge was for illegally shipping birds interstate.

On 'Sixty Minutes' Field recalled one occasion Walker had been busted: 'I remember the headlines in the paper at the time — the busting open of a black market in birds, they said it was . . . But that was all bullshit. Black market in birds? They'd only got on to a bloke who was carting stuff interstate. Happy was no big-time smuggler.'

Field told '60 Minutes', he had given information to N.P.W.S. to have Walker 'busted' seven or eight times and asked 'Why wasn't he knocked-off every time?'

Five years after Field's employment with N.P.W.S., he himself was 'busted' by officers within the department, who took his own birds and formally charged him with wildlife offences.

Rob Dempsey, former head of the Department of Environment, and therefore also in charge of N.P.W.S., was told that Field had been caught possessing birds illegally and he therefore gave the go-ahead for charges to be laid.

Dempsey told '60 Minutes'

'Then some members of the department came to me and said, "We urge you not to do this," . . . The inquiries revealed that a select few in the department had hired Mr Field to work for the department unbeknown to the people who were preparing the case against him, and indeed to most other people in the department.'

After Dempsey ordered an inquiry to establish who had authorised Field's involvement, the N.P.W.S. officials concerned were unable to show any authorisation for Field's activities on the files, nor was there any 'official' budgetary allocation to Field for money he claimed was owed him.

Dempsey again told '60 Minutes', 'I'm reasonably certain in my own mind that what was going on in South Australia is only the edge of a much wider, well-organised and highly lucrative operation.'

The charges against Field were dropped after he gave the media copies of taped conversations with his contacts in N.P.W.S., in particular Eves and Lyons. Some of his seized birds were also returned and he received 'back-pay' of $68 000.

Discussing the number of smugglers or dealers with whom he had had dealings during 'Operation Uncle', Field told '60 Minutes', 'There could have been 15, 20, might have been more different ones that I sold birds to during the period.'

In the South Australian Parliament, allegations were made and Lyons and Eves were named. When they were both questioned by '60 Minutes', the response was 'No comment.'

South Australian Democrat and barrister, Robin Millhouse, alleged a major cover-up and tried to initiate a much wider inquiry. Ian Leslie of '60 Minutes' asked Millhouse 'Is there anything to suggest that someone was in fact lining his pockets, that there was maybe a Mr Big in this operation?' to which Millhouse replied 'Oh yes, I think there is a lot to suggest that. There are these unanswered questions. Why was it allowed to go on? Who did make the money out of the birds that Bert Field trapped? Why now is there such an unwillingness to have an inquiry into it? All those things add up to the gravest of suspicions.' When Leslie suggested a 'cover-up', Millhouse agreed.

When Leslie asked Field if some of the birds had ended up overseas, he replied 'I'm sure some of them did.'

Leslie had asserted quite correctly 'If only 10% of this cargo had reached the destination alive, the smugglers would still have made a fortune.'

Field died of a heart attack while on a fishing trip shortly after '60 Minutes' screened the story about his case. Much of the information about the whole South Australian racket no doubt went with him.

The Results

Following the 'busting' of Field by N.P.W.S. there was a purge in the Service, after which several officers retired or were transferred.

SMUGGLED

Bob Lyons, Brian Eves and two Perth-based Customs officers, Peter Harris and Harvey Latner, faced charges before Adelaide Magistrate's Court of illegally trafficking in fauna (birds) in early 1980. The offences that were the subject of the charges were alleged to have occurred from July 1973 to December 1974, only a fraction of the period when Field was trapping birds on behalf of these men.

The case was unusual in that the prosecution hadn't taken statements from a number of key witnesses and others weren't called. Mr A. E. Schapel even applied for an adjournment so that a statement could be taken from Bert Field. Defence lawyers for the four men on trial successfully argued against this application on the basis that the Crown had been able to interview Mr Field for weeks prior to the case. The presiding magistrate refused to allow for an extended adjournment and so the Crown case was critically disabled. The four accused men had invested heavily in defence lawyers, including a Q.C., which was relatively unusual for a case heard before a Magistrate's Court.

N. Maloney and L. J. Elliott (Q.C.) during the case admitted to the trafficking in birds by their clients. They stated that their clients thought that the issuing of permits to trap and trade in birds was not necessary as they were employees of the fauna or related authorities. No permits had ever been issued by either the South Australian N.P.W.S. or interstate counterparts.

Birds had been caught by Field, with the approval of Lyons in the Northern Territory. No South Australian official had juristiction there and no relevant authorisation from that State was produced at any stage. During the case it was revealed that among the people Bert Field sold birds to was none other than Harvey Latner. Latner had allegedly told investigating police that he had been instructed to trade birds illegally by Jeffrey Arthur Morgan, a senior officer of the Customs Department in Canberra.

During the case it was also revealed that Lyons' superiors, Dr G. Ingliss, the director of the Department of the Environment, and Mr Broomhill, Minister for the Environment, were allegedly ignorant of the fact that Lyons and his associates were aiding and abetting the illegal trapping and trading of birds.

The presiding magistrate, N. S. Manos dismissed the charges on 15 April 1980.

As '60 Minutes' had previously reported, 'No comment from Lyons. No comment from Eves. But Bert said he had taped conversations between his contacts within the National Parks and Wildlife Service.' (A recording of Bert and Eves in conversation is then heard on the film.) 'But neither recordings like this or Bert's diaries have ever been tested in court.'

Why was that material not presented in court in 1980? Although Bert Field is now dead, I believe that his tapes and dairies should be given a complete public airing.

Endnote

In 1990 my secretary contacted Adelaide Magistrate's Court, to research the above case. The clerk at the court said that the court had no record of any appearance by any of the four men named above for any charges during 1980. When asked if the court may have erased the record as a result of 'pressure' by some anonymous official, the clerk replied 'Yes, that does go on.' The clerk cited previous cases where police officers had taken steps to erase their past traffic offence records.

AFTER FIELD

After stemming the trade in illegal birds from South Australia, the flow from South Australia to Victoria reversed. Laundered birds from Victoria, sourced largely from Queensland and the Northern Territory and claimed by dealers to be captive-bred, were transhipped from Victoria to South Australia, presumably before being sent overseas.

In early 1982, Mr. Sid Cowling, assistant director of the Victorian N.P.W.S., stated that about 100 000 birds were imported into Victoria annually. Mr Cowling was quoted as stating that 'as many as 50% of the illegal birds reaching Victoria eventually go on to South Australia.'

The initial appearance of rare orange-bellied parrots (*Neophema chrysogaster*) in Europe in the early 1970s was also allegedly linked to South Australian fauna authorities. Danny Sim, convicted of an aborted smuggling attempt who served a jail term as a result, also told me of high level corruption among South Australian fauna authorities. Sim, who had numerous dealings with well-known Singapore trader Christopher Wee, told me that he'd been shown an interesting series of photos. Among them was one of Christopher Wee and a former South Australian Minister for the Environment standing together 'arm-in-arm' as good friends. A parliamentary enquiry was told that both were allegedly illegally trafficking in birds.

Journalist Dick Wordley played a key role in exposing corrupt South Australian Drug Squad chief, Barry Moyce. Moyce was head of the Drug Squad and widely recognised for his role in promoting the anti-drug scheme, 'Operation NOAH'.

Moyce was found to be a major drug dealer and at the time of writing had just been sentenced to 21 years in prison. More importantly, in the context of this book, Wordley informed me that Moyce had been a very keen aviculturalist and had been allegedly trafficking in birds illegally through a contact in Singapore. It seems therefore that wildlife smuggling in South Australia extends far beyond the confines of the State fauna authority, N.P.W.S.

4
RETAIL SMUGGLING

The operations of exposed wildlife smuggling syndicates and their couriers are widely reported in the media. At one stage no fewer than six major syndicates were supplying a single Asian dealer. Another Asian dealer was known to sell birds in large quantities to European traders. Single consignments in excess of 100 000 birds were common. A few case histories are worth repeating here.

A CHAIN OF EVENTS
A Frankfurt-based businessman Horst Selig was arrested at Sydney airport in November 1988, with two suitcases containing 27 Australian parrots and 11 lizards. The reptiles were cooled with ice-packs to keep them still and included blue-tongue lizards *(Tiliqua* sp.), shinglebacks *(Trachydosaurus rugosus)* and eastern water dragons *(Physignathus lesueurii)*. The birds were drugged with tranquillisers. The mortality rate among both birds and reptiles was very high, indicating Selig's relative inexperience. The man was sentenced to two and a half years' jail at Sydney's District Court in April 1989. No minimum term was set.

Selig told Customs officials that he had been paid $5 000 to be a courier after he had been apprehended trying to board a flight to Bangkok.

Anthony Sommerville, a man of apparently impeccable credentials, had been seen escorting Selig to the airport. Sommerville had long been viewed by authorities as an Australian connection in a Thailand-based syndicate and the sighting with Selig was one of a long line of events linking him to the syndicate.

Sommerville, from the town of Orange in New South Wales, owns a vast, priceless collection of rare and extinct bird species eggs. Some of the eggs date back to Douglas Mawson's expedition to Antarctica. Sommerville, who was highly regarded in avicultural circles, first came to the attention of authorities in 1984 during an investigation into illegal birds' eggs collectors.

Before Selig's arrest, a Canadian had been intercepted by chance arriving at Sydney airport bringing in exotic birds. He was allowed to pass through without realising that airport authorities knew what he was doing. On the way out the same man was stopped and found with Australian natives mainly consisting of Major Mitchell cockatoos *(Cacatua leadbeateri)* and gang gang cockatoos *(Callocephalon fimbriatum)*. On board the plane bound for New Zealand (where smuggled Australian fauna can be given legal export permits), officials searched the courier and discovered an address book containing 'useful' names and addresses in places such as Bangkok and other Asian captitals. Anthony Sommerville's address and phone number were also listed.

The Canadian courier was prosecuted and sentenced in August 1988, receiving 12 months' jail for importing the exotic birds and two years' jail for attempting to export the Australian natives. As a result of this 'bust', and the fact that Sommerville's telephone was being tapped, authorities learnt that Sommerville telephoned syndicate members in Bangkok and elsewhere which confirmed that he was trafficking in wildlife.

Sommerville may have been forewarned of the net closing on him. He had escaped by yacht to West Irian by the time authorities arrived at his home with a search warrant issued by a magistrate. What they discovered was fascinating.

Below the house was a specially excavated room, accessed by a trapdoor in a broom closet. There were found drugs used to sedate birds during smuggling, hypodermic needles, especially made suitcases, tubing and other material used to aid the export of wildlife. After Indonesian police arrested Sommerville, he was returned by them to Sydney where he faced trial on a number of smuggling charges. Sommerville was sentenced to six years' jail, where he remains at the time of writing this book.

SNAKES AND LADDERS

The tortuous smuggling game is sometimes referred to as 'snakes and ladders' and the following cases are good illustrations of why.

On one occasion, an Australian python (C.I.T.E.S., appendix 2 species), was smuggled by a major syndicate from Australia, via Europe to the U.S.A. where it was subsequently sold by a dealer as a legally held captive-bred animal. The purchaser promptly put the snake in a package and posted it directly back to a friend in Australia where it was later licensed as a legally held snake by the N.P.W.S. of New South Wales during an amnesty on illegally held reptiles in 1989. In that case a single animal had been illegally exported at least twice and then 'legalised' on at least two occasions.

In another case in the early 1980s four wild-caught albino Burmese pythons *(Python molurus bivittatus)* were imported into the U.S.A. All were believed to have been captured in Thailand. The first specimen died within a month of importation due to poor health. The next three, two males and single female, were sold by Alfred Ojeda to another dealer, Tom Crutchfield of Herpetofauna Inc. in Fort Meyers, Florida. Crutchfield mortgaged half his house to come up with the US$21 000 purchase price. Unknown to the U.S. traders and the Thai animal exporter, the three albinos had been stolen from Komain Nukulphanitwipat, also known as Deng, a well-known collector of all albino animals, and director of the Siam Farm in Bangkok. The person who'd sold the snakes to the Thai exporter was subsequently accused by Deng of being responsible for the theft of the albino pythons. Deng pursued the matter in

Thai courts and the thief was ordered to pay Deng monetary restitution for the theft of the snakes.

As Tom Crutchfield was three times removed from the theft of the snakes he retained ownership of all three snakes, although he did in due course off-load all three at an asking price of US$10 000 per snake. Snake breeder Bob Clark obtained a single male from the trio and by careful breeding produced a second generation of inbred young. About 25% of those offspring were albinos. Some of these offspring and their offspring have since been sold back to South-east Asia, including to the Sri Lanka National Zoo and Deng himself.

In 1990, price lists for reptiles in the U.S.A. offered albino Burmese pythons for about US$1 000 each, a ten-fold reduction in their original price as the snakes had now become more 'common'. The first specimens were legally exported to Europe late that year selling for about $3 000.

At the same time, the first specimens were being illegally exported to Australia. At a herpetological conference in Sydney, a man offered many of the people present a juvenile albino Burmese python for $2 000. When questioned about the source of the specimens, the man replied 'Don't worry about whose snake it is.' When further questioned about how it could have been brought into the country legally, the man replied 'I've got official connections . . . but for Christ's sake don't try and get a permit for it!'

The 'Game' Continues

In late 1991, a wildlife ranger at Patchewollock in Victoria saw three men acting suspiciously. They were carrying nets, maps and other wildlife collecting equipment. Surveillance led to 'Operation Foil', in which officials from three Government enforcement agencies participated. Eventually a large smuggling operation involving at least six Americans and a Canadian was 'busted'.

On 16 September 1991, three Americans were arrested as they boarded an international flight at Sydney airport. They were carrying more than 100 cockatoo eggs in tight-fitting vests when searched. The vests were designed to prevent crushing of the eggs. Also in their possession were two pink cockatoos and a lizard. Joseph Fred Demanio (aged 21), Ronald Martinolich (24) and Matthew Salvatore Pisciotta (24), were convicted of acting as couriers for a smuggling ring later believed to have been operating for up to five years. The eggs were from Major Mitchells, galahs, grass parrots (*Cacatua* sp.) and West Australian red-tailed black cockatoos (*Calyptorhynchus magnificus*).

About a week later a man and woman were arrested trying to board an international flight at Melbourne airport carrying 24 galah and Major Mitchell eggs sewn into tight-fitting vests. They were also connected with the same racket.

Some of the eggs taken by the smugglers were from nests in the Wyperfield National Park, in Victoria. In that area alone an estimated 200 separate nests had been identified by the gang. The eggs of the birds were valued at $5 500, while adult pairs of birds fetched up to $50 000 overseas.

The eggs were bound for San Francisco and other parts of the U.S.A. It was thought that the organiser of the racket had fled the country before he could be arrested, perhaps because he was warned in advance.

The offenders appeared in courts in Sydney and Melbourne charged with a variety of State and Federal wildlife offences. For the Federal charges, the smugglers each faced maximum penalties of 10 years' jail and $100 000 in fines. Maximum penalties for the State wildlife offences were less.

On 17 December, 1991, John Francis Nichols, 55, a well-known wildlife dealer, was arrested with a friend by Customs officials at Melbourne airport, attempting to board a flight to New Zealand with 74 shingleback lizards and seven bearded dragons *(Pogona vitticeps)*. The lizards were packed into two suitcases, with their feet taped and hidden under a blanket when discovered by Customs officials.

Nichols had arrived in Australia from his home in New Zealand ten days earlier and pre-arranged the purchase of the lizards. Some years earlier, he had lived and worked in Melbourne as a wildlife dealer.

Nichols stated that he was exporting the lizards as a favour for his brother-in-law, although it was clear that the lizards were likely to be transhipped from New Zealand, where export laws are more lax. The lizards appeared to have been caught in Western Victoria or nearby, where they are common and easily caught in huge numbers crossing roads between September and November. The shinglebacks sold for between $900 and $1 200 each in the U.S.A. (1991 prices). The lizards are rare captives there due to their slow breeding rate, usually a maximum of two young per adult female per year, so are highly sought after by smugglers.

When initially arrested and charged, Nichols was remanded in custody, but later successfully applied for bail. On 6 January 1992, Nichols pleaded guilty to the Federal offence of attempting to illegally export native fauna at Melbourne Magistrate's court. He was subsequently sentenced to 18 months' jail.

Peter and Rosaleen Robson of Fremantle, Western Australia pleaded guilty and were convicted on 10-11 November 1986 of three counts of illegally exporting Australian reptiles. They had appeared in Perth District Court on charges brought under the *Wildlife Protection (Regulation of Exports and Imports) Act* 1982.

The couple had posted packages containing live reptiles from the Bentley post office on 16 January 1986, 9 September 1986 and 15 September 1986 to reptile dealers in Denmark and West Germany. The reptiles totalled 57 specimens and included 41 shinglebacks, 2 western bearded dragons *(Pogona minimus)*, 1 western blue-tongued lizard *(Tiliqua occipitalis)*, 8 other skinks and 5 geckoes *(Gekkonidae)*, worth an estimated $20 000 on the European market.

The packages were intercepted before they left Australia.

Peter Robson was given a nine months suspended sentence with a three year good behaviour bond and recognisance of $10 000, plus a $2 000 fine. Rosaleen Robson was also given a nine months suspended sentence with a two year good behaviour bond and recognisance of $5 000.

COURIERS ANONYMOUS

Smuggling syndicates often use couriers to transport fauna on commercial flights. This system has several advantages. Firstly, the principals who run the syndicates don't get caught for actually smuggling. Secondly, if a courier is caught, they will be charged and fined a minimum penalty for a first offence. The penalty, which until recently was rarely more than $1 000, would be paid outright by the syndicate leaders and the courier would not be used again as they now had a record. As couriers are very well paid for their efforts,

SMUGGLED

$100,000 lure in lizard export plot

By BRETT QUINE

A MAN tried to smuggle out 74 native lizards worth up to $110,000 on the US retail market, the County Court heard yesterday.

New Zealander John Nichols, 55, was caught with two suitcases packed with lizards at Melbourne airport last year.

Nichols, an invalid pensioner, has pleaded guilty to the attempted export on December 17.

Judge Nixon remand-ed Nichols in custody for sentencing tomorrow.

The court heard the smuggling ring principal, who also lived in New Zealand, had paid Nichols with a plane ticket and $480.

Authorities in New Zealand were still investigating the ring.

The acting director of the Wildlife Protection Authority, Mr Paul Jewell, said there was a high risk the lizards would die once taken from their environment.

Mr Jewell said the lizards, shingle backed skinks and bearded dragons, were found taped in Nichols' cases.

He said that most wildlife smuggled out of Australia was bound ultimately for the US.

The court heard Nichols had accepted the air ticket and expenses so he could see his estranged daughters in Queensland.

Mr Robert Stary, for Nichols, said his client had not seen his daughters for 15 or 20 years.

He said Nichols' wife in Auckland was a severe epileptic who relied on him for support and urged a bond and a fine for his client.

Customs officer Mr Brett Sanders told Judge Nixon that Nichols was one of two men intercepted with the cases of lizards.

● Rescued ... some of the 74 lizards packed into suitcases that were found by Customs officers at Melbourne airport last year. A court was told yesterday of big profits for smugglers.

there never seems to be a shortage. Thirdly, as syndicates use a courier only once or twice, enforcement officials are unable to familiarise themselves with people likely to be smuggling wildlife on commercial flights.

When a Perth horse trainer appeared in a Sydney court charged with attempting to illegally export ten native birds worth about $23 000 he was fined a mere $500 as it was his first offence. The man pleaded guilty. He said that he was approached at a racecourse while drunk by a man who asked him to take a case to Singapore. He told the court he had not even known what was in the bag. He said 'I don't even like birds. I'm frightened of them.'

Taxi Drivers

It is common practice for smugglers to employ taxi drivers to deliver bags containing wildlife to airports. This is principally due to the difficulty in tracking down a taxi driver and the fact that if traced, taxi drivers tend to respect the confidentiality of their clients.

Schooley recalls a bungled smuggling operation, which although not necessarily directed by a taxi driver, was certainly organised by a group of them. After acquiring headed paper from the offices of Sydney University, the syndicate head enquired with Customs and airlines officials about the export of university equipment to Bangkok University. He was told there would be no problem provided papers and documents were lodged before the flight.

The documentation was lodged with the appropriate airport departments by taxi drivers. The birds were packed in two suitcases marked in large letters 'University of Bangkok' and then taken by taxi to the airport. The taxi driver took the cases to the Qantas airline freight shed where they were booked in. Payment and all other details had already been taken care of.

Due to an alert put out concerning the type of suitcase most commonly used by bird smugglers — the 'hard-shelled' style available from any large department store — it was routinely searched by Schooley in his capacity as a Customs official. Plastic tubes containing a number of parrots were found. The taxi driver told Schooley that he had collected the bags from a man at some steps at Sydney University. The man who had allegedly given the bags to the taxi driver was never found and no arrests in relation to that incident were ever made.

Women

Syndicates using couriers may also choose young attractive females of European origin. Usually syndicates ask a female on holiday in Australia if she would like a free trip to her homeland. Her only task is to take some wildlife home with her in order to cover costs for the syndicate. With an increased number of back-packers coming from Europe, there is no shortage of potential recruits.

SMUGGLING BY AIR

Customs officials have reported that light aircraft movements out of northern Australia cannot be adequately monitored by the authorities due to lack of resources. Michael Schooley has documented several cases in which large numbers of birds and other animals have been exported from remote parts of northern Australia in a single hit.

In the 1970s, Customs officers uncovered, almost by accident, a plan to

TOP END RACKET

In the mid-1980s an illegal export racket in the Top End of the Northern Territory was discovered, involving two Government officials and the Aborigines on a remote mission.

Aborigines on missions and in reserves tend to be exempt from wildlife laws that prohibit the taking or killing of protected fauna, which includes most types of native animal. This exemption is to allow Aborigines to continue their tribal lifestyle. However, few Aborigines today maintain this lifestyle, many having been influenced by social welfare and royalties paid by whites for the use of tourist facilities built on their land or mining royalties.

The fact that Aborigines are allowed to capture and kill any animal on their reserves does mean they tend not to be scrutinised by fauna officials and others likely to detect an illegal smuggling operation.

The operation of this particular racket was simple. Aborigines trapped reptiles and birds which were taken by the two white Government officials by boat out to sea. There they met Indonesian fishing vessels and passed on the wildlife in return for cash and precious stones. The animals made their way through Asian markets to dealers in Japan, the U.S.A. and Europe.

Asked why he participated in such a racket, one Aborigine named Clyde commented 'If white-fellas give us grog for bungarras (lizards), we give 'em bungarras.' Most of the profits enjoyed by the Aborigines were probably in the form of the amber fluid.

It was only by a stroke of luck that the operation was exposed. A visiting museum collector from a southern State was offered specimens in return for grog by a drunken Aborigine. Further questioning revealed the well-established pattern of capturing specimens for export.

The relevant fauna officials were notified of the racket and it was duly terminated. Neither of the white Government officials was charged or disciplined although they were transferred elsewhere. No Aborigines were charged with any fauna offences. Perhaps the prospect of charging virtually a whole tribe with either smuggling wildlife or aiding and abetting the same seemed too daunting to the fauna authority officials.

That the racket had been flourishing for some years soon became well known. The repeated incursions into nearby waters by particular Indonesian fishing vessels, which were detected by coastguard vessels, were probably due to regular contacts made between the operators involved in the racket.

A similar racket was uncovered on a mission in north Queensland, near the Northern Territory border. Among those involved were a medical practitioner and the local priest.

export some 600 native birds by light plane from northern Australia to Singapore. The plan called for the birds to be initially held in Adelaide before being taken by hired truck to a remote airstrip near Katherine, in the Northern Territory where the birds would be collected by the pilot and delivered to the Singapore contact, Christopher Wee, a well-known bird trader, who had allegedly paid off the 'right Customs officials' in Canberra to make sure the operation would be successful.

This operation was complicated by the airforce which was holding training exercises in the Katherine area, so a new departure point near Derby, Western Australia was arranged as a rendezvous. Derby was chosen as it was not in the airforce radar shield and had an airstrip at least 100 m (300') long that a car could drive on at 50 km (30 miles) per hour so the plane could land. The pilot got his lines of communication mixed up with the men on the ground and apparently flew to the wrong airstrip. To make things worse, the pilot got fairly drunk while flying to the supposed pick-up point.

The two men driving the truck were apprehended at Derby before being able to off-load the birds. The apprehending officer was a local policeman who had been disturbed by the men while listening to a radio broadcast of a football match. The mortality rate among the birds was over 50% and at one stage some 350 replacement birds had been flown from Port Pirie to Katherine, to meet the truck and cover the losses. Only about 350 birds were alive when seized by officials. The case was prosecuted by Frank Moran Q.C., and at least one of the operators was sentenced to six months' imprisonment, which he served.

SMUGGLING BY SEA

On one occasion a trans-Tasman bird smuggling operation involving a large yacht was exposed. The entire hull of the boat had been converted into large bird holding cages and the boat took birds to and from New Zealand from a point near Sydney.

During the early stages of the war in East Timor, a number of Australians and Indonesians who smuggled arms to Fretelin forces also became involved in the trafficking of wildlife. It is presumed that some fishermen in north-west Australia are still engaged in some wildlife trafficking.

Also in the 1970s Customs officials foiled a two-way smuggling operation between Broome and Bali, in which at least one load of Australian reptiles and birds worth about $100 000 was taken to Bali, with another return shipment of birds and monkeys being brought into Australia. The operation was badly planned with a high mortality rate among animals at all stages of the operation. When later apprehended in the Northern Territory, the offenders had about 40 surviving birds out of an original several hundred. A similar number of animals had managed to survive the journey to Bali.

HIT AND MISS

A well-known wildlife trafficker had a smuggling attempt foiled when his suitcase full of parrots was picked up off a carousel in Brisbane by an elderly lady. The smuggler and the lady had identical bags and neither knew they had picked up the wrong bag until they got home from the airport. The lady notified the authorities of the birds inside her bag after opening it. The smuggler had apparently flown from Sydney to Brisbane and stopped over for the night before planning to continue with his birds to Singapore.

Schooley reports a second incident involving the same unfortunate man, who attempted to get birds by road from Sydney to Brisbane, before flying out of the country with them. One night, the man carried a box full of parrots through a paddock adjacent to the State border. He had mistakenly believed that there were police searches of cars at border crossings and was trying to avoid being caught with the birds.

While quietly walking in the dark, he startled a cow which suddenly leapt up from under him making him jump to one side and fall into a dam. The box smashed on the ground and all the birds flew into the night.

Another smuggling attempt was foiled, due to a minor error by a truck driver courier. The truck driver had been assigned to deliver two wooden crates on an open-top truck to Trans Australian Airlines air cargo, which was in turn an agent for Thai Airways. The relatively panicky nature of the man attracted the attention of Schooley and another Customs official, resulting in one of them asking what was on board the truck. The driver said kangaroo skins, not realising that a special permit was needed for these. As the man had no permit, the boxes were opened. They revealed some 36 Major Mitchell cockatoos.

Noises coming from boxes or bags are a common cause of failure in smuggling attempts. When noises were heard emanating from some boxes at Mascot airport, destined for Portland, Oregon, U.S.A. and labelled as computer parts, the police were called in. When the boxes were opened, each was found to contain a tea chest with wire across the front. Some 87 parrots were found, all wide-awake and all screeching loudly as they first saw daylight.

In the 1970s a major smuggling operation existed which sent large numbers of reptiles in and out of Australia, mainly from Victoria. It came unstuck when a man at Sydney's Parramatta Hospital refused to respond to snakebite treatment. Medical analysis revealed that he had not been bitten by an Australian snake, so Customs officials commenced a search for the exotic snake responsible.

Eventually a large network of collectors with overseas reptiles was found, holding among other things water mocassins (*Agkistrodon piscivorus*) and broad-banded copperheads (*Agkistrodon contortrix laticinctus*), both from North America and a puff adder (*Bitis arietans*) from Africa or the Middle-east, all of which are deadly. Within a short time, over 300 exotic snakes were found in the care of several individuals. Dick Wordley reported that in the initial raids on these people no live snakes were found. The reason was because a 'mole' within Customs had notified them of impending 'top secret' raids.

After the reptile importing network was broken up, some holders of these prohibited foreign reptiles tried desperately to off-load them before being caught. Some reptiles including a king cobra (*Ophiophagus hannah*) and pair of gila monsters (*Heloderma suspectum*) were unsaleable so the men who possessed them promptly posted them back to the U.S.A.

Another group involved in posting reptiles to and from the U.S.A. fell apart when those at the U.S. end panicked and sent back to Australia the unopened parcels containing snakes. New legislation enacted in certain States together with increased publicity about the C.I.T.E.S. treaty caused the American recipients to back out for fear of detection and prosecution.

The parcels were delivered to return addresses in Sydney. Unfortunately

MYSTERIOUS SOURCES OF WILDLIFE
Another problem faced by those trying to track down sources of smuggled wildlife is that dealers are often loath to divulge their sources, for fear of losing them. This is particularly the case with illegally obtained wildlife. No dealer wants to jeopardise the source of his wildlife and profits, the dealer's sole reason to be in business.

Some interesting cases arise out of this. In 1985, I received a letter from an American who wanted to know where a python he possessed had originated. The man wrote saying that he had purchased the snake from a dealer in the U.S.A. who refused to tell him either who had sold him the snake or where in Australia the snake had originated. Enclosed with the letter was a photo of the snake he had purchased. I was shocked when I saw the photo: it was of a snake stolen from my house in July the previous year.

A few years earlier, Richard Bartlett from Florida corresponded with me after purchasing from a dealer Storr's monitors, a north Queensland species that had been taken from my house by N.P.W.S. officers in 1977. Those monitors along with two carpet snakes had been given by N.P.W.S. officer Tony Alexander to another reptile keeper who lived less than a kilometre from my house; through an import-export business this keeper had apparently shipped the lizards overseas.

Bartlett wrote to me about the lizards because he had difficulty getting information about their habits. He'd been informed by a mutual colleague that I had collected the species in the wild on three separate field trips.

Perhaps more bizarre was the fact that the man who'd been given the reptiles by the N.P.W.S. officer, immediately brought some of them down to my house to show me what he'd just been given, initially not realising that the reptiles were in fact mine.

The same man was later tape recorded twice admitting that he'd been given reptiles taken from my house illegally, including the Storr's monitors.

Richard Bartlett later became the first person in the world to breed Storr's monitors in captivity. His published results in relation to that species constitute much of what is currently known about the species.

people living at those addresses weren't the ones who'd been posting the parcels. Some addresses were entirely fictitious. As a result, the parcels were stored in the unclaimed mail section at the Redfern Mail Exchange where they languished for some months. Eventually some of the snakes within the parcels died. The smell attracted attention and the parcels were subsequently opened. The problem for the mail inspectors was that although some snakes had died, others hadn't and when the parcels were opened, the inspectors were often confronted with one or more agitated snakes.

Inspection of the written contents of the parcels led authorities to prosecute a man named Hewson in the Sydney suburb of Regent's Park for his role in the operation. Hewson's imported reptiles, including a single gila monster, were seized, and he was convicted under Federal law.

SMUGGLED

IDENTIFICATION PROBLEMS

In the early 1980s a fish dealer in Sydney imported a number of piranhas (*Rooseveltiella* sp. probably *nattereri*), native to South America and one of the world's most ferocious fish. The piranhas had been imported through the 'correct' channels and labelled as 'silver dollar fish'. As officials could not identify the fish, they let them through without any problems for the importer.

Customs officials became aware of their identity only when a keeper of tropical fish rang the department to tell them he had been offered one by a dealer. Further enquiries by officials resulted in most, if not all, the fish being later seized.

New South Wales

Act No. 80, 1974.

National Parks and Wildlife.

Corruption.

170. A person shall not, without lawful authority, offer, make or give to an officer of the Service, an ex-officio ranger or an honorary ranger any payment, gratuity or present in consideration that the officer or ranger will do or omit to do any act or thing pertaining to his powers, authorities, duties or functions as such an officer or ranger.

Penalty: $200 or imprisonment for six months or both.

Airport case for beagles

BEAGLE dogs will be used to sniff out banned food and plants being smuggled into Australia at Sydney and Brisbane airports in a five-month trial.

The dogs have a sense of smell 100 times greater than humans and have been used successfully at United States and Canadian airports.

The three Australian Snoopy sniffers have been trained to sit on luggage when they detect illegal imports such as cheese, live birds and plants.

5
PRIVATE SMUGGLING

Cases of private smuggling are commonly documented in the Australian media. These, however, represent only a fraction of what is illegally exported and imported. The reasons for this type of smuggling vary.

SMALL PERSONAL COLLECTIONS
During the last 20 years I have regularly encountered people who have smuggled small numbers of reptiles in and out of Australia either for themselves or as a favour for friends.

Since 1980, I have received, on average, ten solicitations a year, through the post from overseas residents who want me to export reptiles to them. In every case these solicitations have been from private reptile keepers who want the animals purely for their own private collections, usually with captive breeding and research as a prime motivation. Although I have declined every request for assistance in smuggling, no doubt many other people within this country aid and abet overseas enthusiasts.

THE PURSUIT OF KNOWLEDGE
In some cases, individuals are simply keen to further their personal knowledge. If wildlife protection laws in Australia were modified to enable a freer exchange of animals between countries, the following case might never have occurred.

Aviculturalist Daniel Bottlang from Switzerland first came to Australia in July 1988. He came to investigate the possibility of exporting eggs, but was told that authorities in Australia didn't issue such permits to private aviculturalists.

Bottlang, however, was keen to get some birds' eggs to his native Switzerland. He then sent two empty incubators back to Switzerland and when they passed through Customs unchecked he decided to return to Australia in the bird breeding season to get some eggs. Upon arrival in Australia a second time in October 1978, Bottlang was noticed by residents in the Three Springs area, some 250 km (150 miles) north of Perth 'acting suspiciously'. He was then kept under surveillance by local Conservation and Land Management (C.A.L.M.) officials.

Subsequently on 7 October, Bottlang attempted to send two crates via Qantas air cargo in Perth. One crate contained personal possessions, while the other contained a battery powered incubator with eight birds' eggs. Three were of galahs, two from red-tailed black cockatoos and three from little corellas *(Cacatua sanguinea)*.

Bottlang was fined a total of $1 500 on Federal charges and $1 800 on State wildlife charges.

RARE SPECIMENS

The case of Michael Murdian, from West Germany, illustrates a growing trend in illegal imports. On 10 November 1989, Murdian was apprehended when he arrived at Sydney airport from Germany. Concealed inside his jacket were four birds, a pair of rose-ringed parakeets *(Psittacula krameri)* and a pair of princess parrots *(Polytelis alexandrae)*. Now the logical question to ask would be, why on earth would someone bother to smuggle an Australian bird like the princess parrot back into the country from Europe, when they are so common in aviaries here?

The reason was that the birds in question were a 'lutino' mutation and worth up to $100 000 each in Australia. The breeding of 'rare' mutations in captive wildlife is becoming increasingly popular in the U.S.A. and Europe and these animals are invariably the most sought after.

On 27 March 1990, at Sydney District Court, Murdian was convicted and jailed for two years and eight months for wildlife offences and given six months for using a false passport, with a minimum total term of two years.

INVETERATE SMUGGLERS

In late May 1989, a well-known American snake keeper, Ed Celebucki, was arrested at Sydney's Mascot airport with two suitcases containing over 50 reptiles. He was en-route from New Guinea to the U.S.A. Included were Bismark ringed pythons *(Bothrochilus boa)*, white-lipped pythons *(Bothrochilus albertisi)* (both C.I.T.E.S. appendix 2 species), and mangrove monitors *(Varanus indicus)*. All are rare in captivity in the U.S.A. and in total worth many thousands of dollars.

One has to assume that either Celebucki wasn't the only American trapping these reptiles for sale in the U.S.A., or that it wasn't the first time he'd been to New Guinea. Several American dealers' price lists displayed Bismark ringed pythons for sale. Interestingly, almost all the specimens offered were males.

Among other north American herpetologists Celebucki was known to be a trafficker and according to some, it was only a matter of time before he was caught'. He typically kept some of what he smuggled, trading the rest with other reptile keepers for other species he sought.

Celebucki was only fined a small amount for his troubles after his May 1989 'bust'. According to those present at the court case in Sydney, the presiding magistrate failed to take the matter of smuggling reptiles seriously and summed up the case by ordering Celebucki to leave the country.

Celebucki wasn't the first American to be 'busted' taking snakes from New Guinea, via Sydney to the U.S.A. On 24 December 1987, Timothy Donovan was intercepted by Customs officials at Port Moresby airport attempting to

---

WINDFALL FOR MELBOURNE ZOO

In the early 1980s a parcel addressed from the U.S.A. to an Avondale Heights pet dealer was intercepted. A green python in the parcel had died in transit and gave off a very foul smell, so the parcel was opened before delivery. Postal officials were confronted with a highly agitated albino eastern diamondback rattlesnake (*Crotalus adamanteus*) which had its rattle taped up so it wouldn't make noise. Fauna officials seized the rattlesnake and it was passed on to Melbourne zoo. It was held on public display until 1990, when it died.

At about the same time a Keon Park dealer was also busted for illegally importing reptiles. The seized reptiles were shared between the Melbourne Museum and Melbourne zoo.

In 1991, John Nichols was convicted of trying to illegally export 74 shingleback lizards and 7 bearded dragons. The seized lizards also ended up at Melbourne zoo. As the capture locality of the lizards was not known, it would have been reckless to release the lizards. The zoo didn't want most of the lizards so they were put on sale at $30 each through the Victorian Herpetological Society. The profits from the sale were used to educate the public about reptiles.

---

board a flight to Sydney. He had 22 live reptiles in bags in his luggage. These were 12 green pythons (*Chondropython viridis*) 8 Boelen's pythons (*Python boeleni*) and a pair of brown tree snakes (*Boiga irregularis*).

Donovan was charged under Papuan law and fined a total of 160 kina. (He'd faced a maximum penalty of 11 000 kina). Brown tree snakes are relatively worthless as they are certified as a pest in some places such as Guam, a U.S. territory. Green pythons retail for about US$500 each, while Boelen's are estimated at US$10 000 each.

'OPERATION HARNESS'

Sometimes individuals work together in small gangs. Penalties for this type of well-organised operation can be quite severe, unless the individuals escape.

In 1989, three West Germans appeared before a Melbourne court charged with attempting to smuggle 32 birds in 2 suitcases from Tullamarine airport, on 17 April. The 27 long-billed corellas (*Cacatua tenuirostris*) and 5 galahs were worth $6 000 each on the black market according to press reports at the time. A 30 cm (12 in) long baby crocodile was found dead in one of the suitcases. The West Germans had been attempting to board a flight bound for Singapore.

Ludwig Horr, his wife Vera and Albert Mueller were bailed after each agreed to post $10 000 cash deposits and on condition that they appeared in Melbourne Magistrate's Court on 24 July 1989. As well as surrendering their passports, the three had to report to police daily until the hearing date. The three skipped the country in late May after having false passports sent to them by friends from West Germany. They also faced drug charges on top of the smuggling charges, as they had administered local anaesthetic to the birds to quieten them. A Federal police officer stated that the three faced up to ten years' jail if convicted, but due to the unusual extradition treaty between West Germany and Australia, it was unlikely that the trio would ever be prosecuted.

A fourth man, an aviculturalist from the Melbourne suburb of Nunawading also faced charges resulting from the aborted smuggling attempt and was later convicted and fined.

IGNORANCE

Ignorance, or professed ignorance of laws, is a common reason given by those caught smuggling fauna. In July 1985 a couple returned from holiday in the U.S.A. with 40 birds' eggs and six young birds, that they were attempting to smuggle into Australia. An in-flight film about strict quarantine and Customs laws persuaded them to give up their attempt. The birds and eggs were surrendered and destroyed after the couple got 'cold feet'. Lack of education of the public about potential risks and penalties of smuggling no doubt plays a role in many people continuing to bring animals into Australia illegally.

Similarly, West German Dieter Boxheimer was a 33-year-old reptile keeper apprehended on 22 October 1985, by Customs officials after they searched his bags before he boarded a flight from Melbourne to Frankfurt.

Inside were 63 live lizards and a single spotted marsh frog *(Limnodynastes tasmaniensis)*. The lizards were all species common in Victoria and included shinglebacks, blue-tongued lizards, bearded dragons and geckoes, packed in 21 calico bags. Boxhiemer told officials he had visited Australia on seven occasions and as recently as 28 October the previous year, had taken 25 reptiles out of Australia. Boxhiemer told officials 'he believed that because the reptiles were not endangered species he was permitted to take them.'

He was charged under section 22(b) of the *Wildlife Protection (Regulation of Exports and Imports) Act* 1982, and he appeared in Melbourne Magistrate's Court the day following his arrest. He was subsequently convicted.

PARCELS IN THE POST

There are many methods smugglers use to transport wildlife illegally. The main way reptiles and frogs are smuggled out of Australia is through the postal system. These animals are particularly suited to this form of transportation and I have heard of literally hundreds of reptiles being posted without significant mortality. Reptiles can go for long periods without food and water with no ill effects and are usually quiet.

In 1980 a smuggler was caught after a yelp came from a parcel that had been addressed to his parents' house. The parcel was opened by suspicious officials and revealed a number of protected reptiles including threatened species and the juvenile freshwater crocodile *(Crocodylus johnstoni)* that had made the sound.

It is very common for collectors from Europe and the U.S.A. to post reptiles to their home addresses as they collect reptiles throughout remote parts of Australia.

Dick Wordley quoted the case of a South Australian fauna officer stating that he 'had evidence of snakes being posted to Munich wrapped in the Saturday edition of the *Advertiser*', a local newspaper.

Badly-sealed packages can allow snakes to escape with dangerous or frightening consequences. In 1975, an unusual case occurred at a New York

Send it by Python Post!

WANT to send a snake interstate? Then use Australia Post, the national python postal service.

A Cairns man was convicted last week of trying to mail two water pythons and a carpet python to Victoria — and illegal reptile deliveries are on the up.

"Lizards are very commonly sent through the mail, and some of the smaller snakes. Pythons are very popular," said Dr Graeme Suckling, of the Victorian Department of Conservation and Environment's Resource Protection Branch.

"It is quite common for reptiles to be posted. Illegal reptile collectors find it a very easy way to move their stock around."

Unlike Australia's native birds, which are often sent through the mail

By TIM BLAIR

on their way to fetch huge prices overseas, reptiles are ideally suited to mailing.

"Reptiles can be kept at a low temperature and without food for a long time without damaging them," Dr Suckling said.

"Unless they are actually physically damaged in the mailing process, they can survive easily."

Dr Suckling said it vital that snakes be kept cool during mailing, because only when they were warm did they move about and become aggressive.

"If people who keep snakes want to handle them, they will put them in the fridge to cool them down. They cope with that quite well," he said.

"Their body mechanisms are such

that if they are cooled down, their system shuts down.

"But it doesn't harm them. When they are warmed again, off they go."

Dr Suckling said mail carriers and deliverers need not fear a loose snake in their mail.

"The people who send snakes by mail would take precautions with the packaging," he said. "It's not as if there are pythons and lizards floating around in flimsy envelopes."

The value of illegally-trapped snakes varied state by state, Dr Suckling said, but the financial return was "sufficiently high to entice people to break the law".

A spokesman for the RSPCA, Richard Hunter, said Australians loved their snakes and would do almost anything to get one as a pet.

TRUTH, SATURDAY, FEBRUARY 29, 1992—7

mail sorting centre. A highly sought-after Australian diamond python was found loose, having escaped from an unknown postal item, so the addressee was unknown. The fact that the snake was an illegal import didn't seem to worry anyone at the time. Rather, the authorities wanted to know to whom the snake was addressed, so they could simply off-load it. After some publicity, no fewer than 20 people came forward to claim it.

More commonly, however, recipients of mail containing reptiles or other wildlife who are approached by the authorities about these parcels, will deny any knowledge of them as they are well aware of the illegality of posting wildlife.

In 1988, a senior Australian Customs official stated on national television that the policing of Australia's mail system for illegal export of wildlife was effectively non-existent and that those caught smuggling by this means were only caught 'accidentally'. He was at the time denying any knowledge of direct Customs involvement in wildlife smuggling out of Australia.

Contrary to most reports, illegally posted wildlife is not always fed immediately prior to posting. Excess defecation that may occur during transit increases the risk of the parcel being detected. (Most reptiles can survive for many days without water and for weeks without food.)

Posted birds are usually tranquillised (usually with Luminol™ or Valium™) and confined to tubes or other structures when smuggled by private individuals. As birds require frequent feeding and maintainence when confined, they are rarely sent out of the country in the postal system. They are more likely to be concealed on a person or carried in personal luggage on an overseas flight.

OTHER METHODS, OTHER CASES
Apart from using the postal system, smugglers employ many ingenious methods to transport wildlife illegally.

Bags
False-bottomed bags are a favoured method. As birds need to be fed frequently, many smugglers try to take them in their hand luggage and it is common for smuggled birds to be fed in the toilet rooms of planes in mid-flight. According to Wordley, a woman strip-searched by a Customs official at Melbourne was found carrying 16 birds in a compartment of her overnight bag and 8 more in the lining of the all-weather coat that she carried over one arm.

Another person was caught by the South Australian authorities in the early 1970s trying to export two sugar gliders inside a briefcase. The person had intended to feed the gliders on a mixture of honey and glucose added to baby food on the flight to Europe. The market value of the gliders in Europe was several thousand dollars.

Wordley documented a foiled smuggling attempt involving a black 'hand-luggage' bag with false bottom and in-built breathing holes fed by the airvent above the passenger's head. The bag also contained four pocket torches to give the birds the light they needed to feed by and a sponge which the courier dampened in the aircraft lavatory to enable the birds to drink. The Singapore Airlines plane was bound for Singapore when a Customs investigator boarded the flight immediately before take-off. The man refused to leave the plane, saying he was on a 'foreign carrier'. The officer drew a gun and an adjacent woman screamed 'Hijack', sending the plane load of people into a frenzy.

Cassettes and Films
In 1989, a 42-year-old Melbourne labourer was caught trying to smuggle four live birds through Tullamarine airport inside a hollowed-out radio-cassette player. He had been on holiday to Yugoslavia. The maximum penalty for such an offence was $50 000 and/or ten years' jail.

Wordley cited an occasion where a smuggler was caught with an endangered hooded parrot *(Psephotus dissimilis)* squeezed inside the film compartment of a camera.

Mysterious Packages
Birds have also been found in packages labelled as duty-free liquor, in some cases the packaged birds weighing exactly what the container says, e.g. 750 g (24 oz).

One case reported in the American media in 1988, involved a youth illegally transporting a juvenile indigo snake in a cigarette packet. He came unstuck when an airport official saw him smoking and asked him if he could have a cigarette. The youth obliged and reached into his left pocket for the packet

John Nichols, convicted of smuggling 74 shinglebacks and 7 bearded dragons on 6/1/92 in Melbourne.
Photo: Raymond Hoser

Bearded dragon.
Photo: Raymond Hoser

Shingleback.
Photo: Raymond Hoser

One of the ringed pythons seized from Celebucki in 1989. Worth $5 000 in the U.S.A. (1991 prices).
Photo: Raymond Hoser

Oenpelli python. An adult is worth at least $15 000 in the U.S.A. At the time of writing only four specimens were captive in the entire world; all in a Government-owned park in the Northern Territory.
Photo: Raymond Hoser

Gouldian finch. Originally a native of Australia, mutations worth thousands of dollars are being smuggled into this country from Japan and elsewhere.
Photo: Raymond Hoser

SULLIVANS
SOLICITORS

Neil J. Sullivan LL.B.

5th Floor
67 Castlereagh Street
Sydney NSW 2000
DX 524 SYDNEY
Telephone: (02) 233 1966
Facsimile: (02) 233 1841

27 October 1992

The Director
National Parks and Wildlife Service NSW

Facsimile no. 585 6495
PO Box 1967
Hurstville NSW 2220

Dear Sir

RE; PAUL WOOLF
SEIZURE OF REPTILES

We refer to the execution of a Search Warrant at 16 Grenfell Street Blakehurst occupied by the above on 13 October 1992 attended by your Mr Potts, Mr Snook and other officers during which a number of reptiles were seized allegedly in accordance with the National Parks and Wildlife Act.

We wish to point out our that at the relevant time our Client was the holder of a general licence GL 1206 issued 27 May 1992, expiring 31 May 1993. Also at the time our Client was the holder of a permit for movement of Fauna from Queensland number IM 028518, operative from 9 October 1992 to 9 November 1992. Our Client also held an import licence number 9635 from your Service for the period 23 May 1992 to 23 June 1992 and on 6 October 1992 applied for a further extension of that licence with the fee being paid to your office on 8 October 1992. At no time was our Client informed of any impediment under Regulation 10D of the Fauna Protection Regulations and accordingly was entitled to assume in view of his earlier permit that such a permit would issue without qualification.

At the premises at 16 Grenfell Street Blakehurst your Mr Potts informed the writer that he became aware that there were reptiles on the premises after complaints were made by the neighbours surrounding the premises. Our Client has caused inquiries to be made of each and every neighbour in the area and not one neighbour new of the existence of the reptiles nor did they make any complaint to your office. The only neighbour who did state anything informed your agent that she herself did not know of the existence of the reptiles but was informed by her daughter that there may be some reptiles on the premises. This does not amount to a reasonable ground under Section 164(1)(a) accordingly we believe that the warrant obtained by your office under the Search Warrants Act 1985 was illegally obtained and as a result of an illegal search and based on false information.

We are also informed by Mr Paul Cox of Kogarah Municipal Council's environmental Services Department that approximately one week ago he was contacted by an Officer of the National Parks and Wildlife Service who after discussing the keeping of Reptiles at the premises at 16 Grenfell Street indicated words to the effect that; "Mr Woolf has applied for a Licence and we have to give it to him." and there after there ensued a discussion concerning whether or not Council had requirements concerning reptiles. Mr Cox is prepared to come to Court to give this evidence and in support of his allegations enclose a copy of a letter from The Municipality of Kogarah dated 20 October 1992.

Accordingly it is our belief and that of Counsel that you have no grounds to retain the reptiles illegally seized from our Client and therefore formally demand return of the following:

1. 6 Carpet Python

   1 Red Bellied Black Snake

   1 Banded Western Brown Snake

   4 Western Brown Snakes

   4 Black Tiger Snakes

   3 Spotted Black Snakes

   3 Colletts Snakes

   2 Eastern Brown Snakes

   2 Taipan Snakes

   4 Death Adders

   1 Water Dragon

   3 Shingle Back Lizards

   2 Brotched Blue Tongues

   1 Common Blue Tongue

   5 Bearded Dragons

   1 Jacki Dragon

   1 Childrens Python

   2 Bredele Python

Your attention is also drawn to the Governors declaration of 26 March 1995:

Common Blue Tongue

Shingle Back

Eastern Water Dragon

Carpet Snake

Long Necked Tortoise.

Your seizure and retention of these reptiles is illegal and actionable as such.

Unless all reptiles are returned to our Client or made available to our Client for Collection within 7 days we are instructed to approach the Supreme COurt of New South Wales for an Order that the same be removed together with an Order for Costs against your Department.

We require your confirmation that the reptiles will available for collection or returned to our Client by return facsimile.

Yours faithfully
SULLIVANS

N J Sullivan

Storr's monitor.
Photo: Raymond Hoser

Broad-headed snake.
Photo: Raymond Hoser

Hybrid Morelia simacropsilia x Morelia amesthistina.
Photo: Raymond Hoser

Albino eastern diamondback rattlesnake seized by fauna authorities from a Melbourne post office.
Photo: Raymond Hoser

of cigarettes, offering the man a snake instead of a fag. It was the packet in his right pocket that had the cigarettes.

Encounters of a Close Kind

There have been reports on several occasions of snake enthusiasts boarding international flights with small snakes concealed in their underwear. In early 1979, a man was fined in Darwin for attempting to smuggle five live pythons (C.I.T.E.S. appendix 2 animals). Four were strapped to his legs in bags, the fifth was hidden in his underpants.

On 14 December 1989, two German nationals, Wilhelm Furtjes and Gerhard Kammans, were arrested at Sydney airport for allegedly attempting to smuggle four birds into Australia concealed inside a ghetto blaster. One of the men, Furtjes was strip-searched and was found to be wearing a nappy with two concealed and viable parrot eggs.

The birds were two *Charmosyna* species and two African grey parrots *(Psittacus erithacus)*. On 16 March 1990, both men pleaded guilty at Sydney District court to Federal charges laid under section 22 (b) of the *Wildlife Protection (Regulation of Exports and Imports) Act 1982*.

On 1 July 1987, Nako Damcevski, a 39-year-old Melbourne man was caught illegally importing seven live pidgeons. The St Albans man was noticed by Customs officials when he arrived at Melbourne airport from Yugoslavia. Damcevski was acting suspiciously and moving awkwardly when Customs officers decided to search him. The birds were concealed and strapped in pouches on the man's legs below his knees.

The birds had been initially drugged but were fed during the flight. The young adult birds which arrived in good health were to be kept by Damcevski as pets.

Following his apprehension by officials, Damcevski pleaded guilty at Broadmeadows Court to charges laid under the Customs and Quarantine Acts.

RESULTS AND PENALTIES

Poachers of birds' eggs from the wild often inadvertently contribute to scientific knowledge when they are 'busted'. In 1982 an illegal collector of birds' eggs was apprehended after spending several weeks in the rainforests of Iron Range, North Queensland. He had collected the first two clutches of eggs known to science from the green-backed honeyeater *(Glycichaera fallax)*, a bird very restricted in distribution and rarely researched. He'd also taken no less than 14 clutches of the little-studied yellow-footed flycatcher *(Microeca griseoceps)* and other threatened rainforest species.

Another bird egg collector was apprehended after he'd poached some eggs from a nest of red goshawks *(Erythrotriorchis radiatus)* in the Conondale Range north of Brisbane. The hawk, one of Australia's rarest birds, had not been recorded as breeding outside Australia's tropics for most of this century. The nest in the Conondale Range was being studied by ornithologists and the eggs were stolen from their nest before they could hatch.

In order to combat egg collectors, ornithologists and other concerned individuals in areas of heavy poaching such as the Australian Capital Territory, use felt pens to mark the eggs and render them useless to those who take the eggs only for egg collections.

Some cases cannot be charged. Michael Schooley related an interesting case

Spiders in books seize

By BRETT de VINE

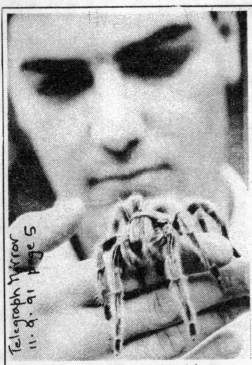

Michael Muscat eyes a tarantula

Jeff Fredrick of Customs with the books

FOUR giant spiders and three snakes are in the care of Taronga Zoo staff after being smuggled into Australia inside hollowed-out books.

Customs officials seized the live imports last week after an x-ray machine at the International Mail Centre at Clyde, in western Sydney, detected three suspicious parcels sent from Florida, bound for Brisbane.

Inside the packages were four tarantulas, two corn snakes and an endangered juvenile ball python.

A customs spokesman said the creatures were hidden inside books complete with creature comforts.

Inside one book were two plastic containers holding the two spiders with a water supply in a sponge.

A second book held two toothbrush containers with a live corn snake inside each, together with water sponges.

The third parcel was a plastic school lunch box with airholes for the python snake, which was in a sock.

After off-loading the cargo at Taronga Zoo, authorities followed the packages to the Queensland address before detaining two men for questioning.

One of the men is a licensed reptile trader but under federal law the species impounded are not allowed into Australia. Charges have not been laid.

54

BIRDS IN A COAT

A racket involving Europeans was 'busted' in Adelaide over Christmas 1973. Authorities received information from Customs that two known traffickers, a gentleman by the name of Van Brommelen and a woman by the name of Wassener, had arrived in Adelaide from Europe. They were in Australia for a five-day stay. They were kept under surveillance during the entire period they were in Australia. The people they visited were mostly of Dutch origin. The blue masked love birds (*Agapomis* sp.) and a particular colour mutation cockatiel brought into the country illegally were sold mainly to contacts in the eastern States. Two other men, Henk Hummen and De Bruin were also involved in planning to export the birds, and these men attracted the attention of the local authorities. Their conversations were 'bugged' so it was possible for authorities to schedule their 'bust' for the most opportune moment.

The smugglers discussed using 'clean-skinned couriers' (without a record), but the idea was discarded. Most, if not all, female couriers used by these men were already well known to Customs officials.

The decision was made that the woman Wassener would attempt to take out the birds. These were concealed in a coat she wore which contained a sausage-like arrangement for the birds. Both Wassener and Van Brommelen chose to leave on Christmas day. The timing was to co-incide with a crowded airport filled with people coming and going. Both were apprehended trying to board a plane and were subsequently charged and fined.

Later Hummen and De Bruin were interviewed by officials, after which they left Australia. It was well known in smuggling circles that both men were financed by a large syndicate with seemingly limitless funds. The two men had been advised that they were now hot properties and as such were no longer suitable for use as the procurers. Both men had been involved in aviculture for many years and were experienced with the breeding and pedigree of birds. In common with other major syndicates they would not accept wild-caught birds for overseas transhipment. They actively sought top-notch, fertile, breeding, captive stock. The birds were conditioned to being smuggled for several days before planned shipment, by exposing them to increasing periods of darkness.

Wassener had also been carrying stock from the eastern States when apprehended. Those birds came from an 'unimpeachable source' with well-established Government protection.

The syndicate involving the four people named above transferred operations to a neighbouring country after their operations stopped here. Other syndicates replaced it almost immediately.

of an Englishman who had illegally imported a South American crocodile (*Caiman* sp.) into Australia. After a tip-off Schooley and another Customs officer visited the house of the man in question in the Sydney suburb of Glenfield. After they entered the house they were 'nearly knocked over by the smell of marijuana', and noted the 'starry-eyed' nature of the occupant presumably from smoking the weed. Numerous reptiles, fish and yabbies were found throughout the house, some in fish tanks but most running loose. One

LAYER UPON LAYER

Another case was documented by Marie McCaskill of the R.S.P.C.A. in Sydney on a 'John Laws World' smuggling documentary. She said:

'I think the most memorable we've had, and they can be amusing, was two Chinese gentlemen who came in from Singapore and of course it was an extremely hot day at Sydney airport, and they were wearing dufflecoats and I mean you do tend to stick out in a crowd if you're wearing a large dufflecoat. And of course they were nabbed fairly quickly.'

When the dufflecoats were opened up they were found to contain a staggering number of slots and holes in numerous layers on the insides of the coats. Inside the compartments were small birds and reptiles 'they were bringing in because they were guaranteed an enormous amount of money'. A large number of the specimens had died.

WILDLIFE AS PROTECTION

An interesting case of smuggling precious stones was uncovered about ten years ago. Smugglers obtained large venomous snakes such as taipans or eastern brown snakes and large dead rats. Each rat was opened, stuffed with gems, re-sewn together and then fed to a snake. Most snakes can be force-fed if they don't take food voluntarily.

The snake would then be posted with the gems to an overseas destination. Should a law-enforcement agent try to open the parcel, he would be confronted by a large, dangerous, potentially agressive snake. About seven days later the gems would be passed out by the snake in its faeces, by which time it would have reached its destination. The aim of the entire exercise was to avoid paying taxes on the gems.

FORGED DOCUMENTS

Another major racket involving forged Australian export documents was stopped in 1974. The racket which was apparently organised by Dutch nationals, involved the forging of Australian and New Zealand export permits. These were sent to Sydney and used by syndicate members to place stock on planes to Europe openly without having to unduly harm or confine the individual animals (mainly birds) being sent. For some time airport officials were fooled into believing the export animals were legal. After the racket was stopped, none of the perpetrators was ever brought to justice. The person who was caught attempting to place a cage full of birds onto a plane was a bona fide courier who had collected them from a large city building as a result of radio dispatch.

It was only as a result of back-checking export documents that the extent of this racket was realised.

room had a number of marijuana plants growing in pots. More than one crocodile was found, including the imported one, it being the only non-Australian reptile on the premises.

When asked how he brought it in, the man said he had declared the crocodile on his Customs form on arrival at Sydney airport. He then just walked straight out with it in his coat pocket. A check of the story revealed its authenticity with the word 'Cayman', the South American name for the animal, being written on top of the Customs form in the man's own handwriting.

The man therefore could not be charged with illegally bringing a reptile into the country as it had occurred only through a Customs' oversight. However, he was charged with other offences relating to his posession of marijuana plants and unlicensed local reptiles.

U.S. Cases

TRAFFIC (an international organisation which monitors trade in animals) reported that on 20 July 1987, Cory Blanc of Longwood, Florida, U.S.A., was convicted of attempting to export four desert death adders (*Acanthophis pyrrhus*) to the U.S.A. without permits at Port Hedland court.

On 28 March the same year, Blanc had been arrested by police at Port Hedland airport after his baggage was found to contain the snakes. He was charged with both State and Federal wildlife offences and on 20 July fined a total of $1 500 plus $331.20 court costs. The snakes in question were worth up to $10 000 each in the U.S.A. depending on size and sex.

On 7 January 1988, Americans Robert Stene and David Rittenhouse of San Jose, California were jailed in the U.S.A. for smuggling wildlife, mainly reptiles into the U.S.A. The wildlife had been obtained on trips to Australia and Mexico and posted in the mail to friends back in the U.S.A. The men were both given three years' suspended sentences and put on five years' probation on condition that they served six months and ten weeks respectively in a community treatment centre. Stene was also fined a total of US$20 200, and Rittenhouse was fined a total of US$4 100 and ordered to carry out 240 hours of community service.

Different Magistrates

Which presiding judge or magistrate hears a given case can have a huge bearing on the penalty imposed. Hans Klein, an Austrian citizen, was originally convicted on 4 October 1988, on Federal wildlife smuggling charges in a Sydney court, after being prosecuted for bird smuggling. He had been sentenced to five years' jail, the maximum penalty under the *Wildlife Protection (Regulation of Exports and Imports) Act* 1982, and two years on a quarantine charge to be served concurrently. On appeal, the sentence was reduced to four months on the wildlife charge and two months on the second charge, to be served concurrently. By this stage Klein had already served his time, so he was released immediately.

In the Future

The future lies in educating the public, a fact that is slowly being recognised as the following cases show.

INFECTIOUS DISEASES

In 1989, an attempt to smuggle some 50 parrots by air from Western Australia to Queensland was foiled by fauna officials. Much of the consignment died of *Chlamydia psittacosis*, a virus peculiar to Australian parrots. The remainder had to be destroyed. To make things worse for the Queensland wildlife ranger who apprehended the smugglers with the birds, he too caught the debilitating and potentially fatal disease and subsequently became extremely ill.

On 12 September 1984, William Robinson and Jonathan Wood were arrested at Los Angeles International Airport trying to smuggle 27 eggs of rare birds from Australia into the U.S.A. The eggs, which were concealed in their clothing, were discovered by an American Customs officer who decided to search the two men. The following year, when sentencing the pair, the American judge not only put the pair on probation for five years, but also sentenced them to pay for the making of a documentary film about the importance of birds of prey.

On 16 January 1985, a 32-year-old Dutchman, Johnny Rinaldo Noordman, was apprehended trying to illegally export a number of snakes and lizards at Melbourne airport. He was later fined $5 000 under Federal law. He later voluntarily appeared on a British documentary about smuggling wildlife from Australia in a bid to deter others.

6
DETECTION OF SMUGGLERS AND SMUGGLING ACTIVITIES

Detection of wildlife smuggling is currently the responsibility of several authorities who in theory co-operate with one another; these include Customs, State and Federal fauna authorities (usually National Parks and Wildlife Services), and Federal and State police.

Although Government officials frequently complain of lack of funds and manpower, official corruption is often the reason for smuggling operations continuing. Rivalries between officials of different departments may also hamper efforts to curtail these activities.

In terms of actual figures, it is hard to be certain how many people are directly involved in trying to prevent the illegal trafficking in fauna. Many officials from wildlife, Customs and quarantine authorities have the control of wildlife trade as one of their many duties. The amount of time devoted to this particular task is difficult to quantify for a given official. The Queensland N.P.W.S. in co-operation with the police force have a two-man full-time fauna squad operating in that State. Licensing officers of the N.P.W.S. also take an interest in smuggling matters. Customs officials, particularly those entrusted with guarding the coastlines, occasionally 'bust' wildlife traffickers. In addition, any police officer may take action against wildlife traffickers. So in Queensland, many people are involved in the effort to detect wildlife smuggling.

Other States tend to have a similar proportion of officers involved in the same sorts of activities.

METHODS OF DETECTION
Small-time smugglers are usually caught as a result of bad luck, when a suspicious official decides to search a person or their luggage. Dead animals give off a distressing odour and this probably accounts for the majority of detections when reptiles are sent through the post. Escaped specimens are almost impossible to avoid detecting.

Sniffer dogs may be trained specifically to detect fauna enclosed in parcels. 'Probing' of suitcases and parcels to see if wild animals are inside is a relatively new method of inspection and has had some success. The probe inserted measures carbon dioxide levels and if the level is abnormally high then an alert is raised. As animals exhale carbon dioxide, such a method of detection may be used for any type of animal.

Snakes are less likely to be detected by sniffer dogs and probing for two principal reasons. Their scent is usually harder for dogs to detect than those of other reptiles, birds and mammals; and as with other reptiles, snakes have a lower metabolic rate than mammals and birds and therefore lower levels of carbon dioxide are exhaled, which may not register on the probe.

Resurfacing Stolen Fauna

Often stolen wildlife will resurface somewhere in the hands of another collector, zoo or dealer after the initial theft. Detection of this 'resurfacing wildlife' is a perennial problem. Bird keepers have developed ringing systems (placing identification rings around one of the legs). Sometimes these rings cannot be removed without mutilating the birds and on the rings is information identifying the owner. Reptile owners resort to scale clipping and similar forms of mutilation in a bid to aid identification of stolen stock. Most reptile owners are able to recognise all their individual snakes and lizards even if they hold hundreds of specimens. Mammals are sometimes branded or tatooed to identify their owner. Fish and frogs, which do not seem to be stolen or smuggled to anywhere the extent of the other groups, are not marked in any way by their owners.

In 1990 reptile keeper Peter Moran, of Mornington, Victoria, was convicted by the local Department of Conservation, Forests and Lands (C.F.L.) officials for having unlicensed reptiles. Some were sent to Dr Hal Cogger, a herpetologist at the Australian Museum in Sydney, for identification. At the time Graeme Gow was visiting Cogger at the Museum and noticed that one of these particular snakes had been stolen from his reptile park at Humpty Doo in the Northern Territory some years earlier.

Despite the number of people involved in keeping wildlife, it should be noted that people who keep reptiles generally don't keep birds and vice versa. Within these two groups, there are relatively well-defined sub-groups who tend to keep particular types of reptile or bird. A similar situation occurs for mammal, bird and fish people. Therefore when something goes missing, potential buyers for the given animal/s are limited.

Although one might assume that if a person has received a stolen or smuggled animal, that person would attempt to keep the fact a secret, this is not necessarily the case. Keepers of wildlife may be secretive with officials but they like their peers to know what they hold. The legality of specimens isn't always questioned. The saying 'possession is nine-tenths of the law' is often believed. Therefore by keeping abreast of who has what, it can be possible to track the movements of stolen wildlife. Dealers in particular are forced to advertise their wildlife holdings and often inadvertently advertise illegally obtained stock.

Zoos, other institutions and major private keepers of wildlife often publish lists of what species they hold, including numbers, in specific inventory-style publications; e.g. a reptile and amphibian inventory is published annually by Frank Leo Slavens, listing the holdings of several hundred collections worldwide. When a few specimens of a given species are held by only one or two people and those animals are stolen, one has only to wait and see who announces they have just acquired a specimen before investigating the theft further. An ant-hill python stolen from my house in 1981 was 'found' after its new keeper boasted to the world that he held the species in an *Inventory of Live Reptiles and Amphibians* the following year.

Specimens stolen from keepers in Australia have repeatedly been re-discovered after having been purchased unwittingly by keepers in the U.S.A. and Europe who believed the purchases to be legal and accordingly publicised them.

By asking the 'legal' purchaser of a stolen animal about its immediate antecedents it is sometimes possible to track down smugglers from the selling end. It is quite common for a particular bird or reptile to pass through the hands of five or six people between the initial theft in Australia and the final sale in the U.S.A. or Europe. Some of those intermediate people may be unaware that they are involved in the illegal trafficking of fauna.

Generally speaking, overseas dealers and keepers who refuse to disclose details about who sold them their wildlife, have something to hide and are most likely to be directly involved in smuggling operations.

Overseas Officials

Co-operation of officials in foreign countries is extremely hard to obtain. In many countries the relevant law enforcement officials have little, if any, interest in Australian wildlife and plenty of problems of their own to worry about. When they do focus on Australian wildlife and illegal trafficking, the officials concerned are just as likely to be involved in smuggling and therefore unlikely to blow the whistle on a racket from which they expect to profit.

Hi-Tech Methods

High-tech means of detecting smugglers or aiding investigations are increasingly used by officials. Genetic fingerprinting, i.e. making an accurate copy of an individual animal's genotype, is a foolproof means of identifying an animal.

Injecting micro-chips subcutaneously into an animal is also a useful means of identification, particularly when it may become part of a large legally held collection. The Roy Philip Pails case is an example of this.

Pails, a snake keeper of Ballarat, Victoria, was convicted of illegally bringing five scrub pythons *(Morelia amethistina)* by plane from their native north Queensland. The shipment was intercepted by Victorian C.F.L. officials at Melbourne Airport on 8 June 1991. The consignment had been labelled 'Engine Spares'. Rather than 'busting' Pails on the spot, the snakes were secretly injected with micro-chips and the consignment was then followed. After monitoring Pails' movements for some time, C.F.L. officials moved in, seized the snakes and charged Pails. The snakes were positively identified from Pails' large number of other snakes by using a scanner, similar to that used to identify barcodes on supermarket merchandise.

Pails pleaded guilty to various wildlife charges. He had imported two of the snakes to replace licensed snakes that had died, while three others were

THE FAT LADY AND THE MILLIONAIRE

The story of English bird keeper Denis Washington typifies the pulling power of rich overseas bird keepers in terms of their ability to get hold of Australian fauna. The people Washington dealt with in order to get what he wanted also typify the illegal wildlife trafficking scene in more ways than one.

The one-legged Washington, a self-made millionaire from the construction business, spent a large amount of money setting up private facilities for keeping birds and mammals from all parts of the world including Australia.

Before Sir Edward Hallstrom's death, Washington visited Hallstrom's home in Australia and saw his extensive private collection of birds and other animals. Hallstrom apparently assisted Washington in getting the neccessary contacts to export wildlife out of Australia.

One of these contacts was a woman known as 'Big Bertha'. She took birds out of the country in a belly band — being a rather large lady, the birds were never detected. Washington also acquired most of his stock through what he called 'the biggest gang of rogues I have ever met in my life', a syndicate of taxi drivers. Consisting of about a dozen individuals, the gang was based in Sydney and individuals were paid $1 000 a trip to fly birds to the U.K. for Washington. Washington also informed journalist Dick Wordley of a 'new' method of tranquillising birds with a higher success rate than the drug Luminol™. He had taught this method to the taxi driving syndicate who were somehow able to source birds from all parts of Australia. Before this, Luminol™ injected into the breast-plate of birds was regarded by many as being the best way to reduce bird mortality when smuggling.

The syndicate of taxi drivers had a leader who never missed a trick when it came to illegal activity and it was this that upset Washington, leading him to eventually terminate business with the gang.

The smuggling out of birds wasn't the problem. The money, however was being 'contra-ed' in Singapore, according to Washington, for bringing into Australia illegal drugs, immigrants and currency. Most of the illegal immigrants were Italians, who were brought in by ship and then dropped off on the coast somewhere near Darwin.

Washington's collection of wildlife was extensive and included a blue macaw *(Ara araruana)*, the world's largest parrot. He also held the only albino penguin in the world. That penguin, a king penguin *(Aptenodytes patagonica)*, had been found by two Inca Indian boys in Peru where the birds were nesting. Washington's agent, who bought the penguin from the boys was the son of an exiled Spanish princess. The agent was paid US$200 into a bank account and Washington had the bird flown to him at Heathrow Airport where he collected it. The bird survived the journey without complications. Washington had obtained the bird very cheaply.

Also in Washington's private collection in his backyard were 35 African flamingos *(Phoenicopterus ruber)*, six other king penguins which apparently died and several other birds from various parts of the globe.

After adverse publicity in the U.K. about Australian birds being smuggled into the country, Washington decided to sell his collection of Australian birds. It wasn't the illegality of the original export of the birds that worried him, it was the possibility of people breaking in and stealing them. He told Dick Wordley 'My wife Grace could not sleep at night and I could not sleep so I sold my collection of Australian birds.'

The birds were sold to other keepers for a total of £25 000. In Australia they could have been bought for a few hundred dollars.

An illegally imported emu *(Dromaius novaehollandiae)* offered by a dealer to Washington for £1 000 had been refused because Washington wasn't sure how it would get on with his flamingos.

Washington offered Wordley £5 000 for a red kangaroo *(Macropus rufus)*. Washington, who himself wasn't directly guilty of any wildlife trafficking offence, even though he had knowingly purchased smuggled wildlife, argued strongly for the controlled export of certain types of animals. For example the type of kangaroo Washington was willing to pay £5 000 for was being shot as a pest in many parts of Australia.

---

for a friend. He imported the snakes for himself in order to retain the C.F.L. licences for the two deceased pythons. Ironically, one of Pails' best mates in Melbourne bred legally held scrub pythons at about the same time, and Pails might have been able to get snakes from him without difficulty.

The Role of the Media
A problem throughout Australia at the time of writing is the general lack of accountability of public officials. This includes law enforcement officials entrusted with policing wildlife smuggling operations. State and Federal Ombudsmen's departments have a low success rate. The *Bulletin* magazine stated that only 8 of the 10 000 complaints against police in Victoria were sustained. Yet all were presumably scrutinised by the Deputy Ombudsman's office as is law in that State. The implication, that the other 9 992 people who bothered to complain about the police were telling lies, is difficult to believe.

The main hope of detecting official smuggling operations is through media exposure which forces departments to take publicly visible action.

For example, virtually every man, woman and child in Brisbane knew that illegal brothels were located in Brisbane's Fortitude Valley, yet the head of police in that city denied their existence. It was only after the Australian Broadcasting Commission (A.B.C.) documented the existence of the brothels and their police protection, that political action was taken. This ultimately led to the establishment of the Fitzgerald Inquiry which brought down the long-established State government.

That the A.B.C. was the only section of the media to expose police corruption in Queensland reflects the unfortunate reality that no commercially owned media outlet wants to risk being sued; defamation laws in Australia have been framed in such a manner that they often protect those who are guilty of corruption. Until these laws are altered, the likelihood of ever publicly exposing the principals of wildlife smuggling rackets is slight.

At the time of writing, it is fair to say that without a Royal Commission into wildlife trafficking and the administration of State fauna authorities, current major smuggling operations will continue unimpeded.

7
THE ROLE OF WILDLIFE AUTHORITIES

Fauna authorities are entrusted with the task of preventing wildlife smuggling and in most cases this does occur. Unfortunately, certain activities in recent years have sometimes had the unintentional effect of aiding and abetting illegal trafficking.

Fauna authorities and officials (usually State bodies) wield enormous powers, regarded by many conservationists as excessive and counterproductive to the conservation cause.

THE 'BAN ON MOVEMENTS'
At the time of writing, the New South Wales N.P.W.S., and some other State fauna authorities have instituted a 'ban on movements' of fauna between holders. The stated rationale behind this is somewhat vague, but its effect has been to prohibit trade or movement of fauna between licensed keepers. Breeders of endangered fauna are unable to off-load surplus stock and so in some cases, have killed it, due to their lack of alternative.

Snake breeder, Brian Barnett, had to reduce his rate of breeding because the New South Wales authorities prohibited him from legally exporting up to 100 captive-bred pythons (C.I.T.E.S appendix 2 species) and other snakes from Victoria to New South Wales. Bob Irwin, a reptile park owner in Queensland, froze eggs of rare and endangered snakes because he was unable to do anything with the surplus young if they hatched. He also kept snakes of opposite sexes separate in a bid to further curtail breeding activity. Bird breeders have been more affected by the ban and have initiated a major campaign to have it lifted, with some limited support among N.P.W.S. officials themselves.

The banning of legal trade between wildlife keepers within Australia simply encourages unregulated illegal trade, both locally and overseas.

CURIOUS COINCIDENCE
In the 1970s, endangered orange-bellied parrots had been bred in a few aviaries

and their future as a species seemed assured. Upon the death of the most successful breeder of these birds, Peter Lewitzker, fauna authorities took and allegedly released his captive-held birds, despite widespread protest from conservationists and aviculturalists. It is unlikely that any of those birds would have survived in the wild, as most aviary-kept birds do not.

Although none of these parrots has ever been legally exported, at least one pair was found by Wilson Wheeler, of the International Council for Bird Preservation, in a collection in Holland at about the same time that Peter Lewitzker's were allegedy released. The possible connection between the two incidents raises questions about what actually happened to the birds. Taking into account the rarity of the species, it is most likely the birds had been sourced from captivity.

Since the loss of Lewitzker's collection, numbers of orange-bellied parrots have continued to decline in the wild. After a recent study, Tasmanian fauna authorities decided to embark on their own captive breeding programme of the parrots. This entails removing more birds from the wild and the programme will require large sums of public money. Previous successful captive breeding was all privately funded.

Meanwhile, the relative lack of orange-bellied parrots in captivity has made the species highly sought by traffickers, being valued at over US$10 000 a bird in the U.S.A.

ABUSING THE LAW

Due to the fact that smuggling prevention and the illegal keeping of wildlife are so closely linked, laws relating to both areas need to be considered. The link is nowhere more clearly demonstrated than in the issuing of permits. Officials may lose incoming correspondence or fail to issue permits by a certain date and then use the lack of documentation to 'bust' disliked people for 'illegally' holding fauna.

The Case of Julian Ford

Perhaps the most widely publicised case occurred in 1985-87. Perth scientist and ornithologist, Dr Julian Ford, applied for a permit to collect native birds in North Queensland as part of a federally funded research project. He lodged a 13 page application with the Queensland N.P.W.S. in November 1985 and also paid them the relevant fee for the permit. In due course Ford's cheque was cashed by the N.P.W.S. and he believed that the relevant permit had been issued.

The following October, while completing his field trip in North Queensland, he was raided by N.P.W.S. officials and all his collected birds were confiscated. What N.P.W.S. officials actually did with those birds after their seizure was never revealed to the public.

When Ford complained to the media about what had happened, Queensland N.P.W.S. repeatedly denied ever receiving an application from him. Ford then faced some 60 separate charges laid by N.P.W.S. officials for illegally capturing fauna, which carried possible fines totalling $100 000. The Ford case attracted attention but not because Ford was wrongly charged or unduly harassed by fauna authorities. The case received nation-wide media attention, including a feature story on '60 Minutes' only after he died of a massive heart attack early in 1987, which his wife said was caused by the incident with N.P.W.S.

After Ford's widow, Jennifer, produced evidence in her dead husband's favour, the N.P.W.S. admitted that in fact they had acknowledged his licence application and cashed his cheque.

'60 Minutes' alleged corruption within the Queensland N.P.W.S., but this was denied by the director. It also became clear that the pattern — of wildlife permit being granted, followed by a raid and seizure of wildlife and a denial by officials of a permit having been issued — was not the first such case to occur in Queensland.

Fauna researchers, breeders and others, in particular bird and reptile keepers, have had so much trouble with beligerent wildlife authority officials that numerous submissions, some longer than 100 pages, have been made to these departments to try and change the prevailing attitudes of enforcement officials and in some cases the laws themselves. These lengthy submissions are produced only at great cost, using funds that otherwise would have been spent on the animals themselves.

CURRENT LEGISLATION

The relevant laws are often drafted by public servants who have no knowledge of the animals in question; consequently certain so-called protection laws have sometimes been counter-productive. Some officials have a fundamental abhorrence to any form of wildlife captivity, while others regard scientific research methods as cruel and therefore display hostility to fauna keepers or researchers.

Excessive red-tape and the officials to administer it clearly cost money that would be better spent elsewhere. For example, one State wildlife authority declared a species of fish an endangered species. The reason for this was not that scientists had decided the fish was rare or threatened; nor was it because of widespread poaching by fish enthusiasts. It was declared rare because a Philippine dealer had put the species on his price list and labelled it 'rare'. A copy of the list had fallen into the hands of the wildlife authority and they acted accordingly.

The New South Wales N.P.W.S. had a nasty habit of declaring common pythons, such as carpet (*Morelia spilota macropsila*), diamond and children's (then known as *Bothrochilus childreni*) as 'rare' or 'endangered' (Schedule 12) allegedly to boost overseas prices of specimens taken by their officials.

The Western Australian N.P.W.S. at one stage seemed to declare any newly described species of animal as endangered. Such a classification effectively prohibited further research on these species, even by scientists from museums and universities who had actually discovered the species. In most cases the species in question were not endangered; they were simply little-known species that previously had been overlooked, which is hardly a difficult feat in a State as large and sparsely populated as Western Australia.

In 1976, before the House of Representatives Inquiry into smuggling, Ronald Strahan gave numerous examples of how bureaucrats and regulations were hampering wildlife research and conservation efforts in general. Overseas museums were reluctant to send dead preserved-type specimens to researchers in Australia because of the possibility that Customs officials would refuse to allow the re-export of these specimens back to their original museums after the researchers had finished using them.

Strahan stated that zoos such as Berlin and the U.S. National Zoo had done more for research and propagation of certain types of Australian marsupial such as the wombat (*Vombatus/Lasiorhinus*) and small carnivorous mammals, than any institutions in Australia. The refusal of Customs officials to allow these overseas institutions to import and export Australian animals was seriously hampering the conservation effort.

The editor of *Australian Birdkeeper* magazine, Nigel Steele-Boyce, sums up problems with fauna authorities faced by those involved in wildlife conservation: 'It seems an issue does not go by without some form of dissatisfaction being levelled at National Parks and Wildlife Services, and unfortunately this issue is no different.'

FALSE CHARGES

Those who accuse fauna officials of wrongdoing are often subject to harassment in the form of false charges being laid. On at least two occasions officers of the New South Wales N.P.W.S. laid serious wildlife trafficking charges against people who had been critical of them in the media. After N.P.W.S. officials had maximised bad publicity against their critics, they quietly dropped the charges. On one occasion, to damage my reputation N.P.W.S. laid 'without reason' a trafficking in endangered fauna charge which was later dropped without explanation.

On another occasion, Sydney bird keeper and trader Ray Ackroyd faced a serious wildlife charge laid against him by N.P.W.S. officials. The N.P.W.S. and Ackroyd had been at loggerheads since Ackroyd had made allegations of incompetence in the national media. The charge was quietly dropped just 24 hours before it was due to be heard. Ackroyd had still lost, however. His legal costs up to that point were astronomical and he was unable to get compensation under New South Wales law.

In 1977, New South Wales N.P.W.S. officials accused a well-known reptile keeper of stealing from a local zoo. The charge couldn't stick because at the time of the alleged offence, that same person had been in Queensland with his father collecting reptiles with the permission and knowledge of other officials in the same department.

The South Australian N.P.W.S. has repeatedly framed legislation in a bid to prevent all legal trade between keepers in that State and elsewhere. This has merely stifled the keeping and research of wildlife in that State. Like laws initiated by other State fauna authorities, the South Australian laws are in violation of the Federal Constitution section 92, which permits free trade between the States. The former director of the Service, Robert Lyons, didn't hesitate to test the effectiveness of his legislation against a keeper who was virtually entrapped into violating the new laws.

The defendant won the case (at great personal expense) because the magistrate found in favour of section 92. The case cost Lyons and N.P.W.S. nothing as their case was financed by the taxpayer. Perhaps bearing this in mind, Lyons further recommended 'Let us go find out in the High Court.' The case would have cost everybody even more money if the State Solicitor-General had not refused to continue the case.

The over-enthusiastic tendency of some officials to drag people involved in wildlife research and conservation before the courts to discredit them was perhaps best documented in a case fought by Sydney solicitor Neil Milne in New South Wales. He fought a case 'on black ducks (*Anas superciliosa*), where

BIRD'S EYES

In the early 1970s it was legal to import into the U.K. all types of bird except for poultry which is dutiable and birds of prey which are illegal. All other birds were legal. In other words birds from Australia or Argentina or anywhere else, might have been endangered and 'protected' where they occurred but it was perfectly legal to bring them into the U.K. without *any* permits. This system (which has now changed in the U.K. but still exists in a number of other countries) simply encouraged smugglers to get their wildlife into those countries where licensing laws did not apply and then to somehow 'launder' their stock.

It was common in the early 1970s for bird dealers to stitch up the eyes of birds of prey. The reason for this was simple. British Customs had no real expertise on birds and had been told that all birds of prey had large eyes. If the bird traffickers sewed up the birds' eyes, Customs officials wouldn't realise that the birds were in fact birds of prey. Journalist Dick Wordley published photos in *Pix People* magazine, of R.S.P.C.A. workers at Heathrow Airport unstitching the eyes of an unfortunate bird of prey.

a little old lady had found two black ducks with their wings broken beyond repair, put them in her poultry yard and cared for them for two years. She was prosecuted for having two black ducks, which were actually shot during an open season. And their attitude was that you can kill during an open season, but you cannot capture and preserve during an open season — quite incredible.'

Surely this 'little old lady' is not the fearsome plunderer of our wildlife that any fauna authority should be dragging through the courts and labelling a criminal, wasting thousands of dollars of public money in the process.

MORE INTERESTING CASES
James Fitzgerald's Expensive Goanna
When wildlife authorities are unable to frame laws that effectively ban the legal keeping of wildlife, they sometimes resort to illegal and semi-legal practices to achieve their aims. A classic case illustrating this attitude occurred with the Canberra fauna authority in 1990, involving well-known A.C.T. herpetologist, James Fitzgerald.

As Ron Campbell of the *Canberra Times* put it, 'A young Charnwood man has spent a small fortune and a good deal of energy fighting officialdom for the right to keep a large goanna in his backyard.'

Mr Fitzgerald went through all the 'proper' channels to import a four-year-old captive-bred perentie goanna (*Varanus giganteus*) from a breeder in South Australia. After applying to the A.C.T. Conservator of Wildlife (C.W.A.C.T.), on 25 July, for a permit to import the monitor lizard, he was asked later to give the service details of the cage to be provided for the lizard. Fitzgerald spent a great deal of time preparing a lengthy submission including relevant reference material regarding the best methods of keeping this lizard in captivity, which was duly given to C.W.A.C.T.

Fitzgerald was refused a permit to import the lizard and no adequate reason was given by the fauna authority officials. Although strongly tempted to go outside the law and attempt to import and keep the lizard illegally without a permit, Fitzgerald decided against that option. Instead he enlisted the support of wildlife breeders, museum staff and others throughout Australia, to help him fight for the right to import and keep the goanna.

Fitzgerald took the matter to the local Administrative Appeals Tribunal (A.A.T.A.C.T.). In the subsequent lengthy case, C.W.A.C.T. officials appeared to rely on gross inaccuracies to support their case.

For example, at one stage C.W.A.C.T. lawyers argued that the species in question wasn't suited to captivity, and went so far as to assert that Royal Melbourne Zoo didn't keep the species for this reason.

That the specimen in question was captive bred should have negated the idea that the species couldn't be kept properly in captivity. Furthermore it was shown that the Royal Melbourne Zoo actually wanted to keep this particular species and the only reason they didn't was insufficient space at their facility.

The C.W.A.C.T. officials when in a 'corner' argued about the so-called aggressiveness of the perentie; (anyone who has dealt with the species knows that in a 'free' or wild state, it would be almost impossible to get within 10 m of the animal due to its extreme shyness). C.W.A.C.T. officials stated that the lizard could break a dog's leg with a swing of its tail. The basis of that allegation turned out to be a piece of anecdotal evidence from a very dubious source involving a wild specimen in 1912. How a dog would have been able to approach a perentie close enough for it to be able to swing its tail and contact the dog, was never explained.

When the C.W.A.C.T. lawyer seemed to have lost the argument about how dangerous the perentie allegedly was he cried out, 'If a goanna, why not an elephant or tiger?' Fortunately for Fitzgerald, the tribunal didn't accept the C.W.A.C.T. line of argument in this regard.

C.W.A.C.T. lawyers also questioned Fitzgerald's competence and ability to successfully keep a perentie. Fitzgerald, however, after consultation with others used to dealing with fauna officials, was prepared for this. He had endorsement from top ranking herpetologists and breeders throughout Australia. Victoria's largest snake breeder, Brian Barnett said that Fitzgerald's perentie would probably be the best cared for goanna in Australia.

At the end of the hearing, the tribunal stated that C.W.A.C.T. hadn't really objected to Fitzgerald's keeping of the perentie on the grounds of Fitzgerald's ability to look after the animal or the characteristics of the animal itself. Rather, the tribunal felt that 'the service's real objection was to the idea of keeping a perentie in captivity at all.' As the case had not been argued along those lines, Fitzgerald won and he was allowed to legally import and keep the lizard.

However, it appeared that the C.W.A.C.T. couldn't take defeat gracefully. Before C.W.A.C.T. officials had even left the tribunal it had been suggested that they should change the legislation of the A.C.T. to prevent a similar case arising. As Rod Campbell put it, in order to combat the 'real objection' C.W.A.C.T. needed to change 'wildlife legislation as it was in most other States.'

C.W.A.C.T. officials also asked their specially contracted lawyer to prepare an appeal against the tribunal's decision. He refused stating that they had no legal grounds for an appeal and to do so would only be a further waste of public money.

Not surprisingly, the whole matter was widely reported in the Canberra media, with general support of Fitzgerald coming in from virtually all sectors of the community. Well-known zoologists wrote to newspapers endorsing Fitzgerald's victory, with Richard Longmore, a Canberra-based zoologist even going so far as to state that Fitzgerald's case should become a legal precedent for all future cases.

C.W.A.C.T. officials subsequently tried to defend their own actions in a press release after the case, to restore their publicly perceived role to 'protect and conserve our native wildlife'. Yet they stated quite emphatically that 'it was not considered relevant to inspect the proposed housing facilities to be provided by Mr Fitzgerald.'

Statements such as these perpetuate the well-founded idea that fauna officials in many States prefer to ban wildlife rather than actually conserve it. The mere fact that C.W.A.C.T. officials reacted so quickly to adverse publicity reveals how loath they are to accept constructive criticism.

Permits Cancelled Without Warning
In New South Wales an interesting case occurred in 1984. A reptile keeper told N.P.W.S. officials that he wanted them to take *all* his reptiles, all of which were held on N.P.W.S. issued permits. A letter was sent to the service on 27 March and they subsequently acknowledged receipt. A condition of the permits was that the reptiles had to be held at the keeper's address, so to have moved the reptiles anywhere would have been an offence.

In the first two weeks of July 1984, N.P.W.S. officials cancelled the keeper's permits without telling him and in violation of all the usual procedures. Officials then broke into the house, took all the reptiles while the keeper was at work and subsequently charged him with keeping reptiles illegally.

The above event was typical of N.P.W.S. in New South Wales and this author has had literally dozens of similar accounts given to him, involving both bird and reptile keepers.

Andrew Norbury
Andrew Norbury of Emu Plains had 'done the right thing', applied for and was issued with a N.P.W.S. permit to hold over 20 snakes. He'd invested a fortune in the best reptile cages he could find.

As is inevitable for anyone in New South Wales who holds a wildlife licence, he was visited by a N.P.W.S. official, in this case Gary Sims, a well-known enforcement officer.

Sims asked to see Norbury's permit. Sims took the permit and declared that he was cancelling the permit on the spot. Referring to Norbury's snakes he said 'We're taking the lot!' According to Norbury, 'He got the permits off me and said "Well, we'll cancel your permits, you can't have them anymore".'

Not only did Sims take Norbury's snakes, he also took the cages they were in. Sims promised to return the cages but never did. A logical question to ask would be, why would a reptile keeper put up with such behaviour from an official? The reason is simple. The officials have so much power, that keepers can be intimidated, especially if the only redress involves expensive litigation.

Sims took all of Norbury's snakes, although in his haste to grab them, two were missed and left behind.

Norbury also held a permit to remove snakes from people's backyards, when they posed a perceived threat to human life or civil order (a capture-release permit). These permits are issued by wildlife departments to reptile people in outer suburbs where there is common contact between people and snakes.

After Sims had taken Norbury's snakes Norbury contacted Sims at N.P.W.S. head office, in Hurstville and said 'Look Gary, I get heaps of phone calls, what's the go? Am I still licensed to go collect them and pick them up or re-release them or what?' Sims replied 'I'll get back to you', but of course he never did. According to Norbury 'the phone's been ringing hot' with people with snakes in their yards wanting Norbury to pick them up. As Norbury wouldn't risk being outside the law by catching them and N.P.W.S. officials wouldn't waste their time looking for a single, most probably common, type of snake, people have invariably tended to take matters into their own hands and kill the snakes. So much for conservation!

Disappearing Snakes
Perhaps most interesting is what actually happened to the snakes that Sims took. Since 1977 at least, New South Wales N.P.W.S. officials have been repeatedly accused of smuggling 'seized' snakes overseas. In order to make these officials more accountable, they are required to issue a 'seizure receipt' which lists everything taken and is signed by both the N.P.W.S. officer and the person from whom the material is taken. No receipt was issued to Norbury and the fate of the snakes is unknown. Lack of documentation makes it easier to smuggle wildlife.

In another case a seizure receipt issued on a raid by New South Wales N.P.W.S. official, Clive Jones failed to disclose all the snakes taken.

Re-appearing Snakes
Sometimes snakes re-appear. The Farmer family of Faulconbridge in New South Wales were told during a N.P.W.S. raid that all reptiles taken from them were to be released into the wild. Some months later, one of their diamond snakes was seen on public display at Taronga Park Zoo. The Farmers were not prosecuted over failure to hold a licence or any other alleged breach in relation to the snakes; if they had been, the snakes would have been held in an 'off-display' quarantine area. What happened to other reptiles taken from the Farmers and other individuals raided at the same time in the Blue Mountains was never publicly disclosed.

A spotted python (*Bothrochilus maculosus*) taken from the Farmers by N.P.W.S. was given to me on 31 July 1981 by N.P.W.S. officials under the direction of the director, Don Johnstone. It was a substitute for an ant-hill python wrongly taken by N.P.W.S. and Customs officials from my house on 8 May 1981 and part of an out of court settlement. Of course I refused to accept the snake.

A SET-UP
In States other than New South Wales, wildlife officials do not appear to be taking reptiles or birds for smuggling purposes, but they can still be obstructionist and dishonest. The case of Paul Orange, which unfolded in 1987-90 is one example.

The Western Australian Conservation and Land Management Department

(C.A.L.M.) has done an excellent job of stifling conservation and captive breeding programmes in that State. In 1991 they managed to restrict the number of licensed reptile keepers to less than ten individuals. This is in spite of a population in excess of 1 000 000 people, hundreds of different species of indigenous reptile species, and the fact that no species is in any way threatened by human intervention such as hunting or collecting.

Unfortunately for the few wildlife licence holders in Western Australia, the need for C.A.L.M. bureaucrats to justify their existence is concentrated on pitifully few people.

Paul Geoffrey Orange was a geologist in his twenties who lived at 2 Kurrajong Lane, Kambalda, about 600 km (300 miles) east of Perth. He had followed C.A.L.M. procedures in applying for a reptile keeping permit in September 1987, and after what could only be described as intolerable delays was finally given one in April 1990. Orange then applied for a permit or extension to allow him to legally display his reptiles to the public.

He was visited by two C.A.L.M. officers, Bob Fitzgerald and Bernie Haberley who inspected his facility and looked at his snakes. Fitzgerald and Haberley visited and 'interviewed' Orange on August 12, 13 and 21 and did a 'record of interview' ostensibly to help him obtain his exhibitor's permit.

Fitzgerald and Haberley stated that they were very impressed with Orange's skills as a herpetologist and asked if they could borrow his research notebook, to demonstrate to their superiors in Perth what a competent herpetologist he was. Orange obliged and the C.A.L.M. officers took his notebook and photocopied it, subsequently returning it to Orange.

It was alleged by Orange that the officers were trying to find anything with which to charge Orange. In his notes, Orange revealed that he had fed one of his snakes four common lizards (2 bynoe's geckos [*Heteronotia binoei*] and 2 dtellas [*Gehyra* sp.] both found in their millions across most parts of Australia). Paul was subsequently charged by C.A.L.M. officials with four separate charges of unlawfully taking wildlife (the geckos) from the wild, under section 14 of the West Australian *Wildlife Conservation Act* 1950. As each charge was on a separate summons, Orange faced a maximum penalty of $16 000.

The case lasted four hours and by the end, the magistrate, Barbara Lane agreed that the 'evidence' against Orange had been unfairly obtained and dismissed all four charges. Orange had told the court he would not have given the officers his notebook had he been told it would be used against him, nor would he have been so open with the officials had he thought they were trying to build a criminal case against him.

An expert witness, Brian Bush, called by Orange's defence counsel, Tom Percy, likened Orange's snakes to the dolphins at Monkey Mia, when he said 'What do you expect small snakes to eat? You don't feed the dolphins at Monkey Mia cabbages!'

Another herpetologist, Robert Brown-Cooper, also spokesperson for the West Australian Society of Amateur Herpetologists (W.A.S.A.H.) made some telling remarks about the case. He said:

'The *Wildlife Conservation Act* had already been interpreted by another magistrate in a previous case as an Act to protect fauna from criminal exploitation ... It should not be used to intimidate, persecute or discriminate against someone making a positive contribution to understanding our fauna more fully. The court action was a waste of taxpayer's money and Paul was a soft target. The ramifications of this type of proceedings are broad. Apart from the fines, a naturalist could lose his or her licence. The life of a naturalist could be shattered at the whim of a bureaucrat with no interest in fauna but who likes wielding a big stick.'

Magistrate Lane agreed, announced that Orange was a victim of blatant entrapment and besides dismissing the charges, directed the C.A.L.M. officials to pay Orange his costs to the maximum legally specified amount.

After the case, Orange said, 'I'd been set up . . . It was a set-up from the start'.

The previous case referred to by Browne-Cooper was one in the early 1980s involving a Pilbara reptile keeper, Peter Tight. He'd been charged by C.A.L.M. officials in similar circumstances to Orange and C.A.L.M. had lost that case too. Probably a major reason why C.A.L.M. officials didn't hesitate to charge Orange when they must have known they were in the wrong was because they weren't spending their own money. They were financed by the taxpayer!

Another Waste of Money

In 1990-91 a reptile keeper appeared in Penrith Court in outer Sydney charged with holding two snakes illegally. The snake keeper had over 20 licensed snakes and the two snakes in question were a rough-scaled snake and an eastern brown snake, both of which are found in their millions in New South Wales and Queensland.

These relatively aggressive and dangerously venomous snakes were removed from people's backyards as a result of calls for help to the keeper. The keeper had agreed to remove them only because they were common varieties and N.P.W.S. had refused to come and get them. Police had referred the residents to the now charged keeper.

The case was adjourned three times before being heard, and the 'fact sheet' given by N.P.W.S. officers Russell and Sims had a large amount of irrelevant information apparently designed to prejudice the case against the snake keeper. To keep everyone guessing, the 'fact sheet' was changed three times by officials during the case.

When the case was finally heard, the magistrate exlaimed 'Bloody snakes' and threw the case out. No fine was imposed, although the keeper paid statutory charge of about $40. The magistrate stated 'This case is a waste of Government money.'

Misinformation

Still in New South Wales, the case of Blacktown herpetologist, Peter Jones, is also worth mentioning. In 1989, he approached N.P.W.S. licensing officer, Gary Ellis for a licence to catch and photograph gecko lizards in western New South Wales. He was searching for *Diplodactylus conspicillatus*, a species common in many parts of Australia, but rarely recorded in New South Wales.

In the words of Peter Jones, 'I suffered because I did what National Parks and Wildlife recommended.' Ellis told Jones 'You don't need a licence and you won't have any problems. Um, if you're worried about getting harassed, ah, just tell the authorities where you're operating, what you're doing.'

Jones did just that. Upon arrival at Wanaaring in far north-west New South

Wales, he visited the local police officer, outlined his intentions and said 'If I'm not back in three days, send in the search parties.' Jones then went in search of his beloved geckos which he duly found and started to photograph. It was at that point that Jones was 'busted'.

Accompanied by a N.P.W.S. officer, the local policeman, complete with revolver and handcuffs, approached Jones and said 'I have reports to indicate that you are involved in wildlife smuggling activities.' The alibi used to 'bust' Jones was both typical and completely unsubstantiated.

The lizards held by Jones were confiscated and Jones was summonsed to appear at Bourke Magistrate's Court on State wildlife charges. This meant that Jones had to make a special trip to Bourke, several hundred kilometres from home. Jones told the presiding magistrate the full story and the charges were dismissed. The whole exercise was yet another waste of taxpayers' money and an abuse of the 'conservation dollar'.

As an epilogue, Jones subsequently approached N.P.W.S. again for a permit to work on geckos in western New South Wales, and was again told he wouldn't need one. This time, however, Jones pressed the point and was eventually issued with the correct permit.

Minor Breaches — Big Fines

Reptile keepers in Victoria charged with petty or technical breaches of the law (in contravention of the intentions of the law) by wildlife officials don't seem to get on as well as their counterparts in other States. Perhaps this raises questions about the quality of magistrates in Victoria.

In 1991, Peter Kruger, a reptile keeper from the Melbourne suburb of Newport, was 'visited' by officials from the Department of Conservation, Forests and Lands (C.F.L.). An extremely close scrutiny of his collection revealed two common skinks (*Egernia cunninghami*) over and above what he was licensed to hold. Skinks include the lizards found in backyards throughout Australia, and the species in question is found in huge numbers throughout the eastern states, including Kruger's suburb. Kruger was unlucky with his magistrate who fined him $600.

At the time C.F.L. officials seemed to enjoy charging reptile people with the most trivial of offences, presumably to justify their existence. Keeper Matt Hingley was dragged through the courts in 1991 for failing to notify C.F.L. of a common bearded dragon he'd rescued as sick from a local kid. He received a bond.

In 1991, keeper Hassan Tiba of Broadmeadows, had a red-bellied black snake (*Pseudechis prophyriacus*) and eastern brown snake die. He placed the dead snakes in the freezer to preserve them and delayed writing up the deaths of the snakes in his C.F.L. record book because his wife was having a baby. That the snakes were in the freezer also meant that he hadn't actually got rid of them.

By chance he was raided by the same C.F.L. officers who raided Hingley and Kruger, although Tiba was also graced by the presence of two armed police. When the officials realised that Tiba hadn't written up the deaths of the two snakes, they decided to charge him with two technical offences, one for each snake.

When Tiba received the summons he saw he was also charged with what he asserted was the fabricated charge of holding one too many black-headed pythons. Tiba queried this with C.F.L. officers and was told that they had accidentally written down the wrong number of snakes in Tiba's collection. That charge was dropped. For the other two he was fined a total of $375 at Broadmeadows court.

More about the C.F.L.
The Victorian equivalent of N.P.W.S. is the Department of Conservation, Forests and Lands (C.F.L.). This department has changed its name no less than three times in recent years, and will in future be called Department of Conservation and Environment (D.C.E.). Another Victorian Government department, Vicroads, has been known under no less than six different names within the last decade. In Victoria, it seems name changes are a popular means of attempting to repair damage to reputation as a result of departmental activities. C.F.L. officers have been noted for some 'unusual' actions.

Wildlife keepers have been asked to forward their permits to the C.F.L. for amendments and then been raided by C.F.L. officers and 'busted' for being unable to produce a permit.

On a number of occasions, C.F.L. take so long to authorise 'movements' or transfers of wildlife from one keeper to another, that the animals in question are long since dead by the time the authorisation arrives.

In co-operation with State-owned zoos, Melbourne, Healesville and Werribee, the C.F.L. has effectively tried to restrict the keeping of many animals to these three institutions, in what appears to be a bid to boost potential gate receipts at the long-term expense of privately owned wildlife parks and the animals themselves.

Several owners of wildlife parks have long been fighting losing battles with C.F.L. to hold certain types of wildlife or to abide by the innumerable regulations C.F.L. imposes.

The Fritz Maaten case is one which demonstrates how a man who has worked all his life for the cause of wildlife conservation has had to fight a brick wall of bureaucracy.

Maaten, who works with another wildlife keeper, Andy Stephens, owns a wildlife park, the Monbulk Animal Kingdom, in the hills east of Melbourne. He not only runs his wildlife park but does over a hundred educational lectures on wildlife with live animals to school children and others each year. He has also been involved in the breeding of rare animals.

Instead of being helped by C.F.L. he has only been hampered at every opportunity. In the early 1980s Maaten was raided by C.F.L. and a licensed scrub python was taken from his facility and placed with Melbourne Zoo. The snake was in excess of Maaten's licensed number and was seized on that basis. However, during the raid Maaten told the C.F.L. officers that the snake was in fact legal and belonged to a man called Nick Gambie, who held it under licence. Gambie had apparently notified C.F.L. and received approval from them to place the snake in Maaten's custody while he moved house.

The raiding C.F.L. officers denied any knowledge of this and took the snake. On the raid were two Fish and Wildlife Service (F.W.S.) officers and the then reptile keeper at the Healesville Sanctuary, Fred Parker. To confirm the legality of the snake, Maaten phoned Gambie during the raid so the officers could speak to him.

The snake was still taken and Maaten and Gambie were charged by the C.F.L. officers. In court the C.F.L. officers and Parker gave one version of events while Maaten and Gambie gave another. The presiding magistrate sided with C.F.L. and fined Maaten $60 on a technicality. Maaten also paid $600 in legal costs. Both Parker and the C.F.L. officers denied that Maaten had phoned Gambie during the raid, and according to Maaten, the C.F.L. officers 'told one lie after another'.

The court ordered that the seized snake remain at Melbourne Zoo. Maaten decided to tape all future encounters with C.F.L., which has embarrassed those officers who have attempted to harass him since.

Other interesting events have occurred since the court case. Early in June 1989, Maaten notified C.F.L. that he had legally obtained some crocodiles and wanted his permit altered accordingly. In theory this is a fairly routine matter. For Maaten it was anything but routine. On 8 June, six C.F.L. officers carrying guns raided Maaten's property. The officers threatened Maaten with pistols after he asked them to leave.

The six officers, namely Griffin (in charge), Zidarich, Grossek, McBride, Heard and Del Peva arrived in three vehicles for the commando-style raid and were extremely aggressive from the outset, apparently not realising their every word was being taped. The six men were unable to produce a search warrant, but this did not stop them from attempting to gain entry to all Maaten's facilities. The officers eventually left but returned the next day in an unsuccessful bid to confiscate Maaten's legally held crocodiles.

The raid was reported in the local newspaper, the *Free Press*, and according to Maaten, C.F.L. initially refused to comment. The Victorian Government then criticised the *Free Press* for running the story on Fritz Maaten without a response from C.F.L. It can only be presumed that the Government didn't want the *Free Press* to run the story at all.

After further bad publicity from the raid, C.F.L. regional manager John Twentyman told the *Free Press* that the incident with Maaten had been a 'routine inspection', the result of a tip-off that Maaten had brought crocodiles into Victoria. The tip-off was Maaten's own letter to C.F.L. telling them that he had legally imported the crocodiles and that he wanted his permit altered accordingly.

After Maaten complained to the State Ombudsman, Norman Geschke, about the raid, C.F.L. admitted that the so-called inspection was actually 'an armed raid before it was found Mr Maaten was not in breach of the law'.

Maaten also claimed C.F.L. had misled him on other aspects of his permits including whether or not he was allowed to keep owls at his park for an educational display.

As a result of the newspaper story, which reported that officials had 'threatened Mr Maaten with a pistol if he did not co-operate', the department's director general, Len Foster, and the Minister responsible announced a review of firearm rules in the C.F.L. This announcement was given wide publicity to allay fears among the public that C.F.L. officers were running amok holding up people at gunpoint. The C.F.L. justified the carrying of guns by enforcement and licensing staff on the grounds that these officers constituted only 40 of 3 000 staff. After the publicity died down, no firearm regulations for C.F.L. officials were in fact substantially altered.

Maaten had complained to the director of C.F.L., N.P.W.S. section, Don

Saunders, about the raid. In his letter dated 14 June 1989, Maaten stated 'The matter which apparently prompted the inspection by the six officers was in relation to permits that your department had neglected to issue. I must say that I found the number of officers required to inspect one permit both intimidating and excessive and I asked the officer in charge at the time, Officer Griffin, to make a note of this. Could you explain to me why six officers, travelling in three vehicles are required to carry out such a menial task?'

Among the reasons given by Saunders to justify the raid was that those on the raid included 'staff under training'.

Meanwhile, Fred Parker (who had been present on the earlier raid) had long since left the Healesville sanctuary and set up his own private reptile park in Ballarat, to the west of Melbourne. After what he described as extreme difficulty, Parker received permits to keep koalas, making him the fourth institution in Victoria to keep koalas legally. C.F.L./N.P.W.S. policy in Victoria as stated has been to restrict the places that hold koalas principally to the publicly owned zoos of Healesville and Melbourne.

Maaten wrote to C.F.L. asking for a permit to keep koalas on exactly the same basis as Parker, including offering to source them from the same place as Parker (French Island) or to obtain legal stock from interstate, and to build indentical enclosures to Parker's. C.F.L. refused the application.

Maaten suspected what seems obvious to any outsider: Parker was being repayed by C.F.L. in return for past favours, while Maaten was being punished for having exposed C.F.L. misconduct and incompetence. Both Maaten and Parker keep their wildlife in excellent conditions.

The possession of koalas is regarded by wildlife park owners as a significant drawcard for visitors. Park owners such as Maaten although operating to make a profit, also, by virtue of their dedication to wildlife, channel a major part of their profits back into the welfare of wildlife in general and should therefore be supported, not hampered. The more people are encouraged to profit from conserving wildlife, the more likely it is that wildlife will benefit.

C.F.L. Raids Again

Maaten is not the only private zoo keeper to have been subjected to the tactics of Victorian wildlife officials. Another well-documented case is that of Bruce Jacobs, who owns a Dingo Park at Chewton, Victoria. He was raided on 5 March 1990.

As a result of information given to C.F.L. officials by R.S.P.C.A. members who personally disliked Mr Jacobs, C.F.L. officials decided to raid the park with an R.S.P.C.A. vet, Dr Hugh Wirth. Unfortunately, much of the information given to C.F.L. officials was blatantly inaccurate, a fact which a cursory investigation would have revealed. The eagerness with which C.F.L. officials took action against Jacobs was questioned by many people, including the State Ombudsman, Norman Geschke, whose report on the raid was released in May 1990.

Before the raid was mounted, C.F.L. officials sought approval from the Minister, presumably in anticipation of a possible backlash. The briefing given to the Minister was inaccurate in several key details, in particular the allegation that Mr Jacobs had failed to comply with C.F.L. regulations and permits. In fact, Jacobs had complied with all requirements and was at the time of the raid fully licensed by them. The briefing failed to mention that the property had been approved by the C.F.L., that Jacobs had been licensed by them for many years, and that he had negotiated with them to upgrade his permit to a wildlife park licence.

The Minister gave C.F.L. permission to mount the raid as requested.

Before the raid C.F.L. officers took the unprecedented step of trying to exclude the media by removing the sign advertising the Dingo Park from the side of the highway.

The raid began at approximately 7.40 a.m. Included were two local policemen, about a dozen C.F.L. officers and two veterinary surgeons. Besides the damage done to the property, such as smashed doors, locks, etc. all of which was unnecessary, five dingoes (*Canis familiaris dingo*) were needlessly shot and 49 dingoes were taken away. The Ombudsman, who subsequently investigated the matter, found that the man who ordered the shooting of the dingoes, Hugh Wirth, had had a long-running feud with Jacobs and it was only when a journalist appeared on the scene that Wirth told Mr Max Kitchell, the C.F.L. officer running the raid, not to shoot any more dogs.

Jacobs enlisted the support of the Melbourne media in his fight for justice. He was backed up by a great deal of public support, especially from the many people who had visited his park over the previous six years.

According to Jacobs, Wirth had wrongly ordered the shooting of the dogs to (a) show that they were uncontrollably aggressive and (b) lend support to his adverse view of Jacobs and his ability to maintain dingoes.

The fact that people had been visiting the park for over six years without incident seemed to negate the possibility of undue aggressiveness by the dingoes and as Jacobs stated, any aggression was probably in response to shouting, excitement and the general nature of the raid.

Having lost his dingoes, Jacobs was effectively put out of business. It was only after a large number of complaints and many media reports that the Ombudsman, Norman Geschke, decided to investigate. A report totalling 161 pages was released about two months after the raid. The report was highly critical of C.F.L. officials and the way they carried out the raid and it further criticised C.F.L.'s dealings with Jacobs during the preceding years.

It appears that C.F.L. officers had actually tried to entrap Jacobs into committing wildlife offences, failing to issue correct permits and giving conflicting advice from various officers.

In the end, Jacobs' dingoes were returned by C.F.L., he was exonerated of any wrongdoing by the Ombudsman and all charges laid against him were dropped.

Given the public outrage, a favourable Ombudsman's report, the support of a number of State Parliamentarians and an effective backdown by C.F.L. and the R.S.P.C.A., it seemed logical that Jacobs should apply for and receive compensation. Although clearly entitled to ask for more, he only asked for $18 000, substantially less than he might have received had he sued for damages.

The Minister for the Environment, Steve Crabb (the man who banned smoking in all Government offices except his own), rejected the claim. Opposition Natural Resources spokesman, Mr Coleman, said 'The incompetence of the Government and one of its departments had severely disadvantaged Mr Jacobs.' The raid which Coleman described as 'Rambo-style' had 'destroyed Mr Jacobs' business'.

Bureaucratic Bungles

The Hall family from the Melbourne suburb of Brighton found themselves in trouble with their local council in 1990-91, when a neighbour, Mrs Shoiket, complained about the noise made by Roger, their sulphur-crested cockatoo (*Cacatua galerita*).

The council launched a legal action against Mr Hall, for causing a nuisance, namely allowing the cockatoo to make 'noisy screeching cries'. The matter did not reach court, as it was resolved at the local neighbourhood dispute centre. Mr Hall agreed to cover the bird at night and build a garage in which to house it.

That was the end of the matter, thought Mr Hall. He then received a summons to appear at a 'mention date' at the nearby Sandringham Magistrate's Court. It was the third 'mention date'. Mr Hall hadn't been informed of the first two. To make things worse, two of the 'mention dates' were after the dispute had been settled.

Council lawyers added insult to injury by demanding $1 500 for their legal fees for the three court mentions. The letter went on to say that if Hall paid them, they would 'consider dropping legal action'. The bird wasn't causing problems at this stage; in fact, Mrs Shoiket told a Melbourne newspaper that the situation was fine and could only improve with completion of the garage.

Ironically, it was discovered that the original problem had been caused by wild cockatoos feeding in nearby Landcox Park. Mr Hall vowed he'd rather go to jail than pay the council and told a local newspaper he was tempted to line his bird's cage with the paperwork generated by the dispute.

At the time of writing, this dispute was unresolved, with council lawyers refusing to withdraw. A similar case in Sydney was resolved only when the local council in question agreed not to press charges.

SUCCESS

Despite these failures it must be said that much of the work undertaken by fauna officials is helpful to the conservation cause. The negative aspects have been highlighted so far only because their ramifications are so far-reaching yet remain relatively unknown to those outside the field of wildlife research and conservation.

Dedicated scientists, rangers, wildlife keepers and others employed by fauna services have played an essential role in preserving species already on the brink of extinction and in preventing others from reaching that stage.

Achievements are many and include the successful rehabilitation of formerly degraded bushland, and the continued maintenance of large national parks in every State. One particularly notable project is the Lord Howe Island woodhen (*Tricholimnas sylvestris*) breeding project, carried out largely by officials employed by New South Wales N.P.W.S., which has been a great success. Without the input by wildlife department officials, it is highly likely that the species would now be extinct.

Fauna authorities also hold a great deal of research material and data which is clearly beyond the capacity of any other organisation, public or private, to collate, and therefore their postive role in wildlife conservation will remain a desirably prominent feature of wildlife conservation in the future.

8

THE FAUNA SQUAD

The history of the Fauna Squad in the 1970s is an interesting one. The work of this group of officers from the Customs department resulted in many wildlife seizures from airports and other places around Australia. However, the failures of the squad were equally notable and eventually led to it being disbanded under the Fraser Government about six years after it was formed.

In December 1972, the Federal Government took responsibility for the export of wildlife, from the various State Governments. The Customs department became the relevant department. In 1973, Australia signed the C.I.T.E.S. treaty which was designed to further restrict legal wildlife trade from Australia. This, together with earlier statutory restrictions on wildlife export being more rigorously enforced, resulted in Australia becoming 'closed off' to wildlife exporters relatively quickly. It was under these circumstances that wildlife smuggling began and grew rapidly.

During the Whitlam Government (1972-75) the then Customs Minister, Lionel Murphy, was asked in Parliament by an opposition Member what Australia was doing to combat the illegal export of our wildlife. Murphy replied that there was a specially appointed Fauna Squad within the Customs department dealing with the problem. The following day at 6 a.m. a fauna squad was started. Mike Schooley recalls 'I went to work at 6 a.m. and was told that as a result of a question in Parliament last night, I was to become part of a new Fauna Squad.'

In Sydney, six Customs officers were appointed to this squad, while the other States got the following approximate quotas of officers: Victoria 3, Western Australia 2, Queensland 2, South Australia 1, Northern Territory 1, Tasmania 1. The squad was controlled by Harvey Bates, head of the relevant section of Customs in Canberra.

McShane had been the principal compiler of the working file 'Operation Doughnut' (see p. 1), a file so sensitive that it had mostly been destroyed (illegally). It appears that as early as 1973 entrenched corruption existed within the Customs department in relation to wildlife smuggling.

THE SHOW GOES ON

Despite reports in the Australian media in the late 1980s that wildlife officials had stopped the export of our fauna, a quick perusal of major bird-keeping journals in the U.S.A. and Europe reveals another picture. For example, the monthly *American Cagebird* magazine with a circulation numbering thousands, carries at least a dozen pages of dealers' advertisements. Although many birds sold are captive-bred specimens, others are openly imported from Australia. One advertisement on page 89 of the April 1992 issue, from a Californian dealer read as follows; 'QUALITY AUSTRALIAN PARAKEETS and their mutations at very competitive prices. We import our own birds and provide best care available. Get to know us. For price list send SASE to …'

When journalist Dick Wordley uncovered some extremely important information about wildlife dealers in Europe and Singapore, he contacted Harvey Bates, who was about number two in Customs at the time. Wordley gave Bates a great deal of information about the rackets he'd seen. Bates told Wordley that he already knew about these rackets and that everything was 'under control'.

When Wordley arrived back in Australia, he met Michael Schooley at the Fauna Squad Sydney office in Waverton. In company with another officer, Schooley told Wordley that he was under instructions not to have any contact with Wordley for any reason. The meeting between the three men had been against more senior directions. Schooley had been told nothing about the various European and Asian rackets and other useful information that Wordley had told Bates.

All Customs/Fauna Squad officials are 'under oath' not to disclose certain aspects of their work. For this reason all the former Fauna Squad members I've spoken to, including Schooley, have been reluctant to talk about the finer details of what happened during their operations or to name which officers were corrupt. Schooley's writings about smugglers in the magazine *Australian Birdkeeper*, have names and other details changed to hide the identities of the people involved. However, in several articles Schooley refers to corrupt officers within his department during his six years of dealing primarily with wildlife trafficking (see Chapter 16). Wordley and others have all noted that they thought Schooley to be a thorough and honest officer in all their dealings with him.

Bates was eventually removed from his position as Head of Prevention and Detection and Narcotics in Canberra after questions were asked about him in Parliament. It has been alleged that Bates was in some way being protected by his Minister who subsequently died, leaving Bates vulnerable to a 'purge'.

One former Fauna Squad member told me that he thought at least two former Ministers administering the Customs department were corrupt and had some involvement in wildlife smuggling. Lionel Murphy was named as one. At the time of writing, after Murphy's death, there is no way in which the allegations can be proved. Furthermore, there is little doubt that Murphy's surviving family members would deny any allegations against him.

Under the Fraser Government the Fauna Squad was threatened with closure unless it increased the seizure rate of smuggled wildlife. In the final year of operation, the squad's seizures included about 600 Major Mitchells and many thousands of other birds, an increase over previous years. However, Schooley and others still noted the recurring white-anting from Canberra. At least one man in Canberra was found to be acting as an informant for the Fauna Squad and the smugglers, making money from both parties.

The squad was disbanded under the Fraser Government, as Schooley noted, just as it was starting to have an impact on the smuggling problem.

Despite its difficulties, the Fauna Squad was responsible for a large number of 'busts'. Most occured at Sydney airport where, according to Schooley, the majority of wildlife rackets seemed to be centred. Schooley thought Sydney was the major centre for smuggling because it has more international flights, more people and it is easier to hide in a large crowd.

A large number of the exotic reptiles and birds seen in Sydney's Taronga Zoo are the result of seizures by Fauna Squad officials in the 1970s; for example most of the North American freshwater tortoises seen in the zoo during the 1970s and '80s were seized by Schooley and others from two collections on the far north coast of New South Wales. So many tortoises were seized by Fauna Squad officials that Taronga Zoo officials had to build a new terrarium-style cage especially for them. Most of these tortoises later died as a result of an uncontrolled outbreak of disease.

New South Wales

Act No. 80, 1974.

National Parks and Wildlife.

Importing or exporting protected fauna.

106. **(1)** A person shall not import into or export from New South Wale any protected fauna.

(2) Subsection (1) does not apply to any protected fauna of a specie prescribed for the purposes of this subsection.

(3) A person shall not be convicted of an offence arising unde subsection (1) if he proves that the act constituting the offence was don under and in accordance with or by virtue of the authority conferred by a import licence or an export licence under section 126.

9
ZOOS AND OTHER INSTITUTIONS

A former director of the Australian Museum, Ronald Strahan, told the House of Representatives Inquiry into smuggling in 1975-76 of how a senior officer of a major institution used his position of influence to traffic in wildlife: 'I have sat in the office . . . his mail came in from all over the world and boxes labelled "Photographs" were opened carefully while the reptiles were let out.' Strahan went so far as to tell the inquiry 'Smuggling tends to be regarded as normal practice and even curators and keepers in reputable zoological gardens may be strangely blind where the acquisition of reptiles is concerned.'

Dr Richard Zann of the Royal Australasian Ornithologists' Union told the House of Representatives Inquiry about a major ongoing scam involving curators at Australian zoos trading birds and reptiles with a particular zoo curator in West Germany. The West German curator used the zoo as a 'recognised reputable authority' to cover his own private smuggling operation. He was not only able to obtain enough Australian reptiles and birds for himself, he had enough surplus animals to swap or sell for other species he wished to acquire.

According to Ronald Strahan, the New York Zoo holds the world record for captive longevity in the platypus. However, at the time of his statement in 1976, no live platypus had ever been legally exported from Australia. A 1960 law prohibited the export of platypus, koalas and lyrebirds (*Menura* spp.) for any purpose.

A number of illegally exported koalas ended up in the San Diego Zoo in the 1970s having arrived from New South Wales. The exporter of these animals was never publicly revealed although it was alleged that officials in the New South Wales N.P.W.S. played a role in exporting these animals. The allegation was never investigated by any authority. The arrival of the koalas in San Diego occurred after a lengthy period of unsuccessful negotiation with the Australian Government to legally import some koalas.

Since then the koalas have bred successfully, initially outbreeding any

Australian captive colonies. Husbandry of koalas in this country has since improved.

In the 1975-76 Inquiry into smuggling, Ronald Hastings of Victoria summed up the competence of some zoos in their conservation effort:

'I am referring to zoos. If birds are getting down into a low state, where possibly in time they will become extinct, I think that a zoo is the worst place in the world for any birds to be bred with a view to keep them going. The simple reason is that the men caring for these birds work eight hours a day and are not there, when they should be looking to see if the parent is going back to the nest at night to cover the youngsters. The bird sits out on the perch and the youngsters die. When Fisheries and Wildlife make a raid, they send a lot of birds out to Melbourne Zoo where a lot of crowding goes on and psittacosis or some disease generally crops up and goes through these valuable birds as well. On the other hand, a competent aviculturalist has got his heart and soul in the job and tends them night and day and can make pretty sure of rearing youngsters from them. That is my idea of conservation of the rarer species.'

Hastings also explained the role of commercial dealers in disposing of excess captive breeding stock from private individuals and zoos by saying:

'Cockatiels *(Nymphicus hollandicus)* and zebra finches *(Peophila guttata)* and all these sorts of things . . . they breed by the thousand. What are you going to do with them? They have to go to the dealer who has bigger contacts and more people coming in, and these birds go out.'

The Carolina duck *(Aix sponsa)* of the U.S.A. was exterminated in the wild although specimens had been smuggled to Holland where captive populations persisted. The U.S.A. Government was forced to purchase ducks on the open market and import them back into the U.S.A. in order to re-establish the species in the wild.

A DIFFICULT POSITION

Zoos can find themselves in the difficult position of being attacked on all sides. Zoos that do their job in conservation terms are sometimes harassed by Australian authorities. In 1970 Amsterdam Zoo was black-listed by the Australian Customs Service for having traded Australian parrots (legally). The parrots had been bred to excess in the zoo and simply had to be off-loaded. In black-listing the zoo, Customs officials gave the reason in simple terms: the zoo had sold Australian fauna; therefore they were trading in Australian fauna. To trade in Australian fauna was regarded by Customs in this case as immoral. They ignored the fact that London Zoo had been selling large numbers of red-necked wallabies *(Macropus rugogriseus)* to a Dutch wildlife dealer because for some reason they could not trade them with other zoos.

Smugglers also attack zoos. In 1978, Taronga Zoo had its two green pythons stolen by David Kerry, a youth of Baulkham Hills. Before he could off-load the snakes he was apprehended by police and the snakes were returned to the zoo. He was caught not because he was seen cutting the glass at the front of the cage and taking the snakes, but because he attended a meeting of the Australian Herpetological Society at the Australian Museum and bragged to a number of people there that he was about to send a pair of green pythons to a friend in the U.S.A. in return for a king cobra. He later pleaded guilty in Parramatta Court to the offence and was let off with a minor penalty.

A model shows a coat with specially made pockets sewn into the lining to smuggle birds out of Australia.
Photo: Australian Customs

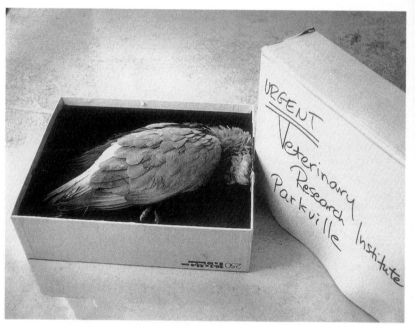

Drugged bird found in 1989, in a parcel at Tullamarine Airport, Melbourne, being smuggled out to Singapore.
Photo: Melbourne Herald-Sun

These suitcases have been especially fitted with compartments for birds. The cases and birds were siezed by Federal fauna officials from a New Zealand ship in 1970.
Photo: Melbourne Herald-Sun

Convicted bird smuggler Happy Walker with an illegally caught cockatiel, part of a cargo of 2 000, worth an estimated $12 000 overseas.
Photo: The Age

Camera seized by Customs officials. It opens to reveal a cage for smuggling birds out of Australia.
Photo: Australian Customs

Birds smuggled in tea chests.
Photo: The Age

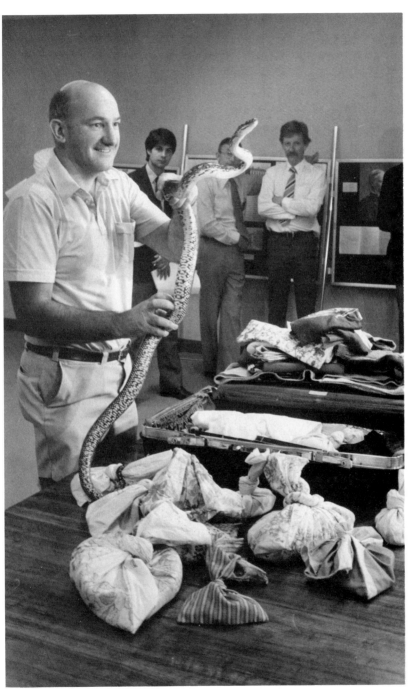

Customs official comes to grips with a tough customer. This diamond python was seized with other reptiles worth an estimated $50 000 at Tullamarine Airport, Melbourne in 1985.
Photo: The Herald Sun or The Herald and Weekly Times

Jack Giles, formerly deputy director of N.S.W. National Parks and Wildlife Service, named in Federal Parliament during an investigation into official corruption. *Photo: Paul Matthews — John Fairfax Group*

Don Johnstone, former director of N.S.W. National Parks and Wildlife Service, named in Federal Parliament during an investigation into official corruption. *Photo: John Fairfax Group Pty Ltd*

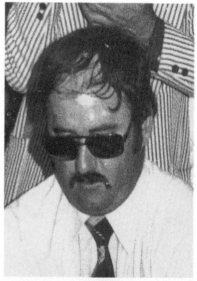

Customs Officer, Peter Marzol, who along with fellow officer Richard Spencer, was charged in 1986 by Magistrate Len Nash with perjury after allegedly perverting the course of an earlier murder inquest. *Photo: Anton Cermack — John Fairfax Group Pty Ltd*

Tea chests used to smuggle wildlife.
Photo: The Age

Photos of U.S. Fish and Wildlife Officers during an illegal armed raid on the premises
of John Brunner, when they spent most of five hours turning the house upside-down.
Photo: John Brunner

The author with his snakes.
Photo: Raymond Hoser

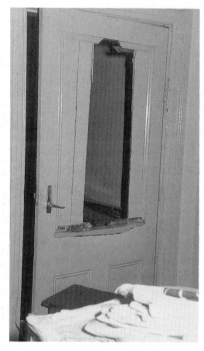

A N.P.W.S. break-in, which resulted in damages to the author's house, furniture, computer, files, books and photographic equipment.
Photo: Raymond Hoser

The problems zoos may face are clearly demonstrated by Taronga Zoo, in Sydney, New South Wales.

TARONGA ZOO

Taronga Zoo has had a colourful history where smuggling is concerned. During the late 1960s, the late Sir Edward Hallstrom was the director of Taronga and owner of a very large private collection of wildlife, which among other animals, included the only colony of albino wallabies in the world. Hallstrom engaged in a number of illegal trading activities that not only landed the zoo in trouble at the time, but made life more difficult for keepers later on.

In co-operation with the head reptile keeper, Uwe Peters, Hallstrom legally imported from New Guinea a great deal of wildlife including over 100 green pythons. The snakes had been allowed out of New Guinea on the understanding that they were to be held at the zoo. Instead, during 'Operation Doughnut', it was alleged that both men sold them to third parties both in Australia and overseas. Green pythons are one of the most sought-after snakes in the world and at the time could be sold for over $1 000. During 'Operation Doughnut', it was alleged that Hallstrom had amassed a large part of his personal fortune from his illegal wildlife dealings.

According to Schooley, Hallstrom had 'front-men' working for him in his wildlife dealings. When people purchased illegally traded wildlife from Hallstrom, they were given receipts marked 'Hallstrom Refrigeration', in reference to Hallstrom's more legitimate business enterprises.

Among the green pythons illegally exported via Australia some apparently ended up in Washington Zoo, where a breeding colony has been established since.

Taronga Zoo was unable to breed the species as for some inscrutable reason the only two green pythons it retained were of the same sex. So the zoo sought permission to obtain more snakes from New Guinea. The authorities refused on the basis that the zoo had acquired more than enough the first time. The Indonesian Government which controls Irian Jaya where the green python also occurs, refused Taronga permission to obtain snakes from its territory, as the Government was attempting to stem the flow of wildlife from its territories. Ironically, being unable to obtain green pythons from any areas where they naturally occurred, the zoo arranged to import a pair from Washington Zoo. Two juveniles were legally imported in mid-1990.

Although in the late 1960s and early 1970s green pythons were smuggled by Hallstrom in considerable numbers from Australia, the illegal trade in this species has since reversed. A number of reptile keepers in the U.S.A. and the U.K. are now breeding this highly desirable snake in large numbers and in 1990 it retailed for as little as US$200 a snake.

Snakes were not the only animals Taronga Zoo was involved in smuggling. During the 1960s an international bird trafficking racket centred on Taronga Zoo, Adelaide Zoo and a fauna trading company. The racket involved the legal export of a few birds and the insertion of extra illegal birds to boost profits for all concerned. After exposure of the racket, Robert Brown of the South Australian Ornithological Association said that 'the main person was a little greedy, and tried to get even a larger order through than he already had permission to.'

SMUGGLED

Mike Schooley recalled a conversation with Taronga Zoo bird keeper Ernie Hargreaves. He said:
'We were talking about Gouldian finches and how the numbers had fallen over the years in the wild. He said we were lucky there were any left at all as the zoo at that time had trapped and sent hundreds to Selfridges in England to be traded in for some giraffes.'

Zoo personnel can use their positions to avoid prosecution for wildlife trafficking and related offences. Uwe Peters attained quite a reputation for wildlife trafficking. After he was 'busted' by N.P.W.S. officials on at least one occasion for doing so, he was approached by N.P.W.S. officers Terry Hill and Tony Alexander to accompany them on raids on private collections. On these raids Uwe was allegedly allowed to take whatever reptiles he wanted for the zoo, regardless of whether or not the person raided held the reptiles legally.

Interestingly, Customs officials were faced sometimes with the choice of either killing illegally imported animals — not a popular choice — or donating them to an 'A' class zoo. The only 'A' class zoo in Sydney was Taronga, so invariably Uwe ended up keeping the reptiles he had imported illegally.

According to Michael Schooley, the only punishment Peters actually received for wildlife smuggling was not being permitted to call himself 'reptile curator' at the Zoo. Instead he had to make do with the title of 'head reptile keeper'. Another possible reason for Peters avoiding prosecution was that his wife was secretary to Premier Askin at the time. The late Sir Robert Askin has been the subject of many corruption allegations investigated by Royal Commissions, detailed in other books.

When I was compiling this book, Victoria's major snake breeder, Brian Barnett of Ardeer, told me he 'knew Uwe Peters was smuggling wildlife . . . everybody did . . . When he came here and saw me, he was always after specimens. But they had to be the right size — juveniles. He obviously wanted to get them out of the country.'

Today, Uwe Peters and Sir Edward Hallstrom have long since departed the scene and public scrutiny of the zoo's operations has increased. How far it goes is a matter of opinion.

In August 1981, a journalist from the *Australian* newspaper was refused permission to enter Taronga Zoo to photograph allegedly illegally obtained reptiles. She was told by the then director Jack Throp, 'The story you are preparing is counter to the interests of this zoo, National Parks and Wildlife Service and conservation.' She got her story without the zoo's co-operation.

ESCAPING FAUNA

A major argument against the trading of wildlife from Australia to other countries or vice versa is the possibility of species escaping from captivity and establishing themselves in the wild. Once established, these 'new' species may displace native animals, causing major environmental problems.

Taronga Zoo's record, for example, is not much better than East Berlin a week after the wall came down. The bushland reserve next to the zoo, Ashton Park, has perhaps the widest diversity of reptile species of any area within the Sydney district. In the period 1977-80, Craig Bennett allegedly caught a carpet snake, blue-bellied black snake *(Pseudechis guttata)*, and Stephen's banded snake *(Hoplocephalus stephensi)* in Ashton Park. None of those species naturally occurs around Sydney or in adjacent national parks. Ashton Park is overrun with peacocks *(Pavo cristatus)* escaped from the zoo, along with a well-established colony of Indian five-lined palm squirrels *(Funambulus pennanti)*, again founded from escaped stock.

Until the mid-1980s the outdoor pits which held lace monitors *(Varanus varius)*, a large tree-climbing lizard that attains 2 m (6′) in length, were about as secure as an open gate. The walls were constructed of cracked concrete which the lizards could easily climb; many escaped. The zoo was able to replace these common lizards fairly easily so the pit always seemed to have plenty of specimens. The lizards which didn't escape tended to be the large, obese males which were probably too lazy or heavy to climb the pit walls.

The outdoor lace monitor cage and other outdoor pits have since been modified to prevent the escape of specimens, predation of smaller specimens by kookaburras *(Dacelo novaeguineae)* and thefts by people who thought that it was easier to go to the zoo to catch a lizard rather than go looking in the bush.

The reptile department in particular has improved and now faces new problems including how to dispose of surplus captive-bred iguanas of a species from the Americas that is endangered. Zoo reptile keepers are currently prevented by Customs officials from exporting these animals legally to overseas zoos which could assist in the captive breeding effort. Likewise the zoo has recently had to curtail breeding programmes for a number of birds because it cannot legally send the offspring elsewhere.

The quarantine facilities at the zoo are also overloaded and seem unable to cope with the influx caused by regular seizures of wildlife by fauna officials. I was present in mid-1990 and saw rare pig-nosed turtles *(Carettochelys insculpta)* in plastic containers in the sun, kept inside by wire held down with bricks. Any wandering peacock could easily have turned over the cages and set the turtles loose. To find this species in Sydney Harbour isn't such a remote possibility.

Of all the waterways in Australia, the one with the highest known species diversity of freshwater tortoises is a lake in Sydney's Centennial Park, near Bondi Junction. The lake is known to have at least eight species of tortoise swimming in it. With the possible exception of one species, the eastern long-necked tortoise *(Chelodina longicollis)*, all are derived from specimens liberated in the area by people who have either kept the species and released them or had them escape.

Liberated Animals

Wildlife parks may also have problems. A park owner in Sydney's western suburbs panicked when fauna officials stated that they were going to inspect his facilities. He took two Nile crocodiles *(Crocodylus niloticus)* that he had illegally imported, to the Warragamba Dam at Wallacia and set them free. They were later retrieved by Customs officials after much media publicity surrounding the incident.

A private keeper in one of Sydney's southern suburbs had four young African Jackson's chameleons escape. He'd illegally imported a breeding pair in the post from the U.S.A. The escapees were assumed to have died until a few years later neighbours started to find green lizards with horns. An intensive campaign eliminated the fledgling colony.

10
THE MAFIA'S INVOLVEMENT

In 1979, investigative journalist Bob Bottom said 'When somebody of the American Mafia reckons a racket is big, it is big.' He was referring to comments made by Vincent 'Big Vinnie' Teresa, a New York Mafia boss turned F.B.I. informer. In a telephone conversation with Bottom in 1979, Teresa said that bird smuggling from Australia had become linked with drug trafficking involving U.S. Mafia interests. He said it was a racket 'that's getting bigger and bigger.'

Teresa had once been a major member of the New York Mafia. He had given evidence before the McClellan Senate Inquiry into organised crime and written a book called *My Life in the Mafia*. After Teresa became an informant for the F.B.I. his testimony led to the successful conviction of more than 50 major players in organised crime.

TERESA IN AUSTRALIA

Less than a week after Bottom published Teresa's statements in the *Bulletin* magazine in August 1979, a truck-load of galahs and sulphur-crested cockatoos, totalling 851 birds in all, were seized by Customs officials in Australia. The birds were allegedly being smuggled to Teresa himself. An American bird-importing agency operated by Teresa was nominated as one of the principals in the racket.

The birds had been legally purchased from a number of Sydney bird dealers for about $3 000 and would have sold for many times that amount in the U.S.A. One estimate valued them at US$3 000 000.

Following the seizure of the birds, Alfred Ferdinham Franz Schmid pleaded guilty to various Federal and State charges. One of Schmid's accomplices, Herbert Stein, was also convicted of State charges. Three others involved in the Australian end avoided all charges relating to the incident.

Schmid, who owned the Old Vienna Inn Restaurant at Kings Cross, was 'unlucky' to come unstuck when near Cairns in north Queensland. Local resident James Kinnear noticed a large furniture van, with New South Wales number plates parked on a disused track beside the main highway. The road was an access road onto his property. Kinnear initially approached the van because he thought the driver might have wanted to camp in the area. After Kinnear heard birds squawking inside the van he was allegedly approached by Schmid, Schmid's young son and Herbert Stein.

Kinnear was told they were wildlife officers and one of them flashed a badge at Kinnear. The badge was later believed to be a Lyons Club badge. One of the two men confused the issue somewhat by stating that they were from Perth, Western Australia, and were driving a New South Wales registered van as their own had broken down in Sydney. Kinnear decided it was unsafe for him to remain so he left and contacted the local Kuranda police. They didn't apprehend the men or their van that day.

Unknown to the police, the men drove their truck to a nearby disused airstrip that evening to meet a DC-3 plane, which was to take the birds to Indonesia.

After seeing the van parked in an adjacent spot near a river bank at about noon the next day, Kinnear again notified the police who decided to investigate. The men were seen cleaning out bird cages, which still apparently contained birds.

Sergeant Jock MacDonald and Constable Philip Grogan searched the area where the van had been parked. Although the van was gone, the officers did find bird feathers, seed and a crumpled cigarette packet which had the Sydney work telephone number of Herbert Stein written on it. That evening the police officers checked local places of accomodation and located the van at the Honey House Motel in Kuranda. The police drove past the motel and summoned re-enforcements from nearby Cairns in the form of Federal police and N.P.W.S. officials, before attempting to arrest the men in the motel room.

When police moved in on the motel, they found a third man besides Schmid and Stein. He was a Customs official who was supposed to have been preventing the very racket he was now caught in. Schmid was unable to produce any permits for the birds and admitted to having none. He allegedly exclaimed 'Oh my God!' when the police opened up the van in his presence to reveal the birds. All three men were then taken to the local police station.

At the police station the third man told the apprehending officers that he was a Customs officer. He stated that he had only met the other men that day in a local pub. As a result he was freed by the arresting officers.

Both Schmid and Stein were charged in Cairns under the Queensland *Fauna Conservation Act* 1974. Both were subsequently convicted in Cairns in early 1981 for 'keeping prescribed fauna without licence'. Schmidt was fined $1 500 while Stein was fined $1 000. The birds and the van, which had been purchased by Schmid and confiscated by the State N.P.W.S. were forfeited to the Crown.

The Phone Call
Although the third man avoided the State charges, a telephone call he had made earlier that day from the Jolly Roger motel in Cairns subsequently cast doubt on his innocence.

On 14 August, Robert Cox, the manager of the motel called Federal police after he monitored an international call. The call had been made by a tenant, presumably the third man, to Vinnie Teresa's unlisted number in Seattle, U.S.A. (206 838 4318).

Smuggling trial aborted because of Herald articles

SMH 15.82

The jury in the trial of four men charged with conspiring to smuggle birds out of Australia was discharged yesterday after two articles in The Sydney Morning Herald on the general topic of fauna-smuggling.

The hearing, before Justice Miles and the 12-man jury, began in the Central Criminal Court on Monday.

The articles appeared in The Sydney Morning Herald on May 7 and today.

Those charged are Rhys Trevor Volkman, 35, former Customs officer, of Glenmore Road, Canterbury; Barry Brian Lowe, 55, self-employed, of Trina Crescent, Canterbury; Herbert Stein, 40, waiter of Springfield Avenue, Kings Cross, and Gunther Opperman, 40, night manager, of Springfield Avenue, Kings Cross,

They had each pleaded not guilty to charges of conspiring to export from Australia prohibited exports — cockatoos and galahs.

When the court assembled yesterday counsel for each defendant joined in an application for the jury to be discharged after the publication of yesterday's article.

Mr John Lloyd-Jones, QC, for the Crown, opposed the application, but Justice Miles agreed that the jury should be discharged.

He called in the jury and told them: "Since we adjourned yesterday something has occurred which has had a monumental effect on the trial.

"You may or may not be aware that this morning there appeared in The Sydney Morning Herald an article headed: The smugglers who prey on our fauna.

"That article has been put to me this morning together with an article reporting a speech made in Parliament last Friday."

[That article was headed: Tough New Penalties for Smuggling Wildlife, and reported a speech in Parliament by the Minister for the Environment, Mr Wilson.]

Justice Miles said: "I have taken the view that it would be unfair to the accused to proceed with the trial in the light of those published articles.

"The issue which arises is whether or not you (the jury) could be expected to free your minds from the matter set out in the articles in the likelihood that one or more of you could have read those articles." It was sufficient to say that the articles were published in a widely circulating metropolitan newspaper.

There was the likelihood that a person reading them might be prejudiced.

Justice Miles said he was not suggesting for a moment that any members of the jury would be affected by the articles. "But the administration of justice has its own reputation to protect.

"If I allowed the trial to continue in the light of these published articles it may well be said that the accused did not receive a fair trial."

Justice Miles allowed the defendants unconditional bail and ordered that they reappear on May 31 for mention.

After discharging the jury, Justice Miles said he was still making up his mind as to whether the Herald was in contempt of court.

He added that the Herald on May 31, if it wished, could make an appearance in court and say whatever it wished in regard to the matter.

90

Teresa was then operating a bird importing business from that address, trading as Seattle Bird Importers Incorporated. It was registered under the assumed name Charles Antony Cantino, a name Teresa had adopted as part of a U.S. Government's witness protection programme after he had testified against other Mafia bosses.

Cox told police that the caller had been upset at having to 'wait another couple of days' and had wanted to 'get out' because of the risk. The pilot of the plane that was meant to collect the birds in the truck at Kuranda, had apparently 'got sick'. According to Cox, the Customs officer and Teresa had talked about a $17 000 payment and how they'd been lucky to get birds out of Australia previously, on a commercial flight.

It became apparent that Teresa and his accomplices in the U.S.A. were confused about what was actually happening. The truck load of birds in North Queensland were just the 'bread and butter' birds; another 200 more expensive birds were still in hiding somewhere on the New South Wales north coast as part of a planned second shipment.

As the birds had been seized from Schmid the same day as the telephone call was made to Seattle, it isn't known what became of the intended pick up flight, although it is assumed that it was cancelled.

Computer Parts

Alfred Schmid, now caught with the illegal birds, had been under surveillance for about two months.

In June, Schmid and a friend had booked an airline container in the name of Computrex Datronmics (Australia) Incorporated, for dispatch to the Philippines, with an invoice for transhipment to the Portland Sales Corporation of Portland, Oregon, U.S.A.

The plan had been to export birds disguised as computer parts in crates. As Schmid and his friend loaded 12 tea chests into the airline container, Schmid pressed five $20 notes into the hand of export clerk David Stewart. Schmid told Stewart not to worry about any noises emanating from the container as they contained cockatoos. Police and Customs officials were called in. They broke into the crates and found 77 sulphur-crested cockatoos and 10 galahs.

The shipment was seized without Schmid's knowledge. The birds themselves had been legally purchased from a licensed dealer for a total of $753. They were worth nearly $500 000 in the U.S.A.

The Customs Officer's Role

After Schmid was finally caught in Cairns, a joint task force between the Federal police and Customs officials was established to investigate the case.

A search was made of two houses in the Sydney suburb of Canterbury, inhabited by the third man and his father-in-law, Brian Lowe. These searches revealed plastic tubes used to hold birds and pieces of wire and wood, underneath one of the houses, indicating previous similar activities in the past.

Although it was almost by chance that Schmid was 'busted' near Cairns with the van-load of birds, Sydney Customs officials had been on the trail of the shipment for some time. It was only by supplying police with false intelligence that the third man had been able to prevent the operation being broken up earlier.

FIRST ZOO

Sydney's first zoo was founded by the Zoological Society of New South Wales on seven acres of land, known as Billygoat Swamp, in Moore Park in 1881. The zoo's area subsequently grew to 15 acres, holding about 500 animals. As the Moore Park site lacked room for expansion a new site had to be found. A harbourside site above Athol Bay with some of the best views in the world was acquired. Taronga Park Zoo was officially opened on 7 October 1916. In 1990 it held about 4 500 mammals, birds, reptiles, amphibians and fish and employed a staff in excess of 150.

It was well known that someone had been after 800 birds, including 60 black cockatoos (*Calyptorhynchus* sp.). A later report to Customs from the bird trade indicated that someone had wanted 500 Major Mitchells and in a hurry. As Michael Schooley said 'When people want that number of birds in a hurry, they only want them for one purpose . . . to smuggle.'

The thwarted plan had involved a pilot known by Schooley and other Customs officials to be involved in wildlife trafficking. The pilot was to fly an aircraft from Merauke in Irian Jaya. From here the birds would be taken by boat to Singapore, then transhipped to Canada, and sent by long-distance truck to the U.S.A. Once there, Teresa would have sold the birds 'legally' as captive bred to other bird dealers and keepers.

At about the same time, Teresa allegedly arranged for 200 rare parrot mutations to be illegally imported into Australia from Singapore, where they were being held in storage at a well-known dealer's premises. Likewise, those birds were to have been laundered before sale in Australia.

Just before the 'bust' in August 1979, no fewer than 16 pairs of gang gang cockatoos had allegedly been shipped about 350 km (210 miles) north of Sydney to a property for 'safe storage', constituting just some of the more expensive birds to have been in the second shipment.

In the week before the Kuranda 'bust' an alert was put out to Customs officials that a large number of galahs and sulphur-crested cockatoos had been purchased from Sydney dealers. Although Schmid was suspected of being involved in the purchase of the birds and of attempting to smuggle them out of the country, increased surveillance at airport terminals revealed nothing. Furthermore, Schmid and his accomplices could not be contacted at home or work, but their absence from these places was seen by Customs officials as suspicious.

The third man's alleged role in the racket was pivotal in several ways. He was the official link in the operation who could try to ensure that investigating officials would never catch the smugglers. He had also spent considerable time in North Queensland and had family there. His intimate knowledge of the area was very helpful.

The successful Kuranda 'bust' led to many other people being visited and interviewed. The other birds 'in hiding' on the New South Wales north coast were never located by Customs or wildlife officials. After meticulous investigation including interviews both within Australia and overseas, four Sydney men were charged with the Federal offences of conspiracy to smuggle protected fauna, namely the galahs and sulphur-crested cockatoos.

ZOO POO

Zoos in their constant struggle to finance their operations sometimes come up with innovative ideas. Victoria's Werribee Zoological Park collects and packs its animal manure and sells it to visitors as garden fertilizer. For just $3 you can buy yourself a three kilo bag of 'Zoo Poo'.

Buying a Case

The charges against the four men were laid in Sydney after Schmid had agreed to plead guilty to all charges in return for indemnity. He had in effect 'rolled over' to become a Crown witness.

The evidence from the earlier attempt to smuggle birds out of the country as computer parts was 'married' to that of the Kuranda case and both sets of charges were laid simultaneously.

The four men were charged in Sydney, where the case was heard. They were Rhys Trevor Volkman, whom Schooley described as 'the mole in our office', of Glenmore Road, Canterbury; Barry Brian Lowe, the Custom officer's father-in-law, of Trina Crescent, Canterbury; Herbert Stein, who had assisted Schmid with the truck, of Springfield Avenue, Kings Cross, and Gunther Opperman, a nightclub manager, who worked with Schmid, also of Springfield Avenue, Kings Cross.

Schooley was forewarned that a large amount of money had been spent on legal representation. The Crown called a large number of witnesses, who had to be flown in from north Queensland and elsewhere. Among them were Queensland police officers, Jock Macdonald and Philip Grogan, James Kinnear, Jim Mealing and another staff member from the Honey House Motel, an officer from the Queensland N.P.W.S., Robert Cox of the Jolly Roger Motel and an F.B.I. agent from Seattle, U.S.A..

The Crown failed to gain a conviction in the case which was finally heard in 1981. The presiding magistrate refused to accept written evidence tendered by the two Queensland police officers, as the police had not issued a formal caution when arresting the men. The lady from the motel who had overheard the conversation with the third man immediately after making the connection was prohibited from giving evidence. The case was immediately appealed and set down for retrial.

Another Failed Attempt

The second trial commenced in early May 1982, at the Sydney Supreme Court and again the same Crown witnesses had to be brought back to Sydney.

On 14 May 1982, the fifth day of the second trial of the four men, counsel for all four defendants joined in an application to Justice Miles that as a result of two articles printed in the *Sydney Morning Herald* newspaper in relation to wildlife smuggling, the jury should be discharged. The argument of defence counsel was that the articles may have prejudiced the jury in making a decision for or against the accused. On the Thursday before the trial, the then Federal Minister for the Environment, Mr Wilson, had referred to the Crown case as if it had already been won, in a speech announcing new wildlife laws. In an article in the *Sydney Morning Herald*, reporter Deborah Hope had quoted Mr Wilson referring to the Kuranda seizure:

'As an example of the illicit trade, Mr Wilson cited the example of a cargo of 900 birds seized in Cairns in 1979 just before shipment. The birds were estimated to have an overseas black market price of more than $2 000 000.'

Mr John Lloyd Jones (Q.C.) appearing for the Crown opposed the application, but Justice Miles agreed with defence counsel and discharged the jury. Justice Miles called in the jury and said,

'Since we adjourned yesterday, something has occurred which has had a monumental effect on the trial. You may or may not be aware that this morning there appeared in the *Sydney Morning Herald* an article headed; "The Smugglers Who Prey on Our Fauna". That article has been put together with an article reporting a speech made in Parliament last Friday . . . I have taken the view that it would be unfair to the accused to proceed with the trial in the light of those published articles.'

Although Justice Miles did not suggest that any members of the jury would be prejudiced by the articles, he said 'If I allowed the trial to continue in the light of these published articles it may be said that the accused did not receive a fair trial.'

Justice Miles gave all the defendants unconditional bail, an unusual step in such a serious case and ordered all to re-appear on 31 May the same year.

In spite of its effect on the trial, no one from the *Sydney Morning Herald* or the company, John Fairfax and Sons Pty. Ltd. was charged with contempt of court. In a bizarre twist of the facts, Justice Miles said on 31 May, that no one from the *Sydney Morning Herald* could be charged with contempt as there was 'no evidence' that any reporter or other representative of the publisher had attended the trial or had any knowledge of the course of the trial.

However, Justice Miles had apparently overlooked the fact that he himself had quoted an 'anonymous' reporter in the *Sydney Morning Herald* on 14 May 1982. Furthermore, the printing of the full names and addresses of the defendants in the *Sydney Morning Herald* on that date, indicated that a reporter must have been present for some of the trial and that the reporter and the editorial staff would therefore have understood the potential ramifications of publishing the two articles.

Interestingly, less than twelve months earlier, staff at the *Sydney Morning Herald* had been accused by members of the A.B.T. and Australian Herpetological Society of deliberately failing to investigate 'new' allegations in a story implicating Government officials in the trafficking of wildlife.

The next trial of the four men, with a new jury of 12, was set down to commence on 13 September. In the words of Jim Mealing,'the whole case was a farce'. According to Mealing, the Crown relied principally on evidence to be given by Schmid. Opperman was aquitted when Justice Miles directed the jury to do so. The trial of the other three men was then set down for 12 October. At the last minute, Schmid allegedly refused to give evidence on very vague grounds. As a result, the Crown case was severely damaged and the trial finished within a day. The three remaining charged men were 'exonerated' and the court file recorded 'not guilty, jury discharged from further duty'. Leaving court, one of the defence barristers told Customs officials that the case should have been won by the Crown.

Michael Schooley later reported 'the one good thing to come from the whole operation was that I was at long last able to establish who the informer, or in current terms the "mole" was in our office.' Schooley then went on to state 'Unfortunately when we had managed to cure that problem we found another one came to light!'. Schooley later elaborated 'This I'm afraid is the reality. The authorities have nearly as much trouble with their own people as they do with the smugglers.'

The third man has been 'quietly retired' from the Customs department. He was just one of several allegedly corrupt Customs officers removed from the department in this way.

What Birds?

Meanwhile, the truck, cages and birds seized by the Queensland authorities had been initially held in a N.P.W.S. compound near Lake Eacham. As a result of the deal reached with Schmid by Crown lawyers in Sydney, whereby Schmid was to have been a Crown witness, Schmid was given back his van and cages in contravention to the earlier court order.

The birds themselves allegedly were destroyed as a result of a mysterious outbreak of disease. Two people involved in the initial apprehension and prosecution of the men, subsequently alleged that the birds were not destroyed but smuggled out of the country in a similar manner to the aborted attempt that had led to their seizure in the first place.

Earlier, in December 1978, U.S. Fish and Wildlife Service (F.W.S.) officials had seized 324 birds from Vincent Teresa. Those birds had been imported from Indonesia with faulty quarantine papers. They were suspected to have been smuggled from Australia in a manner similar to the planned Kuranda operation.

Earlier still, in February 1977, Teresa had made a controversial visit to Sydney to appear before an inquiry into illegal casinos. During his short stay in Australia Teresa spent most of his time visiting bird keepers and traders, presumably establishing contacts he later used in his smuggling operations. His stay in Australia was cut short when the Federal Government ordered him to leave the country.

Within 12 months of the north Queensland 'bust' Teresa was jailed over an insurance fraud in the U.S.A.

Five years later, in 1984, Teresa was again named as the American link in an operation smuggling birds from Australia. In December the same year he was indicted in Philadelphia on charges of conspiracy to smuggle rare birds into the U.S.A.

Mafia involvement in wildlife trade between Australia and the U.S.A. helped by allegedly corrupt officials is thought to continue. Certainly large numbers of birds from Australia are still appearing on the U.S. market.

11
THE SMUGGLING INQUIRY

In 1975-76 a House of Representatives Inquiry was held into the illegal traffic in fauna. About 45 people gave evidence, including fauna officials from various States, Customs officials, aviculturalists, wildlife traders, conservationists, academics, a journalist and a solicitor who had successfully prosecuted the New South Wales N.P.W.S. Since the inquiry, some witnesses have been discredited to varying degrees. However, much of the evidence gave a fairly accurate portrayal of trafficking, official corruption and related matters. At least one witness is believed to have been murdered after allegedly threatening to expose wildlife traffickers.

Athough now 15 years old, the information is still relevant today. Indeed over half the people who gave evidence to the inquiry are in essentially the same positions.

OFFICIALS VERSUS ENTHUSIASTS
Customs figures for seizures and prosecutions relating to wildlife smuggling bear little correlation to the actual volume of trade in wildlife. Furthermore by their own admission, Customs usually do not catch the principals of wildlife rackets.

Aviculturalists who gave evidence before the inquiry repeatedly emphasised that officials appointed to administer wildlife laws rarely, if ever, had previous experience with fauna. The aggressive nature of inspections or raids carried out on licensed bird keepers by these untrained officers was a repeated source of contention.

Dr Lavery of the Queensland N.P.W.S. countered by asserting that aviculturalists had never made a positive contribution to conservation. He ignored the fact that over 50% of all published material on birds has come from people who at some period have kept them. Similarly, every reptile book published in Australia over the last 30 years has been written by reptile keepers or former keepers.

Aviculturalists, like other animal keepers, suffer from a common misconception by the general public that captive animals are not as well off as their wild counterparts. In the modern context, the reverse is usually true. Samuel Dawson of the Australian Avicultural Society gave evidence of how people from the Bird Observers Club had visited him in a most antagonistic fashion and later left quite convinced that the birds were being kept in excellent conditions.

Notwithstanding the above, not all keepers and zoos look after their animals properly. When the death rate is unacceptably high replacement stock is needed, which fuels demand from potentially illegal sources such as smugglers.

Wilson Wheeler of the International Council For Bird Preservation criticised the treatment of birds at a number of Australian zoos including the Healesville Sanctuary in Victoria. He did, however, note pressure on these 'non-performing' institutions to improve and acknowledged improvements in cage designs at Sydney's Taronga Zoo.

Ronald Hastings of the Victorian Avicultural Society noted how the law in South Australia prohibited the sale of birds such as the endangered scarlet-chested parrots (*Neophema splendida*) and princess parrots. This legislation was slowing the breeding of these birds, as aviculturalists who already held them had enough, and being unable to trade offspring, were not putting nesting logs in their cages. Hastings noted that both birds breed readily in captivity but are rarely seen in the wild. He stated 'This is suppressing the increase of two of our rare birds and is criminal to say the least, on the part of those who drew up the legislation.'

Another interesting case raised by Hastings was that of the Cape Barron goose (*Cereopsis novaehollandiae*). The bird is threatened with extinction in the wild, yet it is shot as a pest. It breeds freely in captivity and is found in zoos worldwide. The State fauna authorities in South Australia banned keeping the species in captivity. The resulting temptation to go outside the law to keep this species need never have existed if the laws were more sensitive in the first place.

Avicultural Societies

Robert Brown of the South Australian Ornithological Association gave specific examples of how avicultural societies have in the past directly contributed to the illegal trade in wildlife.

Brown told the inquiry 'In South Australia at least, an avicultural society's practice of awarding medals for bird keeping has undoubtedly encouraged both smuggling and interstate trafficking in protected birds.' Brown also predicted that attempts would be made to 'trap and breed the orange-bellied parrot,' an endangered species, which in the 1970s was estimated to have a wild population of less than 1 000 birds.

Although by 1967 at least 19 orange-bellied parrots were held by various South Australian aviculturalists, and the first captive breeding occurred as early as 1963, no person was ever prosecuted for illegally obtaining the birds. None of the original breeding stock had been legally caught.

The first report of captive specimens in Europe co-incided with two major events: a visit by a well-known English aviculturalist to South Australia and the alleged release of birds by the South Australian N.P.W.S. from captive collections.

It was reported in the 1972 issue of the *Avicultural Magazine*, published by the English Avicultural Society, that the orange-bellied parrot had arrived in Holland. Knowing full well that the birds had been illegally smuggled into Europe, the magazine reported 'One or two pairs have somehow (!) recently reached Europe and J. Posteema of Gieterreen, Holland, acquired a pair.'

In 1971, the Avicultural Society in South Australia abolished its custom of awarding bronze medals for the first breedings of exotic birds within South Australia. This followed the conviction of one of the society's most prominent members for smuggling indigenous birds into Australia. The same member had successfully bred indigenous birds not native to South Australia, such as the regent bower bird (*Sericulus chrysocephalus*) of coastal New South Wales and Queensland, which no interstate fauna authority had issued a permit to collect.

In the U.K., in order to prevent people illegally taking birds from the wild, protected species may be traded only if they are 'close-rung'. Close-rung birds are those which are leg banded as nestlings with a metal ring which cannot be fitted over the foot of an adult without breaking the hind toe. The close-ringing of birds supposedly prevents wild-caught birds being falsely sold as aviary-caught. However, in order to get around the laws of close-ringing, some unscrupulous people have fitted wild nestlings with close-rings before trapping them when they are old enough to leave their parents. The presence of close-rung birds with deformed toes also indicates other traders have been capturing adults illegally and then attempting to trade them as legally obtained birds.

Close-ringing has been put forward as a measure to prevent illegal capture of wild birds by several Australian State authorities, but has been rejected a number of times.

Stanley Sindel, an aviculturalist of New South Wales, told the inquiry that close-ringing of parrots has had problems. Some parents will not accept the ring and will chew the young one's leg off to get rid of it.

Native finches desert their nests immediately if anyone approaches the nest. Therefore close-ringing of native finches is not a viable option. Likewise for soft-bills. Native doves (*Geopelia* spp.) and quails (*Coturnix* spp.) are almost the only captive birds that Stanley Sindel regards as being suited to close-ringing in Australia.

Sindel told the inquiry how the N.P.W.S. had asked him to register with them as a bird keeper some 18 months previously and that he was still waiting to receive his permits and record books. (I registered with them as a reptile keeper in 1974 and received my record books and licence, which was undated and unspecific, in 1977 after numerous representations to the department.)

Lack of Communication

Mr Michael Forster told the inquiry of problems faced by animal keepers in relation to the wildlife authorities, especially the lack of communication.

Forster said 'What we are concerned about is that there is no communication and no apparent treatment of this subject other than to say: "The problem is too hard, let us ban them altogether."'

A total ban on keeping and trading animals would simply turn law-abiding people into criminals.

Forster cited an unusual case in which a number of marine fish were confiscated as illegal imports. The fish dealer in question found it cheaper to supply an Australian scientific institution with these fish by obtaining them in the Philippines rather than catching them in Sydney Harbour, where they could easily be found.

The problem in that case was in deciding whether the fish were native or not. Certainly the species occurred in Australian waters, but the specimens concerned weren't from Australia.

Forster cited another example where it was cheaper to import a particular type of rainbowfish (*Melanotaenia* sp.) rather than catch them locally, even though they were also a species native to Australia. People bringing in the fish illegally, however, would be classified as wildlife smugglers.

Some people who have imported fish into Australia with wrongly filled-out papers have also been charged with trafficking offences.

INTERSTATE MOVEMENTS

Laundering or legalising illegally obtained wildlife doesn't just occur outside Australia. Birds illegally trapped in one State can be taken across the border to another State where it is legal to catch them. These birds may then be 'licensed' in that State, after which, under section 92 of the Constitution which allows free trade between the States, the birds may be imported back to the State of capture where they may be held legally. This works on the assumption that wildlife authorities in each State are co-operative.

Laws making animals of given species the property of the Crown should effectively put a stop to any trading in that species in that State. This also includes the progeny of any legally held animals.

Hastings gave examples of the problems faced by Australians in complying with wildlife laws in different States and why interstate wildlife smuggling occurs. Firstly, there is nobody on State borders to check for wildlife, thereby making interstate transportation of wildlife easy.

Should someone want to 'legally' get a bird from one State to another, Hastings gives a likely scenario of what may happen.

'They are all different. Each State has its own laws. You have to write about ten letters explaining the laws that are used in your State to the fellow in the other State; he writes back and gives you his laws; then you work things out and say we will do this, that and the other; and you find somebody is on holiday and that you cannot get your permit or that you have to wait for it.'

No State Government had made an effort to solve the problems of people trying to legally trade wildlife either interstate or internationally. What Hastings never mentioned was the frequency with which wildlife authorities change their laws or relevant paperwork, thereby making the acquisition of permits even harder. Hastings told a parliamentary inquiry that he was 'accidentally' smuggling birds.

'You could say that I smuggled some birds across from New South Wales. They were only youngsters out of a nest in an aviary, and I forgot all about getting a permit for them, but I could be accused of smuggling on that score.'

Hastings could hardly be described as a big-time smuggler plundering our resources yet it is this type of 'breach' to which officers of State fauna squads seem to be devoting a disproportionate amount of effort.

For example, Gavin Ricketts and Mike Connelly, the two man Queensland Fauna Squad have been 'busting' people for petty breaches for some 13 years, but have yet to expose a single principal of a major official racket. This is in spite of knowledge of large-scale official smuggling from Queensland.

In 1990, the two man squad spent an extraordinary amount of time snaring a North Queensland reptile keeper. After days of surveillance, they caught the man helping a friend transport a single snake without the relevant permit. The herpetologist, Peter Krauss, was woken at 1 a.m. by the officers who searched his house from top to bottom. Krauss, well known as a breeder of rare species, subsequently had all his reptile keeping permits cancelled by the Queensland N.P.W.S. and all his reptiles confiscated, a substantial penalty for his 'misdemeanour'. His vital captive-breeding programmes were terminated for pythons, including Oenpelli pythons, diamond pythons, olive pythons (*Bothrochilus olivaceous*) and woma pythons (*Aspidites ramsayi*).

Ronald Hastings pointed out to the inquiry the absurdity of laws which prevented any Victorian from keeping swift parrots (*Lathamus discolour*) in captivity. This was despite the fact that the bird thrives in captivity and is shot in the hundreds in Tasmania where it is declared a pest.

People who brought these birds across Bass Strait into Victoria could have been accused of smuggling the birds interstate. Overseas the bird sells for about US$1 000 a pair (1990 prices). Why shoot a potential source of income for Australia?

THE ROLE OF SOUTH AUSTRALIA

According to Brian Eves, of the South Australian N.P.W.S., South Australia in particular is used as a transhipment point for wildlife being illegally taken from one State to another. Just as international wildlife smugglers send wildlife through an 'intermediate' country in a bid to make it legal, traders within Australia follow the same practice. Eves obviously had some knowledge of transhipment within South Australia. At the time he gave his evidence to the inquiry, he was himself involved in an illegal bird trafficking and transhipment operation involving Bert Field, Bob Lyons and others (see p. 32).

In one case, the South Australian authorities siezed more than 950 birds that had been illegally taken from the Northern Territory. Although the court case went straight to section 92 of the Constitution, the man who held the birds was eventually convicted because he had caught them illegally in their State of origin. The birds were seized late on a Friday night and were due to be sold in Melbourne the next day for around $6 000. The trailer and vehicle where the birds were found was specially converted for carrying them.

At about the same time, Dick Wordley reported that another South Australian N.P.W.S. ranger had seized numerous birds from a man who'd transported them in a specially constructed semi-trailer from north-west Australia. The man was apprehended in the Adelaide Hills preparing the birds for shipment overseas. Included in the haul were over 60 Gouldian finches (*Erythrura gouldiae*), now listed as endangered, and four different types of parrot.

Many operators arrive in Adelaide with wildlife on a morning flight, complete their transaction during the day and leave on a flight later the same day. It is rare for some wildlife traffickers who trade in South Australia to spend 24 hours in the State.

In one case a man was apprehended at Murray Bridge with a car-load of birds, after having driven from Melbourne to South Australia to buy them with cash before taking them back to Melbourne for sale on the open market.

Some years ago another man arrived in South Australia on a morning flight and purchased some 400 'penny tortoises', juvenile Murray short-necked tortoises (*Emydura macquarii*) for 50 cents each. He flew back to Melbourne on a later flight with all of them in his briefcase and sold them all for $3.50 each. For the cost of his plane tickets he'd made a $3 profit on every tortoise.

As Brian Eves and others noted, recent wildlife smugglers 'have now improved their techniques to such a degree that they seek to move smaller but specially selected items'. As a result, prices have risen for those species not being bred in captivity in large numbers. The trend noted by Eves has accelerated. It is becoming increasingly attractive for wildlife smugglers to source specimens from private and public collections rather than from the wild. A stolen animal can be shifted out of a city within hours of its theft.

One reptile smuggler from South Australia operated for five years before being apprehended. Under surveillance he posted five separate parcels to West Germany in a single day.

When he went before a court, he asked for 72 instances of illegal export to be taken into consideration. The man wasn't registered with the South Australian N.P.W.S.. He didn't keep any reptiles himself but acted solely for a relative in West Germany. The man would go out for a drive on weekends and do his own collecting which, together with reptiles he received in the post from a friend in Queensland, formed the basis of what he sent to Germany. The man also knew of a supermarket in Germany which proudly boasts of being able to supply any species of reptile within seven days, from anywhere in the world including Australia.

TRANSPORTATION METHODS

Joseph Mattinson, a well-known New South Wales breeder of hooded parrots and other rare birds, told the inquiry how Indians traded in wildlife and the cruelty of their methods. He showed the inquiry a photo of 624 parrots sent on consignment from India to the U.K. The consignment was legal but all the parrots were dead.

When asked why laws had not been drafted for dealers to package birds in a certain way to ensure a greater survival rate, Mattinson offered the following response:

'Packaging is not so much the problem, it is the acclimatisation of the bird prior to sending. If you have been to India, as I have, you can go there and buy birds by the thousand of all species. No government should permit what happens to them. To get them quiet, they cut their wings off to the flesh. They just go chop, chop, chop on hundreds of thousands of them, and this is the only way they have of quietening them. There are two ways of quietening a bird: chop its wings off, or do not feed it and it gets tame. I have seen them yarding birds with kids walking around them all day to say that they are aviary-bred birds so they can sell them to dealers in Holland and Belgium as aviary-bred birds.'

The chairman of the inquiry responded 'You cannot sell 624 dead birds, therefore it would seem to be in the interests of the dealer if he is going to collect his cash to deliver a live bird. So where does all this work out?'

Mattinson's reply was 'The Indian dealers are not like that. They do not send the bird until the money is in the bank . . . Cash before delivery with all Indian dealers.'

Mattinson told the inquiry that the top prices quoted for birds are those paid for top quality captive-bred stock and not 'a pair of birds with no tail and no wings in a dilapidated condition coming out of a plane'. In other words only 'professional smugglers' who are able to export birds from Australia in good condition are likely to make large amounts of money from doing so.

Smugglers need only get the birds out of Australia to South-east Asia to launder them and make them legal. The legal export of Australian birds even from Singapore is no problem. Dealers in South-east Asia pay a quarter of the price for stock compared to their European and American counterparts, so the incentive to 'go all the way' for smugglers operating from Australia is usually compelling.

DISEASES

A major reason given for the banning of trade in wildlife is the risk of transmission of diseases by imported animals. Newcastle disease is often given as a prime example of a disease which, if imported, could decimate Australia's poultry industry. What is not mentioned is that although birds may carry the disease, migratory birds not subject to man-made restrictions have not yet introduced the disease to Australian farms.

The limited usefulness of Australian quarantine regulation enforcement was demonstrated by Ronald Hastings when he explained how fruit fly checks are carried out on some State borders. Officials check all vehicles for fruit and vegetables at selected points to ensure that the flies aren't transmitted to new areas where they may do serious damage to crops. The problem is that these officials go home at 6 p.m. and any vehicles that pass check points after that time aren't checked. The flies spread and then it costs millions of dollars to eradicate them.

EXPLOITATION VERSUS CONSERVATION

Dr Richard Zann told the inquiry that he regarded certain species of parrot as being potentially vulnerable to heavy exploitation but at this stage there was no evidence that illegal trapping had in fact reduced their numbers. Most, if not all, species were being bred in captivity at the time. The only exceptions to this were the golden-shouldered parrot (*Psephotus chrysopterygius*) and hooded parrots which he said were being severely depleted by illegal nest robbers. Numbers were believed to have fallen in areas where the birds were once common.

Both species are particularly susceptible to illegal exploitation on the basis of their low natural populations, specialised nesting requirements (in the side of termite mounds), low fecundity and very restricted zone of distribution. The hooded parrot in particular is known in reasonable numbers only in the Pine Creek area of the Northern Territory making it even more susceptible to concentrated trapping.

Dr Zahn cited how illegal trappers of grassfinches in northern and inland Australia were able to ensure that entire populations of these birds could be caught, thereby eliminating them from given areas.

'These birds are caught at the end of the dry period when water is at a premium. The trappers close all the available water holes in the area except one, where they set their nets and traps and capture the entire local population of seed-eaters (mostly grassfinches and pigeons). The drier the season, the fewer the water holes and the easier the birds are caught. Several drought years in succession with systematic trapping must greatly deplete the potential for natural increase in numbers within an area.'

One of the more common cases cited by proponents of captive breeding of wildlife and its usefulness in conserving endangered species is that of the Hawaiian goose (*Branta sandvicensis*). The 'Ne-Ne' as it is locally known was reduced to a mere handful of individuals after white settlement. Since being bred in captivity, the species has now been re-introduced to its natural habitat where it has survived and actually increased in numbers.

SUMMARY

It is this author's view that a far more in-depth inquiry should be initiated. Among its aims should be a complete overhaul of State and Federal laws relating to fauna protection and trade. Fauna smuggling would probably cease to exist if sensible trading laws were introduced.

RAIDS ON BIRD RACKET

Police swoop on international ring

CUSTOMS officers and federal police have questioned more than 20 people in weekend raids aimed at smashing a multi-million-dollar, international bird smuggling ring.

The raids, including eight on Sydney homes and businesses and three in country NSW, followed the arrest in the US of a New Zealand man who allegedly masterminded the Australian operation.

Customs spokesman Alistair Wilson said raids were also carried out in several locations in Queensland and Victoria at the weekend during which "certain evidence" was collected.

Mr Wilson said the raids were part of a three-year international undercover operation by Australian, New Zealand and US authorities investigating the illegal trafficking of exotic and endangered birds.

On Friday, US Fish and Wildlife Service officers arrested the alleged ring-leader of the smuggling operation, Philip Morrison, 35, from Auckland.

He was arrested in the southern Californian town of Costa Mesa, and faces up to 25 years' jail on charges of smuggling thousands of rare parrots, cockatoos and macaws from Australia, New Zealand and the US.

He was allegedly caught in the act of arranging the sale of a shipment of birds.

Morrison, who did not enter a plea during a brief appearance in the Los Angeles Federal Court, was refused bail and will appear in court on February 3.

At the same time as Morrison was being arrested, US authorities swooped on 25 premises in Miami, Florida, New York, Chicago and Louisiana allegedly used in the operation.

Hundreds of live Australian protected and endangered birds valued from $1000 to $27,000 were seized.

They included galahs ($1000), gang gangs ($20,000), yellow-tailed black cockatoos ($27,000), sulphur-crested cockatoos ($3000) and black cockatoos (up to $50,000).

In New Zealand, authorities seized records and live wildlife from several North Island locations.

The Customs regional manager for investigations in Sydney, Mr Lester Hampson, said the operation was a major step forward in international co-operation to thwart the illegal trade in live native birds.

"Our teams have been part of this investigation for some time," Mr Hampson said.

"... We expect our inquiries to carry on for some time yet."

Herald Sun 20/1/92   page 28

103

12
THE AMERICAN SCENE

Although this book is principally about smuggling wildlife out of Australia a summary of recent problems in the U.S.A. is useful. Like Australia, the U.S.A. has plenty of indigenous wildlife, much of which is exported to other countries and has recently been the subject of 'protective' legislation of questionable value. The U.S.A. is also the main recipient of Australia's smuggled wildlife, so a review of their fauna authorities is pertinent.

JAMES WATT

Perhaps one of the most bizarre cases affecting wildlife conservation in the U.S.A was the appointment of James Watt by the Reagan administration to the position of Secretary of the Interior, in January 1981. Watt's position effectively put him in direct control of a number of Federal authorities, including fauna authorities who administered over a third of the land area of the U.S.A. The area under his control included all national parks, wildlife refuges and wilderness areas. His influence extended to many areas of national and local government policy, including those relating to environmental policies.

Before his appointment by Reagan, Watt had been president of the Mountain States Legal Foundation, an activist law firm representing development interests in environmentally sensitive areas. Watt unsuccessfully fought a case to overturn the 1977 Strip Mining Act, introduced by the Carter administration, which was legislation Reagan had entrusted him to administer.

Almost immediately after Watt was appointed, he fired every interior chief down to deputy director level, except for one. At the time of the dismissal announcements, Watt recommended other 'preservation-minded' interior employees should consider working elsewhere. Watt was quoted as saying that America's resources were put here for the enjoyment and use of people now and 'should not be denied to the people by elitist groups' (conservationists). Watt further explained: 'Conservation is not the blind locking away of huge areas and their resources because of emotional appeals.' He was once quoted as saying that his anti-environment stance was motivated by a missionary zeal 'to swing the environmental pendulum back to centre'.

Watt together with Ronald Lambertson, a Watt-appointed associate director of the U.S. Fish and Wildlife Service (F.W.S.) and manager of the endangered species programme, decided to reduce the list of endangered species within the U.S.A. Lambertson was quoted as saying 'Rare fauna can breed themselves off the endangered list if they really want to survive', hardly the attitude one would expect from the director of a conservation authority.

Another of Watt's key men in the F.W.S. was G. Ray Arnett who took pride in prosecuting conservationists. In October 1982, Arnett visited the Cayman Islands where the last 200 grand Cayman parrots (*Amazona leucocephala caymanensis*) were living on the brink of extinction. An American newspaper reported that he had taken it upon himself to shoot two of the endangered parrots. Arnett also kept the sea otter (*Lutra felina*) off the endangered list and was keen to convert the world's only winter refuge of the whooping crane (*Grus americana*) into a commercial development.

As far as habitat destruction was concerned, Watt believed that if an area were not used for some form of human activity, then it ought to be, and 'to hell with the animals that live there'.

Almost immediately after his appointment Watt re-assigned administration of oil exploration on the 3.5 million hectare (8.8 million acre) William O. Douglas National Wildlife Refuge: from the F.W.S. to the U.S. Geological Survey in a bid to reduce environmental safeguards. The residents of the north slope village of Katovik and several conservation groups challenged Watt's plans on environmental and legal grounds. Among the consequences of Watt's plans would have been total annihilation of migratory patterns of the porcupine caribou (*Rangifer* sp.) herd. The District Court Judge in Anchorage found against Watt on the grounds of violating two Federal statutes and the intentions of Congress.

Watt also tried unsuccessfully to lift an American ban on the import of products derived from three threatened species of Australian wallaby, and proposed a subdivision on 8 000 hectares (20 000 acres) of undeveloped land in Nevada that would have wiped out the endangered devil's hole pupfish (*Cyprinodon* sp.) and warm springs pupfish (*Cyprinodon* sp.). This was from the man entrusted to protect these species! The Office of Endangered Species which Watt and Lambertson tried several times to scrap, was forced to prepare emergency listings for two other fish species, three plants and one creeping water bug endemic to the area.

Watt attempted to open up unprecedented chunks of ocean floor off the California coast for oil drilling in spite of Treasury recommendations to the contrary. The environmental consequences were never considered, including the threat to 28 species of marine mammal, some already listed as endangered, a US$1 billion a year fishing industry and a US$6.2 billion a year tourist industry. The risk of earthquakes in the area convinced Congress to halt any development in that area.

Watt was, to say the least, an unusual man. A Christian Fundamentalist, he stated that he believed in setting aside resources for future generations but then asked 'How many future generations can we count on before the Lord returns?' It was also alleged that he misled taxation officials in statements concerning his financial position; many of his assets were allegedly divested to other family members or friends.

Aftermath

Perhaps to non-Americans Watt will be most remembered for his affect on the success of the C.I.T.E.S. treaty, the first concerted effort by nations of the world to tackle the problems of wildlife trade at a global level.

The treaty was initiated by the U.S. Government and is widely known as the Washington treaty. At the time of Watt taking control of American environmental policy, over 70 nations had ratified the treaty. At the March 1981 C.I.T.E.S. meeting in New Delhi, Dr John Grandy, executive vice president of Defenders of Wildlife, was quoted as saying 'The conservationist attitude of the parties was overwhelming . . . Sadly the United States was often an exception.' The U.S. delegation, under directions from Watt, often broke ranks with other nations to vote against proposals for animals which included whales, parrots, rhinoceros, gyrfalcons, bears and bobcats.

Delegates from almost all countries including Australia expressed regret at the change of the U.S. stance under Watt's guidance. *Defenders* magazine likened C.I.T.E.S. (at that time less than 10 years old) to a growing baby; if the mother (the U.S.) decides to kill its child what hope does the child have?

Watt had scrapped the original C.I.T.E.S. delegation and replaced it with cronies. Donald Lambertson headed the delegation, while Fred Jones took a high profile in a bid to push Watt's anti-conservation views. After the third C.I.T.E.S. meeting, Jones went so far as to say he would have taken a more determinedly anti-conservationist stance at the meeting had he thought delegates from other nations would have tolerated it. He even said he had never agreed with the conservationist principles espoused by those attempting to make the C.I.T.E.S. treaty a success.

International opposition to James Watt as Secretary of the Interior gathered momentum but was greater within the U.S.A. Although Reagan was the most popular President in American history, Watt was certainly the least popular Secretary of the Interior within memory.

Many conservation groups pressed for his removal from office. The National Wildlife Federation, a largely Republican group, joined the call for Watt's removal. In 1982, surveys revealed that over 90% of the American population thought Watt's policies were wrong, 99% disagreed with his policies of wilderness exploitation, while over 90% of those who knew of James Watt wanted his immediate removal from office. The Sierra Club collected over 1 000 000 signatures within a matter of weeks in a bid to drive Watt from office.

In spite of public opinion, Watt remained in his job for what seemed like an eternity. In 1982 Watt self-destructed with a speech which included racist remarks against blacks and Jews. He refused to retract the statement and was finally sacked.

Environmental protection departments and fauna authorities formerly under Watt's control still suffer problems stemming from Watt's relatively brief tenure as Secretary of the Interior, although the environmental record of the U.S.A. has improved considerably since his removal.

'SNAKESCAM'

'Snakescam' or what was dubbed by the Northern Ohio Association of Herpetologists as the 'herpetological holocaust' took place in 1981 and was

Atlanta Wildlife Exchange

Robert Stephens, Owner

P. O. Box 48406
Atlanta, GA 30362
(404) 457-3750

USDA License: 57-B-8

Prices Effective September 17, 1980
(Subject to Change)

SNAKES

Qty	Description	Price
1.0	Burmese Python (Python m. bivittatus) 9', captive raised	$150.00
0.1	Burmese Python (P. m. bivittatus) 4', captive raised ...	65.00
0.1	Burmese Python (P. m. bivittatus) 13', captive raised, tame	375.00
10	Burmese Pythons (P. m. bivittatus) babies	40.00 each / 4/35.00 each
1	Reticulated Python (P. reticulatus) 3½', feeding	45.00
2	Reticulated Pythons (P. reticulatus) babies	30.00 each
1	African Rock Python (P. sebae) baby	65.00
1	Guyana Red-tail Boa, 5'	135.00
0.1	Turk's Island Boa (Epicrates chrysogaster) 3', striped phase, long-term captive, feeds good	250.00
1	Yellow Anaconda (Eunectes notaeus) 5'	125.00
1.1	Green Anacondas (E. murinus) 6', captive raised	150.00 each / 275.00 pair
8	Sinaloan Milk Snakes (Lampropeltis t. sinaloae)	100.00 each
2	Mexican Milk Snakes (L. t. annulata) 2' - 3'	100.00 each
1.1	Red Milk Snakes (L. t. syspila) 2'	40.00 each / 75.00 pair
1	Western Milk Snake (L. t. gentilis) 2'	50.00
6	Western Milk Snakes (L. t. gentilis) hatchlings	25.00 each
6	California Kingsnakes (L. g. californae) Banded, small .	20.00 each
1	Yuma Kingsnake (L. g. yumensis) 3'	35.00
6	Speckled Kingsnakes (L. g. holbroki)	6.00/foot
1.1	California Mountain Kingsnakes (L. zonata) 2'	100.00 each
1.0	Blair's Kingsnake (L. mexicana alterna) 3', long term captive	175.00
1	Prairie Kingsnake (L. c. calligaster)	20.00
4	Trans-Pecos Rat Snakes (Elaphe subocularis)	Call
5	Rosy Rat Snakes (E. guttata rosacea) babies	25.00 each
1	Everglades Rat Snake (E. osoleta rossalleni) 3'	25.00
1	Everglades Rat Snake (E. o. rossalleni) baby	10.00
1	Great Plains Rat Snakes (E. g. emoryi) 18" - 2'	12.00 each
5	Fox Snakes (E. vulpina) 4'	20.00 each
5	Fox Snakes (E. vulpina) 2'	10.00 each
10	Sonoran Gopher Snakes (Pituophis melanoleucus affinis) 2' - 4', good color	25.00
5	Bullsnakes (P. m. sayi)	3.00/foot
1.1	Northern Pine Snakes (P. m. melanoleucus)	60.00 each / 110.00 pair
1	Glossy Snake (Arizona elegans) 2'	10.00
20	Glossy Snakes (A. elegans) babies	3.00 each
3	Long-nosed Snakes (Pyllorphynchus decurtatus)	15.00
	Garter Snakes (Thamnophis sp.)	2.00 each / 20.00 dozen
1	Israeli Racer (Coluber ravergieri)	15.00
1	Israeli Racer (C. najadum)	15.00
1	Israeli Racer (C. jugularis)	15.00
1	Israeli Racer (Malpolan monspussalarus)	15.00

LIZARDS

Qty	Description	Price
0.1	Blue tongue Skink (Tilliquia gigas)	$ 50.00
20	Banded Geckos (Coleonyx variegatus) 4"	4.00 each
	Cuban Anoles (Anolis equestris) 8" - 12"	7.00 each
10	Collared Lizards (Crotaphytus collaris)	6.00 each / 6/25.00
	Asian Golden Skinks (Mabuya flavigularis)	3.00 each
	Alligator Lizards	7.00 each
	Flying Geckos, 4"	8.00 each
	Leopard Geckos (Eublepharis macularis)	20.00 each / 3/50.00
	Central American Night Lizards (Bark Lizards) (Lepidophyma flavimaculatum)	8.00 each

TURTLES

Qty	Description	Price
1	Mata Mata (Chelus fimbriatus) 3", real nice	125.00
	Western Painted Turtles (Chrysemys picta belli)	3.00 each
	Ornate Box Turtles (Terrapene ornata ornata)	5.00 each
	Gulf Coast Box Turtles (Terrapene c. major)	10.00 each
	Barbour's Map Turtles (Graptemys barbouri) real nice ..	22.00 each
	Black-knob Sawback Turtles (G. nigrinoda)	22.00 each
	Yellow-blotched Sawback Turtles (G. flavimaculata)	30.00 each
	Alabama Map Turtles (G. pulchra)	20.00 each

Terms and Conditions: Money orders or cashier's checks. Sorry, no personal checks accepted. Send your name, address, phone number, and name of nearest commercial airport with your order. All snake shipments sent Air Freight, Collect, from Atlanta, Georgia. Turtles and lizards may be sent Airmail, Special Delivery, Postage Collect. There is a $5.00 packing charge on all orders under $100.00. All livestock guaranteed live, healthy delivery, provided weather conditions during transit are between the temperatures of 40°F. and 90°F.

All prices FOB, Atlanta, Georgia, while supply lasts. Our stock is constantly changing, so call for items not listed.

PLEASE NOTE: All animals are subject to prior sale, so we may be temporarily out of stock. However, we will do our best to fill your order as soon as possible. Please allow 2 - 3 weeks for processing and delivery of your order.

perhaps the best documented operation in the history of American illegal wildlife trade. It was only after the initial publicity died down that an analysis of the operation was possible.

'Snakescam' was reported in most regional papers, such as the *Los Angeles Times*, and the *Miami Herald*, in national publications like *Newsweek*, and on television programmes including C.B.S. news in mid-July 1981. Assistant Interior Secretary, G. Ray Arnett, called 'Snakescam' 'the largest and most successful Fish and Wildlife law-enforcement investigation ever conducted'.

An editorial in the January 1992 issue of *Notes from NOAH* (the Northern Ohio Association of Herpetologists' Newsletter) described the picture thus: 'overzealous Interior and Customs agents can be seen swarming . . . guns drawn, handcuffs ready, as if Elliott Ness had returned to television'; all for the purpose of arresting a 'handful of questionable suspects'.

Gary S. Casper, a conservationist from Milwaulkie, stated in 1983:

'The aftermath of this event has raised many questions as to the acceptability of the law enforcement techniques employed, which demonstrated a disregard for civil rights and created a huge "black market" for protected wildlife.'

Casper further stated:

'The operation resulted in the destruction of many rare animals and the research being done with them, and has created an unprecedented paranoia among zoological personnel throughout the United States.'

The Atlanta Wildlife Exchange

In 1979-81 officers of the U.S. Fish and Wildlife Service (F.W.S.) operated a wildlife trading business called the Atlanta Wildlife Exchange (A.W.E.). The A.W.E. set up in business in a commercial park in the Atlanta suburb of Doraville, Georgia, soliciting trade in live reptiles from known enthusiasts.

The undercover operation, designed to infiltrate the illegal trade in reptiles, was masterminded by Rick Leach and Bill Zimmerman of the F.W.S. Division of Law Enforcement. It was launched with advertisements in two national wildlife magazines. Printed price-lists were also circulated among potentially interested people. Legal animals such as turtles and parrots were advertised, although A.W.E. appeared to be targeting the reptile market rather than aviculturalists. At the bottom of the price lists A.W.E. added that it was interested in obtaining 'native species' which is often taken to mean rare and prohibited fauna.

Business boomed, with most people dealing with the A.W.E. by telephone. The operator of the Exchange also obtained membership lists of herpetological societies, enabling them to contact reptile keepers and traders throughout the U.S.A. For example the A.W.E. subscribed as a 'member' of the Northern Ohio Association of Herpetologists, one of the largest regional and national herpetological societies. One of the publications of that society was the *White Pages*. This listed almost 1 000 members with names, addresses and interests (what reptiles they kept), as well as a list of most other herpetological societies in the U.S.A. Many of those named in the *White Pages* were immediately targeted by operators of A.W.E.

By advertising for prohibited fauna, the A.W.E. *created* a large market for illegal reptiles where only a small market had existed previously. The A.W.E. also traded in unprecedentedly large numbers of Australian reptiles (up to

10% of traded species on some occasions). Before A.W.E. was exposed as a front for F.W.S. activities, it was repeatedly alleged in several U.S. publications in 1980 that A.W.E. officials were able to source their reptiles directly from known (and named) officials in the New South Wales N.P.W.S. Certainly in the period including most of 1980 and the first five months of 1981, New South Wales fauna officials seized extraordinary numbers of reptiles from licensed and unlicensed keepers and failed to account for the disposal of these animals.

In order to encourage the taking of reptiles from the wild, A.W.E. operators offered financial inducements to gullible people. The prices paid for stock (legal or otherwise) by the A.W.E. were up to four times the prices paid by other dealers. After 18 months, A.W.E. agents had allegedly filled their cages with 10 000 illegal animals, mainly snakes.

In order to entrap formerly law-abiding reptile keepers, A.W.E. officers refused to ship or receive shipments of legitimate animals unless illegal animals were included in the consignment. In other cases the Exchange insisted on accepting animals through illegal channels or not at all. A major portion of the reptiles was sent through the postal system. F.W.S. officials in fact created a black market in native wildlife and effectively contributed to the demise of readily accessible populations.

The first raids, which occurred almost simultaneously on the morning of 16 July 1981, in 14 separate States at no fewer than 45 separate locations, were rarely justified. In virtually all cases, those people raided were well known, high profile herpetologists who'd committed no offence. Some had had no dealings with the A.W.E., while others had returned unsolicited reptiles posted to them illegally by the Exchange.

Legally held reptiles were in many cases seized as were other types of animals not requiring licences. In just two of the hundreds of raids over 100 vitally important, legally held research animals were stolen.

Both before and after the raids, the inability of F.W.S. officers to identify and care for wildlife was often noted. The A.W.E. had gained a reputation for shipping diseased stock long before the raids of July. Some well-known reptile people had legally purchased reptile specimens from the A.W.E. which had broken bones, burn lesions and fatal parasite infestations. Many animals shipped by the Exchange were dead on arrival. This included species listed as endangered.

A.W.E. officials allegedly mutilated captive-bred reptiles purchased from reputable breeders before re-selling them. The mutilation in the form of broken hips, burns and cuts was for identification purposes.

In one raid, a legally held rhinoceros iguana (*Cyclura cornuta*) was seized in mistake for a protected gila monster. Many animals died shortly after seizure due to inadequate holding facilities or care.

On 17 October 1981, several herpetological societies held a conference to specifically deal with the F.W.S. problem. Despite assurances by F.W.S. officials Leach and Zimmerman that they would attend the conference to answer grievances, neither did so. Many cases were cited of abuses by F.W.S. officials. As later reported in *Notes from NOAH* 'there was no lack of discussion about their (F.W.S.) tactics or intentions.' For example Tom Bloomer, of the Association for the Conservation of Turtles and Tortoises in New Jersey relayed his experiences with the A.W.E. His initial contact with the Exchange came when he received unsolicited packages in the mail. These contained snakes including the endangered San Francisco garter snake (*Thamnophis sirtalis terataenia*). The snakes were immediately returned to the sender, the A.W.E. Bloomer was then sent the same snakes a second time. Later he was 'set up' as he put it, in the parking lot of the Holiday Inn Hotel and strip-searched. According to Bloomer, he was interrogated as if he had 'committed the crime of the century!'.

Attempts by F.W.S. officials to off-load seized reptiles to zoos and other institutions were mainly unsuccessful, as after the July raids no one wanted anything to do with wildlife that might have come from F.W.S. officials. Attempts to off-load stock became even more difficult after several reptile keepers won court cases. These victories resulted in F.W.S. officials being ordered to return seized or stolen stock. Some zoos were forced to relinquish reptiles they had received in good faith.

One Individual Case: Terry Lilley

The Terry Lilley case, documented in *Notes from NOAH*, is useful in revealing the tactics employed by A.W.E. and other fauna officials.

On 16 July 1981, Lilley's premises, the Central Coast Reptile Research Centre at Morro Bay, California, was raided. A total of 15 men — F.W.S. officers, officers from the California Fish and Game Department and local police — came in 7 vehicles. Lilley was handcuffed and taken to the local jail, not permitted to be present at his own premises during the search.

The F.W.S. officers showed Lilley a warrant for his files and then with the others ransacked his entire house and adjoining facility for five hours. The men took Lilley's files, filing cabinets, complete scientific slide collection, surfing pictures, bird pictures, all breeding records, all business records, unfinished scientific papers for publication, research documents, permits, bank book, personal phone book, cheques and other material. Without a warrant the California Fish and Game officers took 19 breeding reptiles including fourth generation captive hybrids of California mountain kingsnakes (*Lampropeltis zonata*) and Arizona kingsnakes (*Lampropeltis pyromelana*), Mexican reptiles with documentation, reptiles on loan from zoos and fourth generation captive albino snakes.

The leader of the California Fish and Game contingent, Warden Dutch Huckaby, asked Lilley's wife which reptiles at the facility were native to California. Lilley's wife said she didn't know, so the men took only what was in easy-to-handle containers. Huckaby was the same warden who when invited by Lilley to view his snakes a year earlier, had replied 'I do not know a kingsnake from a horse's ass, don't worry about me.'

Lilley's reptiles had all been held legally, with full knowledge of the relevant authorities. His research was public knowledge and supported by several reputable institutions. All reptiles taken had been bred by Lilley himself at his facility.

During the search through Lilley's files, an entire colony of African Jackson's chameleons was let loose. The longest lived Jackson's chameleon known to science was now roaming through Lilley's suburb.

Lilley's seized reptiles were placed in the care of two men with no knowledge of reptiles or their care. Dutch Huckaby told Lilley he was a law breaker and that if he got mad at them (California Fish and Game or F.W.S.), then they would come down harder on him.

On 31 December 1981, Lilley and Warden Huckaby had an encounter in court in relation to the raid some six months earlier. Huckaby returned a dead baja rosy boa (*Lichanura trivirgata roseofusca*) to Lilley, with its innards hanging out.

Huckaby told Lilley that the snake had been 'mis-identified'. Huckaby had said that he 'no longer needed it anymore'. Huckaby, who'd originally claimed the snake was a California rosy boa (*Lichanura trivirgata gracia*), had kept it in his garage.

The snake had been dead for some two months before it was returned to Lilley. Huckaby told the court that he 'didn't know anything about the care of snakes'. A subsequent autopsy on the snake at San Francisco revealed that the snake had been gravid (pregnant). The cause of death was almost certainly due to intestinal dysfunction, presumably from being abused or moved about too much in its sensitive condition. In court however, Huckaby refused to acknowledge that the snake's death was his fault, nor did he apologise for it. Huckaby belatedly did admit that the snake had not been identified by him and his offsiders when seized on 16 July. That was despite constant objections from Lilley that the snake had been wrongly identified from the start.

The Judgement
Lilley described 28 June 1982 as his 'Independence Day'. In Lilley's words 'After one year of unbelievable harassment, blackmail and even physical violence, I won a court decision to have my reptiles returned by Warden Huckaby.' After six hours of testimony, the judge ordered California Fish and Game officials to return to Lilley all remaining 12 snakes in their custody, which they had kept even after dropping charges against Lilley, on the basis that the snakes were 'contraband'. The judge decided that Lilley had held all snakes legally and that they should remain Lilley's personal property and therefore be returned.

In summing up his long-awaited decision, the judge strongly criticised the California Fish and Game Department and F.W.S. officials. He even said that the last place he would trust a snake of his own would be with the Fish and Game Department. Then the Judge burst out with the comment 'What are you guys doing?'.

Of the 24 snakes taken illegally from Lilley, the following had been killed: 2 California mountain kingsnakes, 1 banded kingsnake (*Lampropeltis getulus californiae*) 1 baja rosy boa and 1 San Diego rosy boa (*Lichanura trivurgata* subsp.).

The Fish and Game officials traded 6 aberrant pattern kingsnakes to the Los Angeles Zoo. Fish and Game officials allegedly gave Harvey Fisher of Los Angeles Zoo the snakes illegally on the basis that Fisher would testify against Lilley in charges that were subsequently dropped.

Fisher later traded three snakes to the Columbus Zoo, illegally again, and another illegally to the San Diego Zoo. The Fish and Game officials needed a court order to give any of these snakes away.

The Fish and Game Department was told by the judge that they had 15 days to return to Lilley all his snakes.

Fish and Game officials subsequently testified that two of Lilley's California mountain kingsnakes taken illegally had been stolen from one of their labs in Rancho Cordova, California. As Lilley said 'They sure come up with some good stories when they are in trouble.'

Of the two baja rosy boas taken illegally, both were returned. One was dead. Two California mountain kingsnakes were also returned to Lilley — both dead. Nine other snakes, some wrongly identified, were also returned. A San Diego rosy boa was not returned. Fisher at the L.A. Zoo had killed the snake and thrown away its carcass.

In relation to the confiscation of fauna by officials, a New Jersey judge had ruled in 1970 that State wildlife officials could not confiscate an animal until the person charged with a complaint had his day in court and was proven innocent or guilty. The judge saw confiscation or seizure as punishment *before* sentencing.

After A.W.E.: The Trials
F.W.S. agents attempted to subvert the course of justice by attempting to have all charges laid by their men heard before sympathetic judges in Atlanta, Georgia, instead of where the alleged violations occurred. In addition, F.W.S. agents were reported to routinely intimidate victims into plea bargaining by using coercion, harassment and the threat of financial ruin. These tactics were designed to minimise the risk of exposing the illegality of F.W.S. agents' methods (through the A.W.E.) and to secure an impressive list of convictions at an early stage, so the whole operation would be judged a success.

F.W.S. agents in some court cases were reported to have produced taped conversations as evidence against particular people. Those tape recordings had in many cases been edited and modified so that portions favourable to the defendant were either deleted or deliberately made inaudible. Outright perjury by F.W.S. officials was reportedly commonplace at a number of trials.

Many defendants were told that they had to prove to courts that their animals hadn't been obtained in violation of any Federal or State laws. In other words they had to prove their innocence. Such was a violation of the U.S. Constitution, which supposedly guarantees innocence until guilt is proven. In a public interview one F.W.S. officer actually stated that the burden of proof was on the defendant. Things were made significantly harder for most defendants as not only had their live reptiles been taken, but their records as well, which could have exonerated those charged.

'Snakescam' in Retrospect
The true failure of 'Snakescam' is demonstrated when one examines what the operation actually did to reptiles and their conservation. Far more reptiles were killed than saved. In some cases the paranoia caused by F.W.S. officials placing themselves above the law resulted in breeders incinerating rare and endangered species or releasing them into unnatural habitats, in a bid to dispose of potentially incriminating evidence.

Gary S. Casper summed up the operation by stating it was
'probably an attempt to justify the existence of an ineffective and overgrown bureaucracy in the face of massive U.S. Government budget cuts and departmental phase-outs. The whole action of the A.W.E. and 'Snakescam' was to create an illegal trade, and entrap otherwise law-abiding people so that a number of fauna officials could continue their employment.'

'The implications of this event are serious and of international concern.

112

The "Snakescam" event is a dramatic example of a bureaucracy "run wild", seemingly concerned only with its own existence and heedless to the consequences of its actions. The wildlife laws which empower wildlife agencies to act in such a manner are clearly unacceptable. These laws are frequently to the detriment of the animals they were meant to protect.'

F.W.S. officials admitted that those ensnared in 'Snakescam' were operating either as individuals or, in a few cases, in small groups — hardly the stuff of organised wildlife trafficking operations. Most violations detected and charges upheld were so petty as to be ridiculous. Alleged mislabelling of parcels and other minor shipping violations were the most common violations alleged. Furthermore the live reptile trade being so vigorously pursued by F.W.S. officials had little if any significant impact on wild populations of reptiles. The trade in skins and other dead reptile products, not the subject of the 'Snakescam' operation, was larger than the live trade by a factor of at least ten.

Even more importantly habitat destruction remains the principal cause of declining reptile populations. Many of the people 'busted' in 'Snakescam' only traded in captive-bred animals and had *never* sourced any of their reptiles from wild populations.

'Snakescam' certainly destroyed the conservation efforts of many dedicated people. People breeding rare and endangered species were forced to euthanise young, being unable to afford the expense of keeping the animals or because of F.W.S. permit restrictions on the off-loading of specimens: endangered Indian pythons (*Python molurus molurus*) were for example being crossbred with Burmese pythons (*Python molurus bivattatus*) to avoid restrictions on trading offspring. The pure-blooded Indian pythons therefore became even rarer.

For fear of running foul of F.W.S. officers in the wake of 'Snakescam', a private keeper was recorded as hiding captive-born offspring of a rare Asian crocodile after a wildlife warden stated he'd kill the animals if he found them. A New York zoo killed 23 captive-born snakes rather than ask for permits from F.W.S. and risk subsequent problems.

The so-called wildlife protection laws that enabled the 'Snakescam' operation to be mounted included three major pieces of legislation: *The Lacey Act* 1900, amended several times, the *Endangered Species Act* 1973, amended several times and C.I.T.E.S., 1973. In addition, often confusing State legislation varies in each American State and changes regularly.

Perhaps the most amazing thing about 'Snakescam' was how it parallelled similar operations in Australia, in particular in New South Wales.

RECENT OPERATIONS
More recently, in late 1987, TRAFFIC (U.S.A.) reported that a senior inspector with the U.S. Fish and Wildlife Service was charged with accepting US$40 000 in bribes in exchange for inspecting and approving illegal imports of more than 50 000 individual live reptiles arriving at Los Angeles International Airport from one or more foreign countries, principally Columbia in South America.

Daniel Noether of Lakewood, California, was charged with 29 counts of accepting bribes from three American wildlife dealers, Steven Lundblad, Axel Roscher and Christine Roscher who, along with another defendant, Miguel

Campo of Barranquilla, Columbia, were charged with conspiracy and illegal wildlife dealing. Campo, who apparently was responsible for shipping the live animals into the U.S.A. via Panama, managed to avoid arrest.

The Roschers operated the business L.A. Reptile, while Lundblad operated Dolphin International. The animals in question were purchased from a Los Angeles wholesaler who was allegedly negotiating with Campo in Columbia and splitting the profits with Noether. The operation was 'busted' after 16 months of investigations and surveillance.

Among the animals illegally imported were iguanas (*Iguana* sp.), tegu lizards (*Tupinambis* sp.), boa constrictors, caimans and mud turtles (*Kinosternon* sp.). The estimated value of the animals in question was US$400 000, the bribes consisting of roughly one tenth of that value.

Import documents falsely stated that the shipments contained animals not covered under the C.I.T.E.S. treaty; there were no export permits. Some of the animals were re-exported to the Far East. The accused all faced possible jail terms and fines up to US$500 000 each.

In examining cases of smuggling, enforcement and detection in the U.S.A., similarities to Australia are clear. Official rackets again appear to be the largest and best organised type of wildlife smuggling. Smaller retail and private operations do occur, with periodic 'busts' and prosecutions. As in Australia, a major part of the problem in the U.S.A. appears to originate with the wildlife laws themselves.

13
SMUGGLING RACKETS IN OTHER COUNTRIES

The detailed documentation of smuggling operations and related wildlife matters in other countries is beyond the scope of this book. However, mention of some cases is worthwhile.

The global trade in reptiles, birds and other types of undomesticated fauna has been estimated at about US$1 billion dollars annually. Not all trade is in live animals however.

EUROPE
When trade is banned in one place it either continues in some form illegally or the operators move to other countries where the trade remains legal or at least easier. For example, when laws relating to wildlife trade were tightened in the U.K. in the early 1970s, traders merely shifted their operations to Europe. As central European countries tightened their regulations, the major dealers moved to Belgium and Holland, and when these in turn altered their trading laws, dealers re-established business in the countries of Southern Europe. Here they import wildlife from tropical countries, including Australia.

An extraordinary contradiction is that as all countries have ratified C.I.T.E.S., it should be no easier to trade protected wildlife in one country than another.

SOUTH AMERICA
French Guiana on the northern coast of South America raises an interesting problem. This country is not run as a colony, but rather as a part of France, like a state or city. French Guiana is therefore considered to be a part of the E.E.C. in the same way as England or Holland, and legally obtained animals in French Guiana may be freely traded throughout the E.E.C., as they are after all already in France.

Formerly, animals were illegally exported from Brazil and other parts of

South America, areas which now have a strict prohibition on the export of all fauna. Today, animals are smuggled over the long unprotected border of French Guiana, where they are locally registered as 'captive-bred'.

From there they are legally exported to France or the E.E.C.. There is a continuous flow of wildlife into French Guiana from other parts of South America: annual exports of some species from French Guiana, such as caimans, actually exceed the total species populations within that country.

ASIA

After substantial pressure, both international and local, from conservation activists such as Marjorie Doggett, Singapore has recently tightened formerly lax laws relating to the illegal import and export of wildlife. The decline in prominence of operations based in Singapore has been matched by a corresponding rise in the relative importance of wildlife trafficking operations based in Thailand and Jakarta. Both Thailand and Indonesia are signatories to C.I.T.E.S., but neither country seems terribly keen on enforcing the treaty domestically.

In Thailand, Hat Yai near the Malaysian border has become as important as the capital, Bangkok in terms of its role in illegal wildlife trade. Due to the rigorous checks on international flights in and out of Bangkok, it is no longer viable to illegally ship wildlife from that city. Instead, consignments of wildlife for illegal export are loaded onto domestic flights at Hat Yai. At Bangkok airport, the consignments are loaded onto international flights and are not checked, as they are an internal transfer for a journey that starts and finishes at points outside Bangkok.

In Thailand and several other countries, Customs work is actually undertaken by airline officials rather than Customs officers. As far as Customs is concerned, airlines themselves should be responsible for what they carry.

Besides being close to the Malaysian border, Hat Yai is one of the closest points in Thailand to Singapore, at the end of the Malay peninsula. A lot of (mainly legal) overland trade in wildlife between Singapore and Hat Yai takes place, particularly in songbirds which are very popular as pets, but protected within Singapore.

The illegal trade in wildlife from some countries is assisted by the sheer vagueness of the paperwork that accompanies legal consignments from certain Third World countries. For example, John Nichol documented the case of a shipment of birds from Burma to Singapore. The export documents simply stated '100 parrots, 100 mynahs . . . ' and so on.

In Singapore and many other countries, the full common and scientific name of each species must be documented with each consignment. So with consignments from the Third World arriving for example, in Singapore, the trader may add on almost any type of bird he wishes: after the word 'parrot', he may write in '10 black palm cockatoos', '10 Major Mitchells' and so on. The species being typed in may or may not have been legally imported from Burma. Illegal birds may be legalised suddenly in this manner.

What cunning traders do is to import large numbers of very common species for local consumption, and then export illegally obtained birds on the basis of the documentation received from places such as Burma. In fact the documents obtained from Burma were often worth more to the bird traders in Singapore, than the birds actually imported. A number of dealers in

Singapore are known to buy and sell blank import documents as cover for newly obtained illegal stock.

In response to pressure from environmentalists around the world, Indonesia has tightened its wildlife protection laws. However, due to local ambivalence towards wildlife in general, little has been done either to protect vanishing wildlife or curb the illegal trade. Laws protecting wildlife and restricting trade were principally enacted to placate world opinion, and were definitely not the result of local environmental pressure. About four major dealers account for roughly half the illegal trade from Jakarta to other countries.

Oddly enough, one of the most senior Government officials in Indonesia charged with the responsibility of protecting wildlife is also the brother-in-law of one of the biggest bird traffickers.

Garuda Indonesia Airways, the national airline, recently got into a spot of bother over a poster advertisement it printed and distributed. The poster showed someone holding a cockatoo, with wording to the effect that when Garuda flew these cockatoos, they were well looked after. The poster was well received by Garuda executives in Indonesia. The poster was not recalled until it was pointed out that it was illegal to carry those birds and international pressure from other airlines was applied. Airline officials were subsequently told not to make further posters like that; they were not directed to stop carrying the birds themselves.

Deng

The story of Komain Nukulphanitwipat, director of the Siam Farm in Bangkok is interesting in more ways than one. Komain is also known as Deng, which is Thai for 'red', because when he was born he was very pink and the name stuck as he grew older. Deng is one of the most famous animal traders in that part of the world, with over a thousand trappers working for him throughout Thailand and nearby areas. Deng is internationally known for his collection of rare, exotic and albino animals including the albino Burmese pythons already mentioned (see p. 37). His fantastic wealth is alleged by many to have come largely from wildlife trade, both legal and illegal.

Deng's contribution to conservation has also been important. Besides being a trader, he is a field naturalist with over 30 years' experience. In the early 1980s Deng was one of those who opposed the World Wildlife Fund in Thailand spending a huge amount of money adopting the kouprey (*Bos sauveli*) which is a large buffalo-like beast, as its emblem. It had already been exterminated by poachers, starving guerilla fighters and others during the politically unstable period of the 1960s and early 1970s. Deng incidentally had the skin and skull of what was allegedly the last living kouprey on his office floor. Certainly Deng, with his army of collectors throughout Thailand and beyond, would have known if there were any kouprey left.

During the 1970s when travelling in Burma, Deng offered natives a large sum of money for live deer of a species he was being fed. From the head of the deer, which had been mounted by the natives, Deng realised that it was probably an undescribed species. In due course Deng purchased from the villagers five deer, which the natives had acknowledged as being of a rare species.

Deng set about breeding them and eventually acquired a sizeable herd. However, in Thailand Deng is not permitted to keep deer, so he has to keep them in a secret location. As the local wildlife officials don't know where the deer are, none can be seized and Deng cannot be prosecuted. In addition, as Deng is not meant to have any deer at all, he cannot even invite scientists to see his new species to formally describe them. A ludicrous situation has arisen whereby a rare and possibly endangered species remains undescribed due to the inadequacy of wildlife legislation.

THE THIRD WORLD
Many wildlife traders in Third World countries are in fact expatriates from Europe, the U.S.A. and especially in parts of South-east Asia, Australians. These men have established thriving wildlife trading businesses relying on cheap local labour and hunters to provide fauna for export.

The position of wildlife in Third World countries is far less secure than in countries such as Australia. Animals so sought after as pets in Europe and the U.S.A. are considered unimportant by local inhabitants. Consequently, if an outsider offers money for a bird or a snake they will be only too happy to catch as many as they can for sale. Most inhabitants of these countries, including Indonesia, are so poor that all extra forms of income, no matter how environmentally destructive, are usually welcome.

ILLEGAL TRADING: WAYS AND MEANS AND PRODUCTS
To be able to ship birds of paradise from New Guinea to Java and elsewhere, natives adopt the procedure of making the birds look like something else. Cock birds, recognisable by their brightly coloured and long feathers, which moult annually, are made to look like crows and mynahs, and are shipped in consignments with them. This is done by carefully plucking out of all long feathers and dyeing the birds black. This treatment does not seem to adversely affect too many of these birds, as 'black' birds of paradise are commonly sold throughout south-east Asia. The black dyes eventually grow out.

Unfortunately many natives don't bother to trap the drab coloured female birds thinking that they're worthless. As a result only males seem to be sold to dealers and keepers, meaning any captive breeding of the species is highly unlikely.

The Crocodile Trade
In French Guiana, there are two locally occurring types of caiman. The black caiman *(Caiman niger)* is strictly protected, whereas the far more widespread spectacled caiman *(Caiman crocodylus)* isn't. Carcasses of both species are regularly sold in markets at Cayenne, the capital. All the stall holders know the regulations very well, so when a complete black caiman carcass is sold, its head is always missing. Without the head, it is very difficult to positively identify a black caiman. If a stall holder were asked to identify a given headless caiman, they would always indicate that it was a spectacled caiman.

The world trade in crocodile skins involves about six species, and some 3 000 000 skins annually. About two-thirds of this trade is legal, while the trade in live specimens is negligible. About three-quarters of those skins traded are of the spectacled caiman. The trail of the skins is interesting in itself. Most specimens are caught in northern Brazil, Bolivia and Paraguay, where they are protected. After being transported overland, skins are taken by boat to French Guiana, where they are laundered and sent on by sea to mainland

France and Italy. There they are made into handbags, belts, wallets and other items, often with designer labels, before being shipped to their points of sale, usually in the U.S.A.

Some U.S. distributers have been fined substantial sums for importing laundered skins. During mid-1985, a Colombian firm, Mendel Hermanos Pty. Ltd., was fined US$6 000 for the illegal export of caiman skins worth an estimated US$32 600 000.

Had crocodile hunting continued unabated in Northern Australia, it is likely that both species found there would have disappeared. Prior to protection of both species in Queensland, large numbers of crocodile skins illegally obtained in the Northern Territory and Western Australia were sent to Queensland where they were illegally sold.

Today illegally obtained crocodile skins from northern Australia are sent to South-east Asia where they are sold legally on the basis that they are from commercial farms.

Some of these farms have up to 30 000 crocodiles at any one time, and are major tourist attractions. According to the *Directory of Crocodilian Farming Operations*, published in 1985, there were about 152 legally operating crocodile and alligator farms in 24 countries, with an estimated stock of over 160 000 animals. Despite repeated denials from proprietors, many continue to source most, if not all, of their stock from the wild, much of which is illegally traded through dealers.

Folk Medicines

The world trade in animal products, although not a major cause of decline for Australian species, is a major worry for many overseas species.

Almost any part of an animal may be used for some form of medicine. Rhinoceros horn is so sought after by Chinese pharmacists, that a single horn sells for thousands of dollars on the black market. The African black rhinoceros *(Diceros bicornis)* has been brought to the brink of extinction by poachers attempting to satisfy demand. Despite new laws in some parts of Africa that allow park rangers to shoot poachers on sight, rhinoceros numbers are still declining. At the time of writing (1990), there were less than 100 black rhinoceros left in the wild.

Should a poacher obtain a single black rhinoceros horn, he may sell it for more than ten years' income. Hence the incentive to risk one's life in order to kill a single specimen. The African white rhinoceros *(Diceros simus)* which looks white only when coated with mud, is also similarly endangered.

It is not just the horn of the rhinoceros that is used by pharmacists. Every part of the animal has a function. In days gone by, a whole village would purchase a single rhinoceros and people would take different parts of the animal. Even the pungent smelling urine is drunk, as it allegedly has health giving properties.

Contrary to popular belief, powdered horn is not used as an aphrodisiac. Other animals or parts thereof are used for this.

Although international trade in rhinoceros products is almost completely banned, it continues with products being either deliberately mis-labelled or exported from countries that have no restrictions on the export of rhinoceros products. These countries, in particular some Arab nations, do not actually have any live rhinoceros themselves. Their governments turn a blind eye to imported rhinoceros materials and then issue legal documentation to allow the export of processed items.

Snakes, in particular cobras (*Naja* spp.) are also used by the Chinese. A common practice in parts of southern China is to confine a snake in a container with just its tail end protruding so the snake cannot curl back and strike anyone. Snake tails are cut off and a person sucks all the blood out of the snake until it dies. The person is meant to have taken the power of the snake into their own body.

No part of the snake is wasted. Various internal organs have different medicinal roles and the skin is usually sold to be made into belts or similar garments for sale elsewhere.

Snakes

Due to severe depletion of serpent stocks in many parts of Asia, farmers have noted an increase in pest rodents and have therefore attempted to curtail the trade in snakes. One part of India has even started to import live snakes and is releasing them locally to control thriving rodent populations.

Stuffed snakes are popular with tourists and a taxidermy industry exists in many countries to cater for this demand. Despite the illegality of importing stuffed specimens into Australia, stalls at Sydney's Paddy's Market and Melbourne's Victoria Market have been selling stuffed cobras for years. In 1990, I saw at Paddy's a stuffed cobra selling for $200, while a stuffed cobra in combat with a stuffed mongoose cost $400.

Recently some enterprising taxidermists in Asia have been marketing 'disco snakes'. For example a stuffed cobra is mounted in a fairly typical position with two small red lights inserted for eyes, with an electrical lead running through the body and out through the cloaca. When attatched to hi-fi equipment, the eyes flash on and off in synchronisation with the music.

Turtles

Marine turtles are poached worldwide, mainly by native peoples for food, although the international trade in stuffed specimens, soup, tortoise shell and other turtle-based products is also large. Recently leathery turtles (*Dermochelys coraicea*) have nested on Malaysia's Trengannu beach only in their hundreds. Just twenty years ago these turtles nested here in their tens of thousands. Large-scale poaching of eggs by local Malays has been the principal cause of declining turtle numbers.

In most parts of South-east Asia, green turtles (*Chelonia mydas*) are hacked up while still alive in order to provide turtle soup. After they are caught, they are usually left on their backs in the searing tropical sun for some time before they are 'processed'. With a small, high-powered electric saw, the turtle's plastron (ventral shell) while still facing up is sliced away from the lower, domed part of the shell. By cutting away at the joining flesh, the flat lower surface is lifted away from the struggling turtle which is then decapitated before its still flapping limbs are also cut off.

Smaller freshwater species are usually killed in a similar manner. In South-east Asia, people do not usually keep tortoises or other reptiles as pets.

Tigers and Other Delicacies

Tigers (*Panthera* sp.) are eaten by rich people in various parts of Asia; people will pay up to $1 000 000 for a tiger to be killed fresh and eaten. In Taiwan, conservationists at great expense have purchased from restaurants tigers destined for banquets and then donated them to local zoos. Many tigers traded in Asia as pets have the bones removed from their paws in order to make them harmless. These bones are also crushed into a powder and sold.

Small monkeys are eaten by wealthy Chinese while still alive. The drugged monkeys are put into a box from which their head protrudes. The skull is cut in a circle just above the eyes and ears so that the top of the head is lifted to reveal the brain. Bread sticks are then dipped into the creamy brain tissue, while the still-living monkey stares and blinks at those who are eating it. When the monkey dies, and the entire brain tissue is eaten, the monkey is removed from the box. The rest of the monkey is then cooked and eaten. The whole exercise is treated as a ritual.

Worldwide, people illegally poach protected birds for the dinner table. Migratory species seem to be particularly vulnerable. The rarer species always seem to be regarded as gourmet species and hence the demand for them rises, putting them at even greater risk.

Restaurants throughout the world offer meat from protected species on their menus. However, it should be added that not all restaurants tell the truth when advertising their food. A 'fried cobra' served in a Hong Kong restaurant to a friend was actually a Russell's viper *(Vipera russellii)*. The same restaurant sold various Komodo dragon *(Varanus komodoensis)* dishes. They actually consisted of material from a far more common monitor species *(Varanus* sp.).

Despite laws to the contrary, there are still some canneries for rattlesnake meat in the southern States of the U.S.A. These operations remain viable concerns despite immense local conservationist pressure.

Although many nations have legislation aimed at preventing people from eating wild animals, few individuals seem to be prosecuted for doing so. In 1984, two Brazilians were jailed for a year and fined about $600 each for holding an enormous wild barbecue which included a main course of 2 400 small birds. That was the maximum penalty for such an offence in that country.

The case went to court only due to efforts of local conservationists and problems with an official. The practice of holding such barbecues in Brazil is apparently widespread and although technically illegal, does not usually seem to worry local authorities.

Not all cases of people eating wild animals relate to hunger. Shortly after the 1990 invasion of Kuwait by Iraqi troops, some Iraqis went to the local zoo and killed, cooked and ate many of the animals. This occurred during the first few weeks of the invasion when Iraqi soldiers looted Kuwait and took whatever they wanted. Species eaten included polar bears, endangered cats, rhinoceros, elephants, various birds and reptiles. According to one media report, at least 40% of zoo animals were killed and eaten within two days.

Animal Products

Throughout the Amazon basin, river dolphins *(Inia geoffrensis)* are killed and eaten by natives. The eyeballs are then sent via traders to tourist shops in Rio de Janeiro where they are sold to tourists for a few dollars each. Thousands of eyeballs are sold annually.

Although the world ivory trade is now substantially more regulated than in the past, many elephants are still ruthlessly plundered for their horns. The situation is particularly bad for African elephants *(Loxodonta africana)* which are not held in a domesticated state and have much larger horns.

In many sub-Saharan national parks, poachers and game wardens play a game of 'cat and mouse'. Unfortunately in many African countries, the money made from illegally trading in elephant horns is so great that game wardens themselves are tempted to kill the elephants.

In many cases, the wardens can take advantage of loopholes in protective laws. Usually sick or disabled elephants may be killed for their ivory. Likewise elephants that die of natural causes may also have their tusks removed and traded.

Game wardens have been known to slowly kill a healthy elephant for ivory. A large splinter of bamboo or rusty metal placed in rotting meat or animal waste is hammered into the sole of the elephant's foot. The animal soon becomes unable to walk, as the infection spreads to the leg and body, so authorisation is given to kill it. The animal is then slaughtered and the ivory sold.

Elimination of elephants through wide parts of Africa as a result of poaching and slow killing is still occurring. Few Western zoos keep the African species as the Indian elephants *(Elephas maximus)* are easier to tame and keep in captivity. Therefore African elephants are under far more serious threat than their Asian counterparts.

The trade in skins of large cats for fur coats and other uses continues. The world's largest consumers of fur coats sourced from large wild cats has been West Germany (now United Germany), where furs made from tigers may still be bought off the rack in most major department stores.

This situation exists despite protection of almost all cat species throughout the world. The effectiveness of legislation can be gauged by the fact that most South American countries have legislation prohibiting export of furs from larger cats, while continuing to do so. In Paraguay, for example, the number of tiger cat *(Panthera tigrina)* skins exported doubled the year following the ban on all commercial trade in wildlife.

As South America suffers less from overpopulation, deforrestation and hunting than Africa, North America and Asia, most big cat furs come from South America.

The trappers of tigers and other big cats take great care when capturing their animals to ensure the furs remain intact. The animals are rarely shot; they are usually caught in traps and then strangled. The strangling is done by putting a noose through the bars of the tiger's cage and then tightening the noose. A damaged skin is worth substantially less than one which is completely intact.

Besides skins, there is a thriving market for the claws and teeth of these animals, mainly for the tourist trade in places such as Bangkok, central America and even Mexico. Places that stock teeth and claws rarely seem to stock skins.

The town of Kastoria in north-west Greece is the centre of that country's thriving fur trade. The trade here is built on the making of garments from the off-cuts of big cat furriers elsewhere. Besides small objects such as wallets and handbags, full-size fur coats are made from off-cuts.

Taxidermists worldwide seem to mainly stuff legally killed game animals. Everyone is familiar with the stuffed heads on walls found in homes of the wealthy in England and elsewhere. An interesting case was reported in a U.S. newspaper some years ago involving a rare peregrine falcon *(Falco peregrinus)*. Cornell University had been running for several years a captive-breeding programme for the species and had released over 200 birds into the wild. A particular hunter shot one of these birds and had it mounted by a local taxidermist complete with leg ring and still operational radio transmitter. The scientists had fitted the transmitter to trace the bird's movements after release and yes, traced the bird back to the man's living room, where it sat in all its stuffed glory. The man was subsequently prosecuted by the authorities and fined. The presiding judge ordered that the US$2 000 fine go to the Peregrine Breeding Fund at Cornell University as compensation for their lost bird.

Tourists fined

Two German tourists were fined $4000 each in the Alice Springs Magistrates Court yesterday for attempting to smuggle geckos out of the country.

Defacto couple Andreas Laube and Andrea Kies attempted to post four common geckos out of Australia when they were intercepted by customs at Yulara on Wednesday.

Magistrate John Manion has given them until March 25 to pay.

If they default they face six months in Alice Springs Jail.

Their passports are also being held.

The two, from Berlin, tried to post two beaked geckos, a knobtail gecko and a Gillen's pygmy monitor in a box addressed to Laube's parents.

Northern Territory News
21/3/92

14
STOPPING THE ILLEGAL TRADE IN LIVE WILDLIFE

To stop the illegal trade in wildlife is easier said than done. The simplest answer is simply to legalise it!

WHY IS IT ILLEGAL?

The commonest major reason given for banning most trade in wildlife both within Australia and to and from Australia, is that unregulated trade in certain wildlife species would result in their demise and ultimate extinction.

This is true of very few species. The conservation status of most species of native birds, mammals and reptiles has been effectively unaltered by laws relating to their conservation. This is because of the animals' relative abundance coupled with the low or non-existent demand for the animals or products derived from them.

Illegal trade in wildlife is a problem mainly because of restrictive export laws coupled with equally restrictive and complicated laws involving keeping and trading wildlife within Australia, which in turn have produced a climate suited to the development of official corruption.

Statutory protection of native animals and the banning of trade in the overwhelming majority of those species, has only a negative result. Fauna officials are employed at great expense to enforce so-called protection laws, which are often highly wasteful of public monies. Bona fide researchers and others dealing with these 'protected' species find themselves having to devote valuable time complying with red tape rather than engaging in research or other useful, more productive activities.

Small-scale wildlife keepers, enthusiasts and in particular children or teenagers who may have a few interesting pets may find themselves charged, fined and even jailed for relatively innocuous activities. These same people may end up with a criminal record for life and suffer long-term difficulty in getting a job, especially jobs requiring Government issued licences.

Another point of view to consider is that keeping wildlife as pets is a harmless occupation, compared with, for example, trashing telephone boxes or taking drugs.

Perhaps the worst thing about the current illegality of keeping wildlife is that banning it does not necessarily stop it, but merely forces it underground.

The idea that making statutory penalties higher for illegally trading in wildlife will remove the incentive is simply inaccurate. Raising penalties dissuades only a few potential players. Rising potential rewards from the trade increase the incentive for organised crime. Furthermore, as the relative power of Government officials to make or break illegal wildlife operations increases, corruptible officials are more tempted by profits, and so the pivotal role of law enforcement officials becomes greater. This has been the clear trend in Australia over the last 20 years.

If open trade were legalised, the price of most species would drop, making illegal trade a largely unviable option. Most people will buy an animal legally rather than illegally if the prices are the same and there is no extra difficulty going through correct channels.

Those species which are genuinely vulnerable or endangered as a result of people catching them for pets, skins or for some other purpose, are relatively few and should not be traded as freely as other species. Few species are actually harvested for food or skins/furs and a discussion of the best methods for doing this is beyond the scope of this book.

Even the rarest of species should be available for trading for any purpose, if it can be demonstrated that long-term conservation of the species will not suffer. For example, if an Australian wishes to export a pair of golden-shouldered parrots that are captive-bred to a potential breeder in the U.S.A., nothing in the form of a blanket ban should prevent this. The fact that the species may be endangered in the wild simply has no relevance in this case.

REGULATED TRADE: A NEW SYSTEM

The main risk from totally unregulated trade in live wildlife is the unacceptably high mortality that may occur when abundant or easily available species may be sold in large numbers through pet dealerships to people who quite clearly cannot or will not keep animals alive for any length of time. Besides the cruelty to individual specimens, such activity can result in local extinctions and long-term declines in species numbers.

Therefore the question arises, how do we regulate the trade in readily available species without banning collection and trade altogether? The easiest solution would be to remove statutory protection for most species other than those for which it is essential to ensure their survival. Then it could be possible to impose a minimum retail price for wildlife traders for each specimen sold. The minimum price for native wildlife should be set at a level high enough to prevent all but the keenest buyers from wanting to buy specimens, e.g. $300 per specimen regardless of species. This would prevent the disposable pet market from becoming a catalyst for the plundering of native species. People collecting wildlife for themselves or close friends would be able to do so, with the exception of the most threatened species. Few farmers or others in bush areas would be tempted to capture wildlife for the trade due to the inability of traders to off-load specimens at anything other than fixed minimum prices.

DOUBLE MONEY

In a remote part of Irian Jaya an Australian expatriate was purchasing birds of paradise from local natives who had caught the birds to sell to a dealer who regularly visited their part of the country. The Australian would release the birds into the wild after he purchased them.

The Australian gave up buying the birds after he realised that the natives were recapturing and re-selling him the same birds!

At the moment, most individuals who see wildlife in the bush leave it alone. This would presumably continue, especially with improved conservation education in schools and through the media.

Captive-bred stock would be exempt from the minimum price requirement and could be traded freely. Although some unscrupulous people might substitute wild stock for captive-bred, such a problem seems impossible to stamp out regardless of what laws are in force. However, no Australian species currently seems to be threatened with extinction as a result of this activity, or would be likely to be threatened under the system outlined above.

Results

Although such alteration to the laws might increase collection of live wildlife from the Australian bush by up to 100 times, the numbers taken from the wild would still be far less than those killed each year by cars on the roads. And this is *before* one considers those specimens killed by farmers and others which die through habitat destruction or other human activities. Natural mortality also needs to be considered when discussing the real conservation equation for a given species.

The increased number of native animal species in captivity would enhance long-term conservation prospects of many species, besides increasing public awareness of native wildlife. The people most concerned with wildlife welfare are those who have most direct contact. The more people who are allowed to have legal contact the better for the conservation cause.

The only major illegal activity which might result from opening up the wildlife trade, is the possible selling of wildlife at reduced prices. Policing that activity would be fairly straightforward and easy to detect when violated on a regular or large-scale basis. Furthermore, as such regulations could and should be enforced by any of several existing Government authorities, the possibility of corruption within a single given department would be reduced.

By removing the need for most keepers to register wildlife with State fauna authorities, with the possible exception of endangered species, the relative power of these authorities in relation to wildlife keepers and traders would be reduced. So, too, would the potential for corruption of officials within these departments.

Instead of banning the keeping of wildlife to make enforcement activity easier and attempt to prevent large-scale wildlife trade, the abolition or reduction of licensing requirements in tandem with a minimum price requirement would control wildlife trade while allowing individuals and institutions to legally hold wildlife for their own purposes.

The lack of a central Government register would also help protect wildlife collections from some of those who wish to steal specimens to send them overseas.

Which brings us to the problem of live wildlife traded to and from Australia. In terms of export, any wildlife should be able to be exported subject to similar conditions that apply domestically. A $600 duty per specimen, including captive-bred specimens, would prevent excessive numbers from being taken out of the country. There would, however, be no minimum price rule applicable to any wildlife exported from Australia.

As an example, such regulations would not prevent a dedicated private snake keeper from the U.S.A. coming to Australia, catching a few Oenpelli pythons and taking them home to keep and breed. No threat would be made to the species in question by this activity and the Government would gain about $1 800 in revenue. If the American chose to import the snakes from a dealer within Australia, he would pay the same amount per snake, before the exporter added his cut. Prices like that would still dissuade many potential buyers, thereby preventing a full-scale pillaging of our wildlife stocks.

As the law stands at the moment, our American friend would be unable to import any Oenpelli pythons for any purpose and would therefore be unable to keep the species, as there are currently none held in captivity in the U.S.A. Should the man choose to import the animals illegally he would risk fines and jail. However, should the man have successfully illegally taken three snakes back to the U.S.A. the wild population of the snake would have been effectively unchanged (the species is very common where it occurs). Furthermore, if the American were to establish captive stocks of the species, further long-term demand for the species from wild stocks would not only decrease (as more captive animals become available) but long-term conservation prospects for this and similar species would be enhanced.

It is only through the efforts of enthusiasts, zoos and museum staff, all of whom must trade and/or trap wildlife, that more can be learnt about animals so that proper long-term conservation methods for threatened species may be devised. Impediments to these useful activities must surely be regarded as counterproductive to the conservation cause.

Quarantine

Quarantining specimens imported or exported is often unnecessary, especially if a given specimen can be certified as disease-free *before* export. This means animals would not have to be held in potentially unfavourable conditions for periods of time in Government-run facilities at vast expense to the taxpayer or importer/exporter.

In my view, current Australian quarantine regulations are being administered in a largely inappropriate manner. It is time they were examined and updated.

Exotic Species as a Threat

The main argument used to prevent the importation of wild animals is the potential threat to the environment should they escape or be deliberately released. However, few species pose this threat; e.g. no ball pythons have overrun the U.S. bush yet, despite thousands being imported annually.

Most long-term captive animals are unable to survive in the bush if

127

accidentally released. In the Australian context, almost all major pest animals, including the rabbit (*Oryctolagus cunniculus*), fox (*Vulpes vulpes*) and cane toad (*Bufo marinus*) were the result of deliberate, if misguided, carefully planned introductions.

Although it would be foolish to import numbers of species that may pose a threat to Australian species should they be accidentally released or escape, there should be few if any major restrictions on importing exotic species which clearly pose no such threat. Trading regulations operating almost in reverse to those for locally obtained stock or species would probably work well.

An import duty of $600 per live specimen (1990 values) and then a $600 minimum sale price for all exotic species by anyone trading the animals within Australia, would prevent large-scale importation of specimens.

PROBLEMS WITH PROPOSED IMPROVEMENTS
One possible problem with the minimum price system is that species held in large numbers in captivity and currently traded freely for just a few dollars, might not fit easily into such a system. However, just as those species are now mostly exempt from wildlife regulations within Australia and elsewhere, they could simply remain so. They could be exempted from local price laws although it would be worthwhile to maintain the duty on import or export from Australia.

Another potential problem is that people within Australia may breed so many specimens of a species in captivity that they may be unable to find buyers for the animals. If the species is sufficiently common in captivity and there is no major drain on wild stocks then the species could be made an exempt species in terms of the minimum price regulations. This could also apply to some exotic species.

The minimum price system might be abused. It would be almost impossible to stop a man selling his best friend an animal for half price or even detect him doing so. However, the system *would* prevent large-scale traders and dealers from doing so. For example, a pet dealer couldn't advertise numbers of a common species sourced from the wild in a newspaper column, at half the minimum price, without coming to the attention of the authorities. It is the potential demand created by these traders and dealers to satisfy the disposable pet market which can pose a threat to populations of given species. Thus the aim of the system would be to profiteer while breeding wildlife rather than to profiteer at the expense of wildlife.

Uniformity Between the States
Although different States within Australia have different local species of wildlife and conditions, fauna protection and trade laws should be drafted on a national basis with every State having uniform laws. The current system of each State and territory having different wildlife protection, licensing and trading laws is bad enough. It becomes even worse when one realises that what may be common in one State is listed as endangered in the next. Such a position is clearly not in the interests of conservation or of the species in question.

As there are no major impediments to the movement of people and goods across State borders, current wildlife laws and restrictions on a State-by-State basis are even more inappropriate. With every State or territory drawing up their own endangered species lists, usually based solely on the numbers of given species within State borders and shaping laws to fit these individual lists, there is a gross duplication of resources and personnel which again is clearly against long-term conservation goals.

Status lists of wildlife as endangered, rare, vulnerable etc., should be based on standardised criteria essentially similar to that used by the International Union for the Conservation of Nature (I.U.C.N.). Species should be included on lists only on the basis of their position globally and not on the basis of single local populations. Many species of wildlife found within Australia are not found elsewhere and so their conservation status here exactly fits that which actually exists. However, where a snake such as the green python may be rare in far north Queensland, but common in New Guinea and Irian Jaya, the species should clearly not be listed as rare for legislative purposes.

When biologically significant populations are threatened, restrictive legislation will not usually save, or have any major effect on, the survival of the population. Other methods such as long-term preservation and management of habitat in national parks are usually the only feasible way to save the population and therefore have no major relevance to the legislation being discussed here.

Wrongly labelling species as 'endangered' can be highly counterproductive. In 1990, conservationist Tom Porter of the U.S.A. said 'Designating an animal as threatened or endangered often assures its demise in the wild, and makes it impossible for qualified private breeders to obtain these animals.' He then went on to cite cases of the accelerated demise of species as a result of this practice.

Labelling carpet pythons in Victoria as endangered is a good example of inappropriate classification. Although the snake is found only in a very small part of the north-west of that State, it is one of the most widespread species in Australia. Even the Victorian subspecies is common across at least half of New South Wales and large areas in Queensland and South Australia. Labelling the snake as endangered has done nothing at all to protect the snakes in Victoria or elsewhere, as no populations, including those in Victoria, have ever been under threat from collecting activities.

This kind of inappropriate designation is a major problem because it diverts attention from those species which really are endangered, such as the orange-bellied parrot, whose total population centres on Bass Strait and at the time of writing, was down to less than 300 birds worldwide. Quite clearly the level of threat facing the two species is not the same.

There is no point in diverting scarce conservation resources into saving species that need no legislative assistance while other species expire through lack of funds.

Law Enforcement
When discussing legislation that will both aid wildlife conservation and stop smuggling, one has to accept that while laws should be kept to a minimum, we still need some laws which have to be administered by someone.

The problem then becomes, how to persuade upholders of the law to do their job in an impartial but fair manner, free of corruption and misconduct. Wildlife authorities and law enforcement officers should be individuals with a long history of wildlife keeping and research, not members of the public service without interest or experience in this area.

CUSTOMS AND PRACTICES

Odd beliefs by smugglers and traders lead to some unusual practices. In markets throughout Third World countries, bird traders split tongues of parrots and mynahs from end to end. These birds are sold to be trained to talk, and for some reason traders believe that splitting the tongue will aid the birds in talking. The splitting, done at time of purchase, involves use of a sharp penknife. The idea is stupid as birds don't use their tongue to mimic speech.

Traders sometimes mutilate stock to make it recognisable as theirs, while large numbers of birds have their wings broken so that they cannot fly away.

The methods used to capture wild animals by traders and smugglers in many countries are too varied to cover here. However, one particularly widespread and sometimes cruel method used is birdlime. Essentially it is a sticky substance used to prevent birds from flying away. The material may be derived by many means, but usually involves a long period of cooking holly, mistletoe or other locally occuring plants.

It is usually applied to landing positions or perches used by birds, which they then stick to. Birdlime may also be used to catch small mammals and reptiles, particularly species that tend to hide in inaccessible rock crevices. In many countries birdlime is banned, but that does not seem to prevent its use.

The substance is so sticky, it is often difficult to remove from birds and they may be damaged when attempts are made to do so. What is perhaps a greater problem is that trappers neglect to remove birdlime from places where they have been trapping. Birds that get caught in these limetraps invariably die if they cannot escape. Many are eaten by predators including aggressive tree-dwelling ants. In some cases predators enticed to the trapped birds, themselves become trapped and may also die. Predatorial lizards are particularly susceptible.

Within Australia, bird trappers rarely use birdlime, preferring nets, traps and other methods. Birdlime is not commercially available in Australia.

Wildlife officers do not need to carry guns as they often do now. This merely increases the hostility between officials and members of the public. In theory, Government officers and wildlife traders and researchers should co-operate to the fullest extent. Should an alleged offender become violent when apprehended, there is nothing to stop officials calling in re-inforcements at that stage.

OUR CURRENT SYSTEM

Current laws in most States allow wildlife officials to enter a licensed keeper's premises at any time without a court-issued warrant and without a reason. Such laws must be repealed as they are perhaps one of the most important ways in which corrupt officials play a role in illegal wildlife trafficking operations.

The fact that wildlife officials may 'legally' break into a person's house without permission and see what wildlife and facilities they have, virtually gives those officials licence to take wildlife if, once inside, they feel they are unlikely to be caught.

That wildlife officials can easily invent an alibi for taking fauna from a facility if they are caught, and subsequently be immune from prosecution, enables them to continue this activity. As long as this legal position continues, the incentive for wildlife officials to illegally traffic in wildlife will remain.

Wildlife department officials must have their regulatory powers restricted to a more reasonable level. Furthermore, these officials must be at least as accountable to the public as wildlife keepers and traders are to the Government officials.

Whistleblowers
State and Federal Ombudsman's departments run by public servants are often more concerned with maintaining the status quo rather than actually investigating crime and misconduct by other public servant colleagues. The failure of State Ombudsman's departments throughout Australia to control organised crime within the public service, including State fauna authorities is demonstrated by the recurrence of Royal Commissions into Government misconduct. Had the New South Wales Ombudsman actually been the 'public watchdog' it was meant to be, there would never have been a need for the Greiner government to create a 'super ombudsman' in the form of the Independent Commission against Corruption (I.C.A.C.).

Public watchdogs against corruption are essential to enable laws to be passed and then administered fairly. We need a truly independent and effective means to deal with official misconduct to guarantee long-term protection of wildlife, the environment and the public.

Money
One common problem that arises when a law-enforcement officer is charged with corruption is that their department usually foots the legal bill. I believe that officers should pay their own legal costs in the same manner as any other member of the public. Should the officer be unable to afford to do so, they would presumably be free to apply for 'legal aid' like anyone else. Currently, a certain amount of taxpayers' money is used to defend corrupt individuals. I believe this money would be better spent elsewhere.

Any person wrongly or maliciously sued by vindictive Government officials should be able to recover costs incurred in fighting their defence as well as other damages. Anyone acquitted of charges that were wrongly laid should be awarded these costs at the time of case dismissal.

People who steal wildlife should be liable for the full value of whatever was stolen, payable to the victim, as well as for the fines payable for having committed the offence. This would discourage 'official style' rackets.

The Courts
The current legal system within Australia was summed up in a story in the *Bulletin* magazine on 11 September 1990, titled 'Police Misconduct':

'The legal system is such in this country that when a magistrate or judge is confronted with opposing evidence from a single accused person and one or more police, and there is no "hard evidence" one way or the other, the magistrate or judge will, all things being equal, support the police case and convict the accused. With police being able to convict almost anyone of any minor or moderately serious offence, it becomes easy for corrupt police to discredit potential critics. They can destroy their finances and lifestyles as well. In recent years in Australia, the number of innocent people charged and convicted — after attempting to expose police misconduct and corruption — who were later found to be innocent, either upon appeal or the appearance of "new" evidence, is too numerous to list here.'

Corrupt fauna officials and smugglers are able to similarly exploit the system.

The Victorian legal system does not even take tapes and/or transcripts of most cases. This is ludicrous. With no ability to accurately scrutinise cases or evidence given by court witnesses, it is impossible to weed out corrupt magistrates or judges on the basis of decisions they make in particular cases. Some Victorian magistrates don't even take notes during cases.

It is little wonder that many people doubt the future apprehension and fair trial of corrupt public servants, smugglers or other individuals. Seeing corruption in high places makes many people afraid to speak out.

Until the legal system is overhauled, any new laws introduced to prevent the illegal trade in wildlife or rout official corruption are unlikely to have the full, desired effect.

15
SAVING OUR NATIVE ANIMALS AND THE FUTURE

Although wildlife smuggling and related problems constitute a long-term threat to some of our wildlife, there are other threats worth mentioning briefly.

THE HUMAN ANIMAL
The problem for wildlife is often people: too many of them. Most other problems stem from this.

About 96% of Australia's land surface is used for some form of human economic activity. It is therefore not surprising that most types of native animals throughout Australia suffer from habitat destruction or alteration. A minority of species actually seems to benefit from these changed conditions, but a quarter of species found within Australia is thought to be in either moderate or serious decline.

Habitat destruction or alteration is the single most important cause of decline for most native animals. Although certain habitat types, usually the most scenic, are being preserved in the form of national parks and similar reserves, other habitats and their representative wildlife are not being similarly protected. Species restricted to these unprotected habitats are at high risk of long-term extinction.

Approximately 100-200 species of native Australian animals are currently thought to be endangered and likely to become extinct if factors causing their decline continue. Other species will no doubt become endangered or known to be endangered, in the future.

In grazing areas removal of dead trees to be burnt as firewood may seem like a minor utilisation of resources but can have a dramatic effect on some local species. Birds that use tree hollows to nest in may be deprived of nesting sites and forced to leave the area, resulting in local extinctions. Small mammals and certain reptiles may be similarly affected.

Wiping out wildlife may have adverse economic effects. The removal of birds and reptiles from farming areas may allow pests such as mice and rats to breed in large numbers and destroy valuable crops.

It is introduced pest species which are without doubt the second greatest threat to Australia's wildlife. Cats *(Felis catus)*, foxes and rabbits have been directly responsible for the elimination of many mammal species and the decline of many more. Cats and foxes prey on them, while rabbits compete for food.

Numbats *(Myrmecobius fasciatus)*, bilbies *(Macrotis* spp.) and stick-nest rats *(Leporillus* spp.) are three examples of mammals which have suffered at the hands of these introduced mammals. All were widespread and common at the time of European settlement; they are now endangered. Numerous other birds, mammals and lesser vertebrates have also been introduced to Australia by Europeans with similarly catastrophic results for local wildlife. All vertebrate groups are affected. Of the major vertebrate groups reptiles seem least affected by human activities, including introduced species. On a percentage basis, fewer species of reptile are endangered than for the other major groups (excluding marine fish).

The preservation of potentially threatened habitat seems to be an easier task than the elimination of well-established pest species that also pose a threat to native wildlife. As an increasing proportion of habitat for remaining rare and endangered species becomes incorporated within reserves or is similarly protected, the need to contol pest species threatening native species will become increasingly important.

So far there has been little desire to restore already destroyed habitat on a large scale, and this is an expensive and unattractive conservation alternative compared to not destroying habitat in the first place.

Trapping and killing wildlife has threatened Australian species in the past but is not a major threat at the moment. For that reason, wildlife trafficking out of Australia must be kept in perspective as not being the major threat to our wildlife right now.

However, related to the smuggling problem is that of corrupt wildlife officials and counterproductive regulations. These are a major threat to wildlife in that they tend to divert scarce conservation resources away from more urgent wildlife conservation problems and discourage individual conservation efforts.

Many species of wildlife no longer able to survive in the wild will survive only in captivity. Many people believe that it is better for an animal to survive in captivity than become extinct. Captive breeding continues to be the key to survival for a number of species otherwise doomed to extinction. These include the Lord Howe Island woodhen, orange-bellied parrot and western short-necked tortoise *(Pseudemydura umbrina)*.

Restrictive actions by wildlife authority officials in Western Australia have demonstrably hastened the decline in numbers of the western short-necked tortoise, to less than 100 individuals so that any recovery in that species will be more difficult. The orange-bellied parrot has suffered similarly in south-eastern Australia.

Modern methods allow almost any species to be bred in large numbers in captivity, provided the money and desire to do so exist. The efforts of people such as Richard Bartlett, of the Reptile Breeding Centre, Fort Meyers, Florida, U.S.A., Brian Barnett of Victoria and others, have demonstrated how captive breeding of Australian fauna can actually provide specimens in large numbers

YOU CAN BUY ANYTHING AT PADDY'S

Until 1974, animal dealers at Sydney's Paddy's Market openly traded reptiles with their other animals. These were the famous pet stalls selling dogs, cats, goldfish and caged birds. Rarer parrots and other species were also traded. With the tightening of regulations governing wildlife trade in New South Wales, dealers appeared to relinquish their former trade in reptiles and rare birds.

As recently as July 1990 at Paddy's I realised this wasn't true. In company with a Sydney herpetologist I approached a pet dealer and asked what 'herps' he had today. The trader was on friendly terms with my companion and led us behind his stall where he removed a bag from underneath a table with a sheet covering it. Inside there was a large, 2 m (6') Queensland carpet python. Even at a glance I could see that the snake had some form of respiratory infection. The asking price was $250.

We were then shown bags containing apparently healthy diamond pythons, Queensland children's or spotted pythons, and a single large grey death adder. All were $200-500 per snake. We weren't shown the contents of another bag allegedly containing about six eastern brown snakes. When I enquired about the legality of keeping snakes (knowing full well that one needed a N.P.W.S. permit to hold those reptiles in New South Wales), the old man said 'Hey, these are below board, but if ya wanna make 'em legal I got connections who may be able to help ya.'

While we were talking with the dealer about other Australian reptiles and his ability to obtain them to sell to us, a Chinese customer came up to the stall. He muttered something about a snake. The dealer retrieved a bag containing a large 2.5 m (8') diamond python and allowed the customer to peer into the bag. He indicated he wanted the snake and paid the dealer $200. The dealer sealed the bag and handed it to the Chinaman who thrust the bag back and said 'I want head off!'.

Without a moment's hesitation, the dealer grabbed the python by the head and wrenched it from the bag. Pulling a large sharp knife from a sheath on his belt he promptly decapitated the snake and then placed the still writhing snake back into the now bloodied bag. The evening's dinner was now secured.

Diamond pythons are protected both in New South Wales and Victoria, where they occur and were at one time listed as rare by the New South Wales authorities. They are a C.I.T.E.S. appendix 2 species.

I found it hard to believe that a man I'd thought was an enthusiastic herpetologist trading a few snakes on the side, could so cold bloodedly kill a snake to provide some delicacy or aphrodisiac. Apparently dozens of live snakes are sold at Paddy's market (all illegally) and bought by Asians for food or medicine each week. The most commonly traded species are red-bellied black *(Pseudechis porphyriacus)*, eastern brown and tiger snakes which are usually sold for about $100 a snake. All are common around the Sydney area.

A second animal trader I was introduced to told us he had some 'hot' (illegal) 'sliders' (an American freshwater tortoise) he was anxious to get rid of. He kept his reptiles at his house and brought specimens to the market only to fulfil pre-arranged sales. The whole activity was conducted very discreetly.

Not all traders are so cautious. A China Town trader, known as the Live Craft Shop at 84 Dixon Street, Sydney, sold hundreds of young and adult, illegally imported red-eared sliders (*Chrysemys scripta*), which were openly advertised in the shop and sold to all takers in 1989-91. No Australian tortoises were sold in the shop. A second shop nearby also sold red-eared sliders and painted turtles (*Chrysemys picta*), apparently sourced from the same importer.

which may ultimately be released to replenish depleted wild stocks.

At the time of writing, there has been a 20 year trend by Government officials to thwart captive breeding efforts by large zoos, other institutions and private individuals.

These efforts have been motivated by a combination of factors. Ignorant animal rights lobbyists have misled the public and the politicians about the supposed cruelty of keeping animals in captivity. Public servants have regulated everything to an increasing extent to justify their own existence in ever greater numbers. Corrupt officials know that restrictive laws guarantee potential profits, and so have perpetuated the system.

These contributing factors are currently under threat. The animal rights lobbyists are largely discredited and regarded by many as being on the lunatic fringe.

There is also an increasing public and political awareness that we cannot support huge numbers of relatively unproductive officials. 'De-regulation' has become a catchcry for many politicians, and although not always appropriate to conservation, wildlife regulations are being increasingly questioned both by those who work under them and by department heads forced to cut costs and unnecessary activities, including paperwork, which have to be administered by staff.

Perceived corruption has affected the popularity of various governments around Australia. Corrupt officials are now under fire from Royal Commissions, media reports and new authorities created to combat official corruption. Although most organised crime activities, including wildlife smuggling, are largely untouched by these initiatives at this stage, public disapprobation will probably increase as we become better educated about all related issues.

All these changes are a good omen for the future of Australian wildlife. The sharp decline in numbers of many species in Australia over the last two centuries is hard to reverse, but the rate of decline is likely to decrease. In some cases, catastrophe has been averted. The case of the Lord Howe Island woodhen whereby the species was brought from less than 20 individuals back to a healthy Island population, is likely to be repeated in the future.

The global decrease in the rate of population growth, although nowhere near enough, is at least a slightly encouraging sign. In an Australian context, the rate of population growth in this country is still far too high.

As the membership of conservation organisations increases, so too will the pressure on authorities to stop wildlife smuggling. Already these organisations have lobbied hard to change wildlife laws so the wildlife in question receives the greatest possible benefit. Victoria recently amended laws to make captive breeding more attractive to wildlife keepers, while in 1990 Canberra-based wildlife researchers lobbied the Western Australian Government to stop illegal wildlife trade in that State by making legal trade easier.

Wildlife conservation relies upon the free flow of information. Bona fide freedom of information which actually makes Government departments accountable and willing to share all information they have, will ultimately be a key to preserving as much of our wildlife as possible.

No doubt there will always be some corruption and some illegal trade in wildlife. It is, however, essential that Australians work together to preserve our heritage. Doing so will ultimately benefit our wildlife and our planet.

Smuggle link probe

THE seizure of prohibited reptiles from a Geelong home yesterday might lead to a huge smuggling racket, wildlife officers say.

Two king pythons from Africa, two huge tarantulas and a Colombian bird spider were seized after quarantine and Conservation and Natural Resources Department officers raided the house about 7am.

Department spokeswoman Lisa Borthwick said officers would try to track a man who sold the reptiles to the 21-year-old Geelong man about three months ago.

She said the Geelong man would be charged on summons with possessing prohibited wildlife, an offence which carries a maximum fine of $5000 and/or two years' jail.

Herald-Sun, Friday, December 4, 1992—Page 5

16
SELECTED BIBLIOGRAPHY

Anonymous (1973), *Convention on International Trade in Endangered Species of Wild Fauna and Flora, (C.I.T.E.S.),* Special Supplement to I.U.C.N. Bulletin, 4 (3), 12 pp.

Anonymous (1977), 'Smuggling Rare Animals: Latest Global Racket', *US News and World Report,* September 26, p. 50.

Anonymous (1978), 'Death Adder Loose in St. Ives', *Daily Telegraph* (Sydney), October 24, p. 1.

Anonymous (1980), 'Bird Business — International Notes', *African Wildlife,* 34 (1), p. 32.

Anonymous (1980), 'Bird Smuggling Charges Dropped', *Age* (Melbourne), April 16, p. 17.

Anonymous (1980), 'Fined Again — International Notes', *African Wildlife* (International Edition), 34 (2), p. 39.

Anonymous (1980), 'Skin Trade — International Notes', *African Wildlife* (International Edition), 34 (2), p. 39.

Anonymous (1980), 'Reprehensible Trade — International Notes', *African Wildlife* (International Edition), 34 (5), p. 29.

Anonymous (1980), 'Blown to Bits — International Notes', *African Wildlife* (International Edition), 34 (5), p. 29.

Anonymous (1980), 'Fine Sentences — International Notes', *African Wildlife* (International Edition), 34 (6), p. 35.

Anonymous (1981), 'Parrot Racket — International Notes', *African Wildlife* (International Edition), 35 (3), p. 17.

Anonymous (1981), 'N.W.F. Asks Reagan to Fire Watt', *International Wildlife,* May, p. 28-B (also printed in most other issues in 1981).

Anonymous (1981), 'Wildlife Trade — Wildlife Digest', *International Wildlife,* May, p. 24-A.

Anonymous (1981), 'Wildlife — The Habitat Hemorrhage', *National Wildlife,* February/March, p. 30.

Anonymous (1982), 'West: Thumbs-down on Watt! — Wildlife Digest', *National Wildlife,* 20 (2), p. 24-A.

SELECTED BIBLIOGRAPHY

Anonymous (1982), 'Watt loses in Alaska — Wildlife Digest', *National Wildlife*, 20 (2), p. 24-A.

Anonymous (1982), 'Snake Collector in Court', *Sydney Morning Herald*, April 9, p. 3.

Anonymous (1982), 'Smuggling Trial Aborted Because of *Herald* articles', *Sydney Morning Herald*, May 14.

Anonymous (1982), 'Fish and Wildlife Facts: The U.S. Endangered Species Act', (FWS-F-010), U.S. Department of the Interior — Fish and Wildlife Service, May.

Anonymous (1982), 'Fish and Wildlife Facts: Regulations to Enforce the Convention on International Trade in Endangered Species of Wild Fauna and Flora (C.I.T.E.S.)', (FWS-F-006), U.S. Department of the Interior — Fish and Wildlife Service, May.

Anonymous (1982), 'Fish and Wildlife Facts: Federal Laws Restricting Commerce in Wildlife: *Lacey Act* 1900, *Endangered Species Act* of 1973, *Migratory Bird Treaty Act* 1918, *Marine Mammal Protection Act* of 1972', (FWS-F-025), U.S. Department of the Interior — Fish and Wildlife Service, May.

Anonymous (1982), 'Judge Recommends no Action Against *Herald*', *Sydney Morning Herald*, June 2, p. 3.

Anonymous (1982), 'Bird-racket Smugglers Reap Millions', *Daily Mirror* (Sydney), November 22.

Anonymous (1983), 'Poaching Penalties Heavier', *Sydney Morning Herald*, March 21.

Anonymous (1983), 'Sydney Snake Man', *City Express* (Sydney), May 25, p. 3.

Anonymous (1984), 'Man Had 350 Reptiles in Home: Police', *Sydney Morning Herald*, June 12, p. 15.

Anonymous (1984), 'Animal Acts' *Sydney Morning Herald*, October 26, back page.

Anonymous (1985), 'Reptiles in Case Earn $5 000 Fine', *Sydney Morning Herald*, March 2, p. 5.

Anonymous (1985), 'Airport Check Traps Snake Smuggler', The *Daily Telegraph* (Sydney), March 2, p. 19.

Anonymous (1985), 'Snakes Alive in Suitcase', *Sydney Morning Herald*, January 18.

Anonymous (1985), 'Snake Man is Seething', *Daily Telegraph* (Sydney), March 3, p. 5.

Anonymous (1985), 'Jail for Taking Snake to Queensland', *Sydney Morning Herald*, April 12, p. 5.

Anonymous (1985), 'Grounded, 63 Lizards and a Frog with a Ticket to Fly', *Age* (Melbourne), September 24, p. 5.

Anonymous (1986), 'Two on Perjury Charge over Addict's Death', *Sydney Morning Herald*, March 12.

Anonymous (1986), 'Customs Officers Charged', *Age* (Melbourne), July 20, p. 5.

Anonymous (1986), 'Zoo Knight "Was Fauna Trafficker"', *Daily Telegraph* (Sydney), May 7, p. 13.

Anonymous (1987), 'Dead Bird Expert "Innocent"' *Times on Sunday*, February 8.

Anonymous (1987), 'A Two-man Hit Squad Polices Bird Poachers', *Sunday Sun* (Brisbane), July 23.

Anonymous (1987), 'Australian Shell Trade', *TRAFFIC Bulletin*, 9 (1), p. 5.

Anonymous (1988), 'Rare Bird Smuggler Jailed for Two Years', *Sun* (Melbourne), August 20, p. 13.

Anonymous (1988), 'Wildlife Prosecutions in Australia', *TRAFFIC Bulletin*, 10 (1-2), p. 12.

Anonymous (1988), *Monitoring Wildlife Trade — The Traffic Network*, (Factsheet of 14 pp.), World Wildlife Fund, Washington, D.C., U.S.A..

Anonymous (1989), *Convention on International Trade in Endangered Species of Wild Fauna and Flora, Annual Report for Australia 1988*, Australian National Parks and Wildlife Service, Canberra, Australia.

Anonymous (1990), 'Snakes and Cannabis Land Couple with a $1 400 Fine', *Age* (Melbourne), Jan 20, p. 17.

Anonymous (1990), 'Herp-net Lists "Herp-crimes"', *NOTES FROM NOAH*, 17 (4), p. 7.

Anonymous (1990) 'Cruel Reality at Chewton/Editorial', *Herald* (Melbourne), May 30, p. 8.

Anonymous (1990), 'Gambler on Bird Smuggle Charge', *Sun-Herald* (Sydney), June 3, p. 11.

Anonymous (1990), 'Seizures and Prosecutions (Compiled by Traffic Oceania)', *TRAFFIC Bulletin*, 11 (4), p. 69.

Anonymous (1990), 'CALM Case Thrown Out', *Kalgoorlie Miner*, November 11, p. 6.

Anonymous (1990), 'Snakes Alive They're Angry', *Sunday Times* (Perth), December 2, p. 20.

Anonymous (1990), 'Trying to Keep Snakes Alive', *Guardian Express* (Perth), December 11th, p. 5.

Anonymous (1991), 'Smuggle-bid Counts', *Herald-Sun* (Melbourne), October 2, p. 5.

Anonymous (1991), 'Dingo Park Raid Compo Bid Refused', *Herald-Sun* (Melbourne), October 28, p. 29.

Anonymous (1991), 'Customs Swoop on Lizards in Suitcase', *Herald-Sun* (Melbourne), December 19, p. 11.

Anonymous (1992), 'Two Face Charges after Reptile Raid', *Herald-Sun* (Melbourne), January 18, p. 21.

Anonymous (1992), '18 Months for Lizard Smuggler', *Age* (Melbourne), March 5, p. 3.

Anonymous (1992), 'Poachers Trapped — D.N.A. testing used on birds', *Herald-Sun* (Melbourne), April 27, p. 29.

Antram, F. (1986), 'The Australian Sea Snake Industry', *TRAFFIC* Bulletin, 8 (3), p. 51.

Antram, F. (1987), 'Papua New Guinea Suspends Exports', *TRAFFIC Bulletin*, 9 (2/3).

Antram, F. (1988), 'Wildlife Prosecutions in Oceania Region', *TRAFFIC Bulletin*, 9 (4), pp. 78-79.

Antram, F. (1988), 'Australia to Lift Live Bird Import Ban', *TRAFFIC Bulletin*, 9 (4), p. 65.

Antram, F. (1989), 'Australian Sea Snake Utilisation — an Update', *TRAFFIC Bulletin*, 10 (3/4), p. 31.

Antram, F. (1989), 'Wildlife Prosecutions in Australia', *TRAFFIC Bulletin*, 10 (3/4), pp. 45-46.

Associated Birdkeepers and Traders (1989), 'N.S.W. Aviculture in Crisis —

Again', *Australian Birdkeeper,* 2 (10), p. 388.

Ballantyne, T. (1982), 'The Smugglers Who Prey on Our Fauna', *Sydney Morning Herald,* May 14.

Bartlett, R. D. (1982), 'Okeetee Update', *Notes From NOAH,* 9 (9), pp. 3-6.

Bartlett, R. D. (1987), 'Some Random Thoughts on Hobbyists', *Notes from NOAH,* 14 (6), pp. 3-6.

Begley, S. and Hagar, M. (1981), 'The "Snakescam" Sting', *Newsweek,* 27 July.

Behler, J. (1981), 'Snakes Under Seige/Lost Habitat and Booming Trade Head The List Of Serpent Woes', *Notes From NOAH,* 9 (3), pp. 10-13.

Belmore, B. (1981), 'Fish and Wildlife Scam Snares 25', *Pet Business,* 3 pp.

Best, P. (1990), 'Out at Last, and Freedom Tastes Good' *Herald* (Melbourne), May 31, p. 3.

Blair, T. (1992), 'Send it by Python Post!', *Truth* (Melbourne), February 29, p. 7.

Bloomer, T. (1982), 'More Snakescam', *Notes From NOAH,* 9 (6), pp. 5-8.

Bottom, B. (1979), 'Riches in Wildlife Smuggling', *Bulletin,* August 21, pp. 28-30.

Bottom, B. (1984), 'Rustling Feathers', *Australian Penthouse,* February.

Bottom, B. (1985), 'Organised Crime Swoops on Bird Smuggling Racket', *Sydney Morning Herald,* July 22, p. 9.

Bottom, B. (1985), *Connections: Crime Rackets and Networks of Influence Down Under,* Sun Books/Macmillan, South Melbourne, Australia.

Bottom, B. (1987), *Connections 2: Crime Rackets and Networks of Influence Down Under,* Sun Books/Macmillan, South Melbourne, Australia.

Bottom, B. (1988), *Shadow of Shame,* Sun Books/Macmillan, South Melbourne, Australia.

Bottom, B. (1988), *The Godfather in Australia,* Shepp Books, Hornsby, Australia.

Bottom, B. (1988), 'The Double Life of a Drug Runner', *Age* (Melbourne), June 29, p. 11.

Bottom, B. (1989), *Bugged,* Sun Books/Macmillan, South Melbourne, Australia.

Bouts, T. (1987), 'Thieves Swoop on $140,000 in Rare Birds', *Herald* (Melbourne), June 4.

Brown, R. (1990), 'Jurong, the Wonderful World of Birds', *Australian Birdkeeper,* 3 (1), pp. 30-33.

Brunner, J. C. (1981), 'A Letter to Interior Secretary James Watt Re: Snakescam', *Notes From NOAH,* 9 (3), pp. 3-7.

Bullfinch (1989), 'Mynah Mutterings', *Australian Birdkeeper,* 2 (10), p. 373.

Bullfinch (1990), 'Mynah mutterings', *Australian Birdkeeper,* 3 (1), p. 14.

Bullfinch (1990), 'Mynah mutterings', *Australian Birdkeeper,* 3 (5), p. 201.

Bunting, B. (1985), 'Heavily-traded Latin American Species', *TRAFFIC (USA),* 6 (1), pp. 7-10.

Burgin, S. (ed.) (1984), *Endangered Species: Social, Scientific, Economic and Legal Aspects in Australia and the South Pacific,* Total Environment Centre, Sydney, Australia.

Burton, R. and Burton, M. (1978), *The World's Disappearing Wildlife,* Marshall Cavendish, U.K..

Butler, J. A. and Shitu, E. (1985), 'Uses of Some Reptiles by the Yoruba People of Nigeria', *Herpetological Review,* 16 (1), pp. 15-16.

California Government (1982), 'Action no. 55812 — Lilley v. California Department of Fish and Game', (Court and associated documents), March 29 and June 28.

Campbell, R. (1990), 'An ACT man who had a go for a Goanna — James Fitzgerald at Home Yesterday with his South Australian Goanna . . . his Victory over Officialdom', *Canberra Times*, November 13, p. 3.

Cann, J. (1986), *Snakes Alive! Snake Experts and Antidote Sellers of Australia*, Kangaroo Press, Sydney, Australia.

Caras, R. (1966), 'Last Chance on Earth, a Requiem for Wildlife', Chilton, U.K.

Casper, G. S. (1983), 'A Study in Wildlife Law Enforcement: The United States "Snakescam" of 1981', *British Herpetological Society Bulletin No. 6. 1983*, pp. 23-26.

Chapman, C. (ed.) (1986), 'Associated Birdkeepers and Traders Update', *A.B.T. Newsletter*, No. 1, A.B.T., N.S.W.

Chisholm, A. (1972), 'The Case For Freeing the Birds From Their Cage of Rules', *The Australian Aviculture*, September, pp. 156-7.

Clark, B. (1988), 'Breeding the Albino Burmese Python', *The Vivarium — American Federation of Herpetoculturists*, 1 (1), pp. 18-21.

Clark, V. S. (1977), 'A Report on Rattlesnake Roundups in Oklahoma and other parts of the United States', *Bulletin of the Oklahoma Herpetological Society*, 2 (4), pp. 70-80.

Clarke, M. (1988), 'Legislative Action', *The Vivarium — American Federation of Herpetoculturists*, 1 (1), p. 13.

Claydon, C. (1990), 'Bavaria, Beer, BMWs . . .' *Australian Birdkeeper*, 3 (3), pp. 116-118.

Cleveland, A. (1974), *Man Kind? Our Incredible War on Wildlife*, Harper and Row, U.K.

Craig, O. (1989), 'Wildlife Kept on Ice: Judge Jails Smuggler', *Sun-Herald*, (Sydney), April 30, p. 9.

Cumming, F. (1981), '"Snakies" Feel Bite of Tough New Stand', *Australian* (Sydney), August 25, pp. 1-2.

De Graff, T. (1974), 'The Import and Export of Birds', *Australian Aviculture*, May.

DeLisle, D. (1988), 'Python Piracy', *The Vivarium — American Federation of Herpetoculturists*, 1 (1), p. 20.

Dickie, P. (1988), *The Road to Fitzgerald*, University of Queensland Press, Australia.

Dixon, R. (1990), 'Department Slaughter of Dingoes Unnecessary, says Ombudsman', *The Age* (Melbourne), May 30, p. 15.

Dodd, C. K. (jnr.) (1986), 'Importation of Live Snakes and Snake Products into the United States', *Herpetological Review*, 17 (4), pp. 76-79.

Dodd, C. K. (jnr.) (1986), 'The Status, Conservation and Management of Snakes', in *Snakes: Ecology and Evolutionary Biology*, ed. by Seigal, R. A., Collins, J. T. and Novak, S., Macmillan Publishing Co., New York, U.S.A.

Donnelly, M. (1984), 'Things are Sliding in Lawson St, Redfern', *Daily Telegraph*, (Sydney), Australia, June 21.

Ehmann, H. and Cogger, H. (1985), 'Australia's Endangered Herpetofauna: A review of Criteria and Policies', in *Biology of Australasian Frogs and Reptiles*, ed. by Gordon Grigg, Richard Shine and Harry Ehmann, Royal

SELECTED BIBLIOGRAPHY

Zoological Society Of New South Wales, pp. 435-447.

Ehrlick, A. and Ehrlick, P. (1982), *Extinction: The Causes and Consequences of the Disappearance of Species*, Victor Gollancz, U.S.A.

Epis, M. (1991), 'Roger Flap Runs into More Flak', *Herald-Sun* (Melbourne), July 4, p. 4.

Fife, R. J. (1981), 'Our Legal Rights as Herpetologists', *Notes From NOAH*, 9 (2), p. 3.

Fisher, J. and HRH Prince Philip (1970), *Wildlife Crisis*, Cowles Book Co., U.K.

Fitzgerald, G. E. (1989), *Report of a Commission of Inquiry into Possible Illegal Activities and Associated Police Misconduct*, S. Hampson, Government Printer, Queensland.

Fitzgerald, S. (1989), *International Wildlife Trade: Whose Business is it?'*, World Wildlife Fund, Washington, D.C.

Forbes, M. (1985), 'Criminals Slip Past "corrupt" computer', *Sydney Morning Herald*, August 9, p. 1.

Foster, M. (1983), 'High Price for Birds Heads and Other Natives', *Finch Breeders Review*, (Newsletter).

Frail, R. (1984), 'The Profit is Worth the Risk as Smugglers Feather Their Nests', *The Sydney Morning Herald*, March 10.

Frith, H. J. (1973), *Wildlife Conservation*, Angus and Robertson, Sydney, Australia.

Fuller, K. and Swift, B. (1985), *Latin American Wildlife Trade Laws*, (2nd edition), TRAFFIC, Washington, D.C., U.S.A.

Gans, C. (1985), 'Comment on Two Checklists', *Herpetological Review*, 16 (1), pp. 6-7.

Geschke, N. (1990), *Report — The Investigation Of The Raid by Department Of Conservation Forests And Lands Officers and R.S.P.C.A. Staff on Mr. Bruce Jacobs' Dingo Farm, May 1990*, The Ombudsman Victoria/ Government Printer.

Gilroy, T. (1986), 'On Banning the Importation of Exotic Birds', *Watchbird* (American Federation of Aviculturalists), December/January.

Glascott, J. (1988), 'Australia's Scandalous Trade', *Age* (Melbourne), June 6, p. 15.

Grandy, J. W. (1981), 'Defenders View', *Defenders of Wildlife*, June, p. 56.

Gregg, S. S. (1988), 'Of Soup And Survival', *Sea Frontiers*, September/October, pp. 298-302.

Grigg, G. C. and Shine, R. (1985), 'An Open Letter to all Herpetologists', *Herpetological Review*, 16 (4), pp. 96-97.

Groombridge, B. (1983), *World Checklist of Threatened Amphibians and Reptiles*, Nature Conservancy Council, U.K.

Halliday, T. (1978), *Vanishing Birds of the World*, Holt, Rinehart and Winston, U.K.

Hamm, R. (1987), 'Egg Thieves of Playa Grande', *Sea Frontiers*, January/February, pp. 27-33.

Haupt, R. (1973), 'U.S. Strikes at our "Swiss connection"', *Sydney Morning Herald*, pp. 1 and 3.

Heatwole, H. (1985), 'Letter to the Editor', *Herpetological Review*, 16 (1), p. 6.

Hickie, D. (1985), *The Prince and the Premier*, Angus and Robertson, Sydney, Australia.

High Court of Australia (1986), *Malcolm Raymond Ackroyd — Plaintiff, and The Honourable Peter Richard McKechnie, Minister For Tourism, National Parks, Sport and The Arts for the State of Queensland and Another — Defendants* Court Transcript, August 6.

Holmes, P. (1981), 'Editorial', *Defenders*, April, p. 54.

Hope, D. (1982), 'Tough New Penalties for Smuggling Wildlife', *Sydney Morning Herald*, May 7.

Hoser, R. (1977), Transcript of telephone conversation with Paul Ludowici (Re-N.P.W.S.), October.

Hoser, R. (1981), Transcript of Australian Herpetological Society Meeting, September 25.

Hoser, R. (1989), 'Smuggling Snakes Out Of Australia . . . How The System Works', *Litteratura Serpentium*, 9 (1), (English Edition) pp. 15-35.

Hoser, R. (1989), 'Australian Reptile Conservation Update', *Herptile*, 14 (4), pp. 146-154.

Hoser, R. (1989), *Australian Reptiles And Frogs*, Pierson and Co., Sydney, Australia.

Hoser, R. (1991), *Endangered Animals of Australia*, Pierson and Co., Sydney, Australia.

House Of Representatives Standing Committee on Environment and Conservation (1976), *Trafficking in Endangered Species*, Report, Australian Government Publishing Service, Canberra, A.C.T. (Report is 76 pp; transcript of evidence given is 1080pp, including evidence given in camera).

Iker, S. (1982), 'The Great American Snake Sting — and Other Tales of Intrigue', *National Wildlife Magazine*, 20 (2), pp. 12-15.

Iker, S. (1982), 'A Year of Reckoning for Endangered Species', *National Wildlife Magazine*, 20 (3), pp. 4-11.

Inskipp, T. and Wells, S. (1979), *International Trade In Wildlife*, Earthscan Publication. International Institute For Environment and Development and the Fauna Preservation Society, London, U.K.

International Union for the Conservation of Nature (1973), 'Convention on International Trade in Endangered Species of wild Fauna and Flora', (C.I.T.E.S.), Special supplement to the I.U.C.N. Bulletin, 4 (3), 12 pp.

Jewell, P. (1990), 'International Trade in Wildlife — Australian Responsibilities', *Australian Birdkeeper*, 3 (4), p. 170.

Johnson, P. (1991), 'Dealer got Stolen Rare Birds Cheap, Court Told', *Age* (Melbourne), August 8, p. 15.

Johnson, P. (1991), 'Stolen Rare Birds Cost Dealer $3 000', *Age* (Melbourne), August 21, p. 5.

Kennedy, M. (1981), 'Endangered Species are Big Business', *National Parks Journal*, Sydney, Australia, pp. 12-13.

Kennedy, M. (1984), 'The Failure of Protection', *Australian Penthouse*, February.

Kennedy, M. (ed.) (1989), *Australia's Endangered Species*, Simon and Schuster, Sydney, Australia.

King, F. W. (1976), 'Slaughter of the Wild', *Animal Kingdom* (New York Zoological Society), April/May pp. 28-32.

King, F. W. (1978), 'The Wildlife Trade' in *Wildlife and America. Contributions to an Understanding of American Wildlife and its Conservation*, ed. by Brokaw, H. P., U.S. Government Printing Office, Washington, D.C., U.S.A.

pp. 253-271.

King, M. and Miller, J. (1985), 'Letter to the Editor', *Herpetological Review*, 16 (1), pp. 4-5.

Knowles, D., Maryan, B. and Browne-Cooper, R. (1991), 'The Role of the Amateur Herpetologist in Western Australia', *Herpetofauna*, 21 (1), pp. 1-4.

Leslie, I. (1983), 'The Man from Uncle', pp. 72-75 in *60 Minutes, The Book*, Angus and Robertson, Sydney.

Lilley, T. (1981), 'The Sting: who Really got Stung', *Notes From NOAH*, 8 (2), pp. 1-3.

Lilley, T. (1982), 'Herpetologist's independence day', *Notes From NOAH*, 9 (10), pp. 16-17.

Livingstone, T. (1987), 'Scientist on Fauna Theft Charges Dies', *Courier Mail* (Brisbane), February 3.

Livingstone, T. (1987), 'Parks Service Admits it Took Scientist's $10', *Courier Mail* (Brisbane), February 10, p. 2.

Lochen, K. (editor) (1984-87) *TRAFFIC BULLETIN*, (multiple issues), Wildlife Trade Monitoring Unit, U.K.

Longmore, R. (1990), 'Conservation of Wildlife' (letter to the editor), *Canberra Times*, 16, Nov, p. 6.

Lucas, C. K. (1972), 'Please, Mr. Chipp! (Editorial)', *Australian Aviculture*, October, p. 1.

Lyster, S. (1981), 'U.S. Stance in New Delhi Worries C.I.T.E.S. Conferees', *Defenders of Wildlife* June, pp. 44-45.

Mackey, D. J. (1980), 'Turtle Traders/World-wide Commerce in Turtle Products', *Oceans*, 13 (4), PP. 59-61.

Macmillan S. (1990), 'The trade in Cruelty/Overseas Traffickers will pay $20 000 for Just one Parrot to the Gangs who are Pillaging Australia's National Heritage', *Australian* Weekend Supplement, April 21-22, pp. 1 and 4.

Manoharan, M. (1991), 'Trade Booming in Vanishing Species', *Age* (Melbourne), November 16, p. 15.

Martin, R. D. (ed.) (1975), *Breeding Endangered Species in Captivity*, Academic Press, U.S.A.

Maryan, B. (1991), 'The Amateur Herpetologist in West Australia — A Rare and Endangered Species', *Monitor — Bulletin of the Victorian Herpetological Society*, 3 (2), pp. 47-50.

McShane, J. (1970), *Operation Doughnut: Report and Papers*, Federal Customs Department, Canberra, Australia.

Messel, H. (1980), 'Rape of the North', *Habitat* (Australian Conservation Foundation), April, pp. 3-6.

Miles, W. (1992), 'Skin Trade', *Australian Penthouse*, January, pp. 34-41, 104-106, 128.

Miller, M. (1981), 'Not Stung, but not Taking any Chances', *Notes From NOAH*, 8 (12), pp. 8-9.

Miller, M. et. al. (1982), 'Notes re "Herpetological Holocaust"', *Notes From NOAH*, 9 (5), pp. 1-9.

Miller, S. (1982), 'Letter re Reptile Smuggling', *Notes From NOAH*, 9 (4), pp. 7-9.

Millington, J. R. (1989), 'Importation — The Countdown Begins!', *Australian Birdkeeper*, 2 (12), pp. 484-486.

Moor, K. (1989), *Crims in Grass Castles*, Pascoe Publishing Pty. Ltd., Apollo Bay, Victoria, Australia.

Muller, D. (1990), Government Rejects Call to Broaden F.O.I. Laws', *Age* (Melbourne), May 31, p. 5.

Murdoch, L., (1991), 'Thailand to get Tough on Wildlife Trade', *Age* (Melbourne), April 18, p. 7.

Myers, N. (1979), *Sinking Ark: a New Look at the Problem of Disappearing Species*, Pergamon Press, U.S.A.

Nichol, J. (1987), *The Animal Smugglers*, Christopher Helm (Publishers), London, U.K.

Nilsson, G. (1981), *The Bird Business* (2nd Edition), Animal Welfare Institute, U.S.A.

Nilsson, G. (ed.) (1982), *The Endangered Species Handbook*, Animal Welfare Institute, U.S.A.

Noble, T. (1989), *Untold Violence/Crime in Melbourne Today*, John Kerr Pty. Ltd., Richmond, Victoria, Australia.

N.S.W. Government (1982), *N.P.W.S.* v. *Raymond Hoser*, court transcript and associated documents, dated April 8.

N.S.W. Government (1984), *N.P.W.S.* v. *Raymond Hoser*, court transcript and associated documents, dated July 6.

N.S.W. Government (1984-5), *N.P.W.S.* v. *Raymond Hoser*, court transcript and associated documents, dated July 25, September 25, December 7, 1984, March 20 and 20 June, 1985.

N.S.W. Government (1985), *Ackroyd* v. *N.P.W.S.*, court transcript and associated documents, dated June 26.

N.S.W. Government (1985), *Raymond Hoser* v. *N.P.W.S.*, court transcript and associated documents, dated September.

O'Gorman, B. (1981), 'The Corella Conclusion!', *Australian Aviculture*, December, pp. 272-73.

Orders, R. and Bondy, A. (1988), 'Animal Traffic/Out of Australia', video documentary, Cinecontact, London, U.K.

O'Shea, M. (1982), 'The Great American Snake Shake Out', *The Herptile* 7 (2), pp. 32-33.

Pacholli, J. (1990), 'While the Pigs are Away', *Toorak Times* (Melbourne), November 28, page 3.

Pena, R. D. L. (1990), 'Reward Offered (Stolen Snakes)', *Notes From NOAH*, 17 (2), p. 7.

Penberthy, J. (1982), 'Bugs /Coming in From the Cold', *Business Review Weekly* (Sydney), June 26-July 2, pp. 8-11.

Platt, C. (1974), *Transport of Live Animals by air from Calcutta and Bangkok Airports*, International Society For The Protection Of Animals, U.K.

Porras, L. (1978), 'A Reptile Dealer Speaks Out', *National Association For Sound Wildlife Programs Newsletter*, 2 (1), pp. 70-76.

Price, R. (1990), 'From the President', (Editorial), *The Long Island Herpetological Society Bulletin*, October/November 1990, pp. 1-2.

Pritchard, P. C. H. (1986), 'In Defence of Private Collections', *Herpetological Review*, 17 (3), pp. 56-58.

Purcell, R. (1978), 'Stolen Death Adder Unlikely to Bite', *North Shore Advocate Courier* (Sydney), (week unknown).

Quinne, B. (1992), '$100 000 Lure in Lizard Export Plot', *Herald-Sun*

(Melbourne), March 3, p. 5.

Reddacliff, G. L. (1981), 'Necrotic Enteritis in Reptiles at Taronga Zoo', in *Proceedings of the Melbourne Herpetological Symposium* (ed. Banks, C. B. and Martin, A. A.), Zoological Board of Victoria, Melbourne, pp. 124-126.

Roberts, G. (1982), 'Big-time Egg-nappers Threaten the Survival of Rare Wild Birds', *The National Times* (Sydney), May 23-29, p. 7.

Robinson, D. (1991), 'Amateur Collectors have Little Impact on Fauna Numbers/Letter to the Editor', *North-West Telegraph* (Western Australia), April 3.

Robinson, P. (1990), 'Smuggling Fighters Discover a Powerful Enemy', *Sunday Age* (Melbourne), April 15, p. 4.

Rosenberg, M. (1979), 'Restrictions Lifted on Captive Breeding of Endangered Species', *Notes From NOAH*, 7 (1), pp. 1-2.

Rosenberg, M. (1981), 'E.S.H.L. gives a Party . . . and the Guests of Honour Don't Show' and 'Australian National Parks and Wildlife Outdoes U.S. F. and W.', (Editorials), *Notes From NOAH*, 9 (1), pp. 1-7.

Rosenberg, M. (1981), 'Corruption in Fauna Authorities', (editorial), *Notes From NOAH*, 9 (3), pp. 1-13.

Rosenberg, M. (1982), 'A Different Solution to "Snakescam"' (editorial), *Notes From NOAH*, 9 (6), pp. 1-4.

Rosenberg, M. (1987), 'Fisheries Service Proposes Fatal Experiments on Endangered Turtles' (editorial), *Notes From NOAH*, 14 (12), pp. 16-17.

Rosenberg, M. (1988), *NOAH Battle Package*, Northern Ohio Association of Herpetologists, Cleveland, Ohio, U.S.A.

Rosenberg, M. (1988), 'Herp' Smugglers get Stung', (editorial), *Notes From NOAH*, 15 (5), p. 1.

Rosenberg, M. (1990), '$2 000 Reward!', *Notes From NOAH*, 17 (12), p. 17.

Rosenberg, M. (1990), 'Herp Buyers/Sellers: Beware of This Dealer!', *Notes From NOAH*, 17 (12), p. 17.

Ryan, K. (1989), 'Bird 3 Fly the Coop', *Sun* (Melbourne), July 25, p. 3.

Ryan, T. (1981), 'Snake Raid', *Telegram Tribune* (California), December 19.

Schooley, M. (1989), 'Smuggling — Continuing the Exposé of Illegal Bird Traffic in and out of This Country', *Australian Birdkeeper*, 2 (8), pp. 300-302.

Schooley, M. (1989), 'Bird Smuggling — Continuing the exposé of Illegal Bird Traffic in and out of This Country', *Australian Birdkeeper*, 2 (9), pp. 352-4.

Schooley, M. (1989), 'Bird Smuggling — The Dealer Decides to Make a Financial Killing', *Australian Birdkeeper*, 2 (10), pp. 398-399.

Schooley, M. (1989), 'Fauna Smuggling — Mr. Fun Fair', *Australian Birdkeeper*, 2 (12), pp. 490-491.

Schooley, M. (1990), 'Fauna Smuggling — The Austrian Connection', *Australian Birdkeeper*, 3 (1), pp. 40-41.

Schooley, M. (1990), 'Fauna Smuggling — the Austrian Connection and one of the Largest Seizures of Parrots Bound for Illegal Export', *Australian Birdkeeper*, 3 (3), pp. 135-136.

Schultze-Westrum, T. G. (1971), *Conservation in Papua New Guinea*, Final Report on the World Wildlife Fund Mission, Mimeo, P.N.G.

Sikora, N. (1991), 'Live lizards N.Z.-bound in Export Scam', *Herald-Sun* (Melbourne), December 24, p. 5.

Silvester, J. (1991), 'Bird Ring Smashed', *Herald-Sun* (Melbourne), October 1, p. 5.

Slavens, F. (1980-89), 'Inventory of Live Reptiles and Amphibians in Captivity', Frank. L. Slavens, Seattle, U.S.A. annual publication.

Sleuth (1975), 'The Smuggling of Birds', *Australian Aviculture*, May, pp. 77-78.

Smith, H. M. and Chiszar, D. (1990), 'Snakes Guarding Illegal Substances: a Request for Information from the Herpetological Community', *Notes From NOAH*, 17 (6), pp. 11-12.

Smithers R. (1990), 'Biologists ask Crabb for a Fairer Hearing', *Age* (Melbourne), May 30, p. 15.

Stonehouse, B. (1987), *Saving the Animals*, Weidenfield and Nicholson, U.S.A.

Storey, T. (1985), 'Murray Farquhar Guilty', *Sydney Morning Herald*, pp. 1 and 9.

Strohm, J. (1982), 'A Scam with a Real Sting', *National Wildlife* 20(2), p. 1.

Tedder, B. (1981), 'Highland Pet Shop. Some advice to Stingees', *Notes From NOAH*, 8 (12), pp. 7-8.

Teese, P. (1985), 'Snakes at $600 a Metre /Large-Scale Smugglers Slip Through Customs', *Sunday Telegraph* (Sydney), February 3, p. 141.

Tilbrook, K. (1980), 'S.M. Queries Charges on Fauna', *Adelaide Advertiser*, April 15, p. 16.

Tilbrook, K. (1980), 'Undercover Customs Officers', *Adelaide Advertiser*, April 15, p. 16.

Tilbrook, K. (1980), 'Bird Smuggling Charges Fail', *Adelaide Advertiser*, April 16, p. 6.

Thompson, S. (1989), 'Armed Officers Raid Park: Owner', *Sherbrooke and District Free Press*, June 21, p. 1.

Thompson, S. (1989), 'Department on Defence over Crocodile Raid', *Sherbrooke and District Free Press*, June 28, p. 1.

Thompson, S. (1989), 'C.F.L. "misled" Park Owner', *Sherbrooke and District Free Press*, July 5, p. 1.

Thompson, S. (1989), 'Free Press Initiates new Firearm Review', *Sherbrooke and District Free Press*, September 13, p. 1.

Tollis, K. C. (1976), 'The Smuggling of Birds', *Australian Aviculture*, February.

Toohey, B. (1983), 'Phone-Tap Scandals', *National Times* (Sydney), May 20-26, pp. 1, 3-7.

Tyler, M. J. (1985), 'Nomenclature of the Australian Herpetofauna: Anarchy Rules O.K.', *Herpetological Review*, 16 (3), p. 69.

Various Authors (1973), 'The Import and Export of Birds', *Australian Aviculture*, April.

Various Authors (1984), *Export of Native Birds, (A Submission to the Minister for Primary Industry The Honorable John Kerin M.P., Parliament House, Canberra. A.C.T.)*, Associated Birdkeepers and Traders, Sydney, Australia.

Various Authors (1976-89), *International Herpetological Symposium on Captive Propagation and Husbandry*, Richard A. Hahn, Maryland 21788, U.S.A.

Various Authors (1977-90), *Red Data Books*, (Vols. 1-4), I.U.C.N., Glans, Switzerland.

Various Authors (1960-90), *International Zoo Yearbook*, Zoological Society of London, U.K.